MW00582787

LONG JOURNEY
—— WITH ——
MR. JEFFERSON

Related Titles from Potomac Books

Bernard Fall: Memories of a Soldier-Scholar
—Dorothy Fall

The Meinertzhagen Mystery:
The Life and Legend of a Colossal Fraud
—Brian Garfield

Broadcasts from the Blitz: How Edward R. Murrow
Helped Lead America into War
—Philip Seib

LONG JOURNEY
—— WITH ——
MR. JEFFERSON

The Life of Dumas Malone

William G. Hyland Jr.

Potomac Books
Washington, D.C.

Library of Congress Cataloging-in-Publication Data
Hyland, William G., 1956–
    Long journey with Mr. Jefferson : the life of Dumas Malone / William G. Hyland, Jr.—1st ed.
        p. cm.
    Includes bibliographical references and index.
    ISBN 978-1-61234-197-2 (hardcover : alk. paper)
    ISBN 978-1-61234-198-9 (electronic)
    1. Malone, Dumas, 1892–1986. 2. Jefferson, Thomas, 1743–1826—Friends and associates. 3. United States—History—1783–1865. 4. Historians—United States—Biography. 5. Presidents—United States—Biography. I. Title.
    E175.5.M34H95 2013
    973.4'6092—dc23
                                2012039778

Printed in the United States of America on acid-free paper that meets the American National Standards Institute Z39-48 Standard.

Potomac Books
22841 Quicksilver Drive
Dulles, Virginia 20166

First Edition

10 9 8 7 6 5 4 3 2 1

To my loving mother, Evelyn Virginia Hyland,
who gave me a passion for reading and history.
And to the memory of my father-in-law, Leo Ruffini,
one of the few men I truly respected.

I meant to go through life and history with him step by step, starting precisely where he did. I'm more or less resting at the moment, because it's been a long journey.

—DUMAS MALONE

The Malone volumes constitute the best biography of Jefferson ever written.

—SAMUEL ELIOT MORISON

Contents

Preface

A teacher affects eternity; he can never tell where his influence stops.

—HENRY ADAMS[1]

A faint, misty rain fell over the University of Virginia Cemetery as I snapped pictures of Dumas (pronounced *DEW-mah*) Malone's granite headstone. In the stillness, I studied the marker and then strolled the peaceful glen of this 180-year-old cemetery. A mound of red, freshly turned soil appeared just beyond the wall, another grave being dug. Glancing at the famous, departed figures of the university, I realized that this stone-bordered ground radiated history, a time capsule as hallowed as that of Monticello, the site of Jefferson's grave. But within its quietude, here rested a man of exceptional accomplishment who had come to know and understand Jefferson better than anyone. Malone grasped more about Jefferson than even the third president's own family. He amassed every unvarnished fact of Jefferson's eighty-three magnificent years, from boyhood to death.

I never met Professor Malone, but as a native Virginian, I have long had an interest in his work. I was a senior in high school when he won the Pulitzer Prize in 1975, yet thirty years would pass before our lives crossed again. As I researched and wrote my own book on the Jefferson–Sally Hemings controversy,[2] I became immersed in Malone's volumes on Jefferson. I grew curious about Malone as a man, teacher, and historian. How did he spend nearly forty years of his life consumed—some would say obsessed—with writing about the same man without breaking his sanity?

I have attempted to recover the authentic man so many knew only by reputation, to catch Malone at propitious moments in his life, to pry open his thoughts and actions during those extended moments, through a vast array of materials. This is a life sketch of Dumas Malone, chronicling his devastating struggle with blindness, his rural upbringing in Mississippi, his experience in World War I, his advancement to the highest levels of academia, and his recognition by the White House. And, finally, this account covers the culmination of his thirty-eight-year "labor of love," the Pulitzer Prize–winning, six-volume biography of Thomas Jefferson. Within the gallery of great figures among the Founding Fathers so often mythologized, Jefferson is recognized as *primus*. A large part of this stature is attributable to Malone. In the pages that follow, I trace his search for historical answers that lay buried within the folds of the most ambitious personality of the Age of Enlightenment. This book also explores Malone's struggles with many notables, including famous scholars, academics, and revisionists, whom Malone thought guilty of historical sacrilege.

A genteel southerner born and bred, Malone had the look of a favorite uncle, a man who had seen much, yet had retained some of the joy of youth. He was "the best possible company," one reporter noted, "a funny raconteur in relaxed Southern style, a genuinely friendly man who talks about his close friend, Thomas Jefferson, with a lifetime's knowledge and unabated liking."[3] Malone appeared both rugged and gentle, with a large, square face framed by long ears, a high forehead, and a full mane of snowy hair. Except for his eyes, which, in his later years, were hardly visible behind thick, scratched glasses, his face seemed bright and expressive. A man of infectious cheerfulness, he often chuckled to himself as he talked. Like Jefferson, Malone emanated a courtly, persuasive charisma and never seemed rattled. Born in Mississippi, he grew up in the Deep South and forged his youth in Georgia. One of his interviewers said he was "magnanimous, the best single word to describe him as a man. Of course, he [was] learned, witty, charming and urbane—a true democrat and a gentle man."[4]

Malone had the charm of an exquisite character that emerged as inseparable from his personality, and epitomized an unsurpassed, southern graciousness. Yet, his genuine warmth did not prevent him from academic debate, be it in the realm of ideas, in the trenches of university life, or with an intransigent television network over the Sally Hemings controversy. He did not heed criticism, not because he was a callous man, but because he cared, first and foremost, about his motto: *veritas*. The historical facts mattered and all else became secondary.

In his habit of welcoming students into his home, Malone emerged as a vivid reminder of the old South, a place quieter, smaller, and more traditional than the wealthy, expansive colleges of today. He was of the old school when it came to camaraderie and service to the University of Virginia; if President Edwin Alderman asked you to do something for the institution, you did it. And if you were a famous professor, nearly blind, you did not use that as an excuse to be relieved of the grind of committee work. You worked harder, you were a part of the institution, and when it needed your services, you gave them.

Dumas Malone was not only one of the great historians and biographers of modern times, but he achieved that distinction in spite of handicaps that would have daunted a lesser man. Almost blind for the last fifteen of his ninety-four years, he nevertheless managed to complete the sixth and final volume of his masterful biography of Jefferson in the same graceful and scholarly style that characterized the entire work. In the bright lexicon of Malone's life, the word "surrender" did not exist. He was the same witty and modest man in his final years that he had been before his eyesight began to fail. Even after he finished volume 6, Malone's determination kept him writing, although his process involved a complicated regimen of putting down words in longhand and having them transferred to a mechanical reading device with a large screen.

Educated at Emory College (now Emory University) and Yale, Malone later became a member of the faculties of Yale, the University of Virginia, and Columbia. As editor in chief of the *Dictionary of American Biography* (*DAB*), he brought that monumental work to completion and later served seven tumultuous years as director of the Harvard University Press. In 1959 Malone returned to Mr. Jefferson's "Academical Village," the University of Virginia, and finished his "long journey" at the place where it all began.

The more I learned about Malone, read his articles and books, and studied his interviews, the more he reminded me of my own father: a serious scholar who took life and academic pursuits in earnest, yet never lost his sense of humor or of family. I felt the reader of this biography would come to know Malone as both a man and a teacher. Professor Malone exuded modesty, but his deep scholarship, genuine understanding, and good common sense became apparent throughout his work and his personal life. He also successfully mastered the temptation, faced by every scholar, to clutter his pages with the evidence of his diligence.

It is said that America loves Abraham Lincoln and venerates George Washington but remembers Thomas Jefferson. Hundreds of books have been written about Jefferson, who has been, at various times in history, worshiped, feted, loathed, mocked, and synthesized. For most of the twenty-first century, it seems, our response to Jefferson in particular and the Founding Fathers in general has been littered with legends and lore, oscillating between idolization and evisceration.

Yet, the six most comprehensive and richly nuanced volumes on Jefferson belong to Malone—a revered professor, historian (he held four degrees, three from Yale, including a master's and a PhD), teacher, biographer in residence, U.S. marine, and oldest winner of the Pulitzer Prize for *Jefferson and His Time*, which is currently in its sixteenth printing.[5]

Quite simply, Malone's biography of Jefferson is a balanced literary gift. If it is true that the past is beyond retrieval, Malone's *Jefferson* is, in the end, a masterly interrogation of the past by the present. His breadth and storytelling propels the volumes into the twenty-first century and beyond, while offering an interesting education in American history. Malone renders Jefferson more human, more vivid, more intimate, and certainly more connected to ourselves in a democratic republic. As Emerson contended, "There is properly no history; only biography."[6] Perhaps Malone had these words in mind when he first thought about sculpting Jefferson from the murky wells of history, as early as 1923. By the age of ninety, Malone had written more than a million words about "Mr. Jefferson."[7] When the sixth and final volume of the biography appeared in 1981, critics praised his life's work as "perhaps the greatest presidential biography ever written."[8] Historian M. E. Bradford commented, "After a labor of almost 40 years . . . Dumas Malone has brought to a distinguished conclusion, what will be for our time, the standard biography of Thomas Jefferson."[9]

In the opinion of some friendly critics, Malone concentrated on Jefferson's milieu to the neglect of his character. Events smothered ideas, some historians protested, and Malone's conventional method became inadequate to achieve sharpness in a biographical portrait. Malone recognized the problem, especially in the middle volumes. Ideally, he retorted, employing a favorite metaphor from music, "The biography of a public figure should be neither a solo performance nor an orchestral symphony but a concerto." Examining the subject at length in an essay, Malone confessed, "Biography is personalized history. Its advantage over history lay in its focus on a single and great human subject with whom the reader might identify and follow through historic time." Malone believed that the biographer's principal obligation was to tell what the man did, along with who, when, and where. Questions of why and how were secondary, although they could not be dismissed. He rejected psychological interpretation, insisting that he was not writing Jefferson's personal life story. "He had no fondness for that genre," one historian commented, "which he associated, to his horror, with Fawn Brodie's *Thomas Jefferson: An Intimate History.*"[10]

Malone was accused by some of blandness, but most critics became absorbed in his detailed, constructed narrative, which captured even the shadows of Jefferson. Walter Clemons of *Newsweek* wrote, "Malone's is the biography on which later biographers [will depend], even in disagreement. For the general reader it has the attractions of grace, calm judgment and uncluttered fullness. It is a very long biography one never wishes shorter." Garry Wills, in the *New York Review of Books*, offered his assessment of *Jefferson and His Time*:

> I write in the happy knowledge that nothing I (or anyone) can say will diminish the size of Malone's achievement. Monuments make easy targets, but survive whatever small misgivings are expressed about them. The material for reflection on Jefferson is given us by Malone even when we use it to criticize some of his findings. Allowance will be made for the man's hero worship, since the hero is so worthy of the worship—as this book and its companions prove for all time.[11]

Malone's death left a large void both in Charlottesville and American historiography. At the age of ninety-four, Malone had come to be seen as absolutely permanent, partly because few figures generated such affection from those who knew them and even from those who did not. I, like others, thought most of Malone's adult life was consumed by the Jefferson volumes. This proved a mistaken assumption. As Malone always pointed out, he did not publish his first volume on Jefferson until he was fifty-six. Yet, the theme that ran throughout Malone's personal and professional life, before and after Jefferson, was simple: to present a figure in his own historical time frame, that is, to view him as his contemporaries would have and as Jefferson saw himself. In the introduction to his first volume, Malone wrote, "My main purposes for this work are that it shall be comprehensive, that it shall relate Jefferson's career to his age, and that it shall be true to his own chronology." Seldom has an author so well fulfilled his intentions. *Jefferson and His Time* is comprehensive, not only in fullness and detail, but in treating the whole of a many-sided man. It always relates Jefferson to his age, and that is what makes it a work of history as well as biography. And it is true to Jefferson's own chronology. This, in fact, is Malone's greatest achievement.

To most previous biographers, Jefferson was elusive, a stone figure of paradox and contradiction, "a portrait on the wall." But Malone converged this Mount Rushmore image of Jefferson into a living, growing, changing man. It is this dynamic that Jefferson's life assumes a clarity scarcely written before or after. Malone's *Jefferson* transformed both his legacy and the field of biography itself. He excelled at this detailed method of writing history and provided a consummate model for present-day biographers. His first and main concern was to get the facts right. His second was to record events in the context of their own time. But the underlying theme of his work, and, one could say, his life, was always to be honest and fair-minded about his subjects, never the prosecutor or defender of them. His portrayal of Jefferson conveyed not a social, political, or cultural commentary, but it instead transformed a penetrating and woven fabric of historical intricacies into a human portrait. By utilizing these principles and themes, Malone has set the highest standard for twenty-first-century biographers, which, in my view, will be unequalled in our time. His Jefferson has stood the test of time and will influence our understanding of the "Sage of Monticello" for decades to come.

A French diplomat once commented on his tour of Monticello, "There will never be another man like Thomas Jefferson in 500 years." And, I dare say, there may not be another biographer like Dumas Malone. So authoritatively did Malone conjure up the day-to-day details of Jefferson's life that the reader practically forgets that his books are based on thousands of researched facts. Indeed, Malone's *Jefferson and His Time* has the organic intimacy of a novel that has sprung full-blown from the imagination of its creator.

In 1981, toward the end of his life, scholars and laymen interested in history agonized over whether Malone would be able to complete the series with a volume on Jefferson's last seventeen years. They were rewarded with

The Sage of Monticello, the final book. Malone, nearly blind and requiring the help of two assistants and a machine to write, finished the work. Even though he was eighty-nine years of age, he had retained the standards of exhaustive research and of a graceful style that he had set for himself in volume 1.

Sigmund Freud, commenting on his own biography of Leonardo da Vinci, warned that biographers often choose heroes "out of their own special affection." Freud observed that biographers often, "devote themselves to a work of idealization." Intolerant of anything in their subject's inner or outer life that smacks of human weakness or imperfection, biographers then give us a cold, strange, ideal form instead of a man to whom we could feel distinctly related."[12]

Nothing could be further from the truth with Malone's portrait of Jefferson. Biography will always be a collaboration between the author and his subject, and there must be the reflection of one temperament in the mirror of another. The danger in such collaboration, of course, is that the author will confuse himself with the subject, intruding his own opinions, forcing his own personality into the book, until it becomes autobiography. But Malone had always been too good a scholar and much too strong a person to fall into that trap. The collaboration was founded on a basic empathy, a harmony of ideas and feelings. He believed that empathy was properly an aid to understanding. It became necessary to a full and fair representation.[13]

No doubt Jefferson presented a grand subject for a biography, one in which both Jefferson and Malone seemed worthy of each other. But that assertion is deceptively simple because both Jefferson and Malone were complex and fascinating men. Jefferson is, perhaps, the most important figure in all American history. Malone is equally worthy of our attention because he ranked among the three or four most profound writers of history during the twentieth century. Great figures in history live long after death through their writings, but even longer in the lives they touched, the values they imparted, and the example they set. So it was with Malone, mentor, colleague, husband, father, and friend of so many who now strive to emulate him. His numerous books and no less important articles are a staggering corpus of work. But they represent only a portion of his legacy. Malone left behind him a vast array of professionals in government, history, journalism, and business who forged their careers because of him. Some of them followed his path to academe—they include professors at the University of Virginia, Columbia, Yale, Harvard, and many other institutions—because they were inspired by an academic ideal that he embodied. Yet Malone's distinctly southern kindness and charm embraced everyone, from presidents to timid graduate students.

"I flattered myself that sometime I would fully comprehend and encompass Jefferson," Malone once said. But Jefferson's character, many traits of which he shared, proved the basis for the scholar's affection for his subject. "I considered him my friend," he confessed.[14]

Given what I now know of Malone's life story and work, I realize his task was staggering and its completeness overwhelms. In its majesty and soothing prose, Malone's portrait of Jefferson comes from another time and place. Historians shy away from using the word "definitive" to describe any biography. Malone would have been the first to agree. He began his quest looking for the man rather than the statue on a pedestal. His tightly braided work allowed neither celebration nor dismissal, but mapped out an "explanation" of Jefferson for generations to come. Fortunately, historical scholarship allows newly scrubbed historians to stand on the shoulders of their predecessors. When they are on the shoulders of such giants as Malone, fresh scholarship can stand high indeed. Malone's lavishly detailed portrait will not be matched. If it ever is, that future biographer will have to make the long journey with both Thomas Jefferson and Dumas Malone.[15]

ACKNOWLEDGMENTS

This book could not have been written without the valuable assistance of three outstanding people: Steve Hochman, whose memories and insights provided a blueprint for this work; Dr. Ken Wallenborn, friend, mentor, and leading Jefferson authority who personally knew Dumas Malone; and Gifford Malone, Dumas's son, who fully cooperated from the beginning of this project. His comments saved me from various errors and contributed immensely to improving my rough manuscript.

I am also grateful to several valuable colleagues and friends who lent their time in critically reading all or part of the manuscript. I have benefited from their comments: Art Downey, Helen Cripe, Tom Faulders, Tom Fleming, Clyde Wilson, Eric Petersen, Eddie Leake, and Kay Sargeant. I am also grateful to Professor Robert Turner at the University of Virginia for his kind comments and scholarly insight. Similar gratitude is owed to the staff at the Alderman Library at the University of Virginia (Special Collections Department), who provided me with valuable research material and access to Malone's massive collection of personal papers.

No book is complete without the assistance of a passionate editor. I was fortunate to have one of the best, Elizabeth Demers, who took a rough manuscript and shaped it into a readable biography. I also am indebted to all the fine people at my publisher, Potomac Books. I also wish to thank my literary agent, Jane Dystel, who did not give up on the book.

Finally, I am indebted most of all to my loving children, Victoria and William, who provided me with encouragement and inspiration and who always put a smile on my face. I hope they gain a sense of the most comprehensive, richly nuanced historical record of Thomas Jefferson left to their generation.

CHRONOLOGY

1892	Dumas Malone is born.
1902	Malone family moves to Cuthbert, Georgia.
1906	Malone enters Emory College.
1910	Graduates Emory College with AB degree.
1914	Begins teaching job at Randolph-Macon Woman's College.
1916	Receives bachelor of divinity degree from Yale Divinity School.
1917	Enters the Marines.
1919	Is discharged from the Marines.
1919	Becomes instructor of history at Yale University.
1921	Earns master's degree from Yale.
1922	Accepts professorship at Yale.
1923	Earns doctoral degree from Yale.
1923	Is awarded the John Addison Porter Prize from Yale University.
1923	Accepts professorship at University of Virginia (UVA).
1923–29	Teaches history at UVA.
1925	Marries Elisabeth Gifford.
1929	Accepts assistant editor position at the *Dictionary of American Biography* (*DAB*).
1931	Is appointed chief editor of *DAB*.
1936	Accepts editor position at Harvard University Press.

1938	Signs contract with Little, Brown for Jefferson biography.
1940	Publishes biography of UVA President Edwin A. Alderman.
1942	Resigns from Harvard University Press.
1943	Attends Jefferson Memorial dedication in Washington, D.C.
1943	Receives Rockefeller grant for Jefferson biography.
1945	Accepts position at Columbia University.
1948	First volume of *Jefferson and His Time, Jefferson the Virginian*, is published.
1951	Second volume, *Jefferson and the Rights of Man*, is published.
1951	Is awarded Guggenheim fellowship.
1953	Becomes managing editor of *Political Science Quarterly*.
1959	Resigns from Columbia to teach at UVA.
1962	Becomes biographer in residence at UVA.
1962	Third volume, *Jefferson and the Ordeal of Liberty*, is published.
1967–68	Becomes president of the Southern Historical Association.
1970	Fourth volume, *Jefferson the President: First Term*, is published.
1972	Is awarded John F. Kennedy and the Wilbur L. Cross medals.
1974	Fawn Brodie publishes *Thomas Jefferson: An Intimate History*.
1974	Fifth volume, *Jefferson the President: Second Term*, is published.
1975	Malone wins Pulitzer Prize.
1977	Becomes almost totally blind.
1981	Sixth and final volume, *The Sage of Monticello*, is published.
1983	Is nominated for Presidential Medal of Freedom.
1986	Dies in Charlottesville, Virginia.
1992	Malone's wife, Elisabeth, dies in Charlottesville, Virginia.

1   The White House

It's a great satisfaction . . . that somebody thinks you've
done something for the country.

—Dumas Malone[1]

The task was staggering. I do not see how Malone could
accomplish it at all, much less do it with such style
and balance. For that matter, I do not see how Jefferson
had time to live the life it took Malone three decades
to narrate.

—Garry Wills[2]

The White House
February 1983

The White House telegram arrived in Dumas Malone's book-lined office at the Alderman Library on the campus of the University of Virginia. The content was succinct:

It is my pleasure to inform you that you have been selected to receive the Medal of Freedom from the president of the United States for your contribution in the field of history and letters. This is the highest civilian honor that the country can bestow on one of its citizens. The award ceremony and lunch will take place at the White House at 12 noon on February 23, 1983.

You may bring four guests. Michael Deaver, Assistant to the President and Deputy Chief of Staff.[3]

Two weeks later, under a warm drizzle, a stream of black limousines, bearing the recipients of that year's Presidential Medal of Freedom, drew up to the White House. Each of the honorees received a military aide upon arrival. Attendants whisked away coats, umbrellas, and scarves. The crowd flowed up the spiral staircase. The U.S. Marine Band played as guests milled around, greeted each other, and tried to spot the men and women who would receive the nation's highest civilian award in an hour's time.

Clare Boothe Luce, U.S. ambassador to Italy and wife of Henry Luce, publisher of *Time*, *Fortune*, and *Life*, swept into the East Room. She was petite and marvelously chic in a gray suit, gray stockings, and pumps, a single sweet-smelling American Beauty rose pinned to her lapel. She spoke to Richard Clurman, former chief correspondent at *Time*. Tish Baldrige Hollensteiner, who served as Mrs. Luce's secretary in Rome, explained that her husband was late, "as always." Tish, having served as Jackie Kennedy's social secretary, was no stranger to the White House.

A receiving line formed, and the guests passed down it into the dining room, where they sat at round tables for eight decorated with gardenias. As they finished their lunch of chicken Veronique, tiny peas with fresh mint, and lemon mousse, waiters poured steaming coffee. A gaggle of photographers gathered at the end of the room as the Marine Band wound up its program with a flourish. President Ronald Reagan, wearing a gray-brown glen check suit, formally buttoned, strode to the dais. He adjusted an inch of crisp cotton that protruded from his shirtsleeves before he spoke.

At precisely 1:12 p.m. Reagan began his remarks, his tone smooth.

Ladies and gentlemen. One of the greatest privileges and the most distinct pleasures of my job is the duty that I perform today, awarding our nation's highest civilian honor, the Presidential Medal of Freedom. This medal is given to those who have risen to pinnacles of achievement in their fields. It is recognition of their accomplishments, hard work and dedication for America and for humanity. The men and women that we honor today come from across our land. Some children of immigrants, some immigrants themselves, many from humble beginnings. But they all share a quality that Carl Sandburg once summed up so well when he wrote, "Man is born with rainbows in his heart."

Reagan paused a beat, his brilliantined hair gleaming dense and dark. As the president called each name, the recipient or the person accepting for the recipient walked to the podium to receive the civilian equivalent of the Congressional Medal of Honor and remained on the stage: Paul "Bear" Bryant (posthumously), Reverend Billy Graham, Clare Booth Luce, Jacob K. Javits, and finally,

> Dr. Dumas Malone. And the medal will be accepted by his son, Gifford Malone. As one of the foremost historians, authors and scholars of this century, Dumas Malone has recounted the birth of our nation and the ideals of our Founding Fathers. Among Dr. Malone's most notable accomplishments is his biography of Thomas Jefferson, now regarded as the most authoritative work of its kind. Dr. Malone's contributions to our national lore will remain invaluable to succeeding generations as each takes up responsibility for the heritage of freedom so eloquently described in his articles and books.

Reagan glanced down at his notes. "Well . . . that concludes the presentations," he said. "By the achievements of their lifetimes and by their presence here today, in person or in spirit, each recipient has brought honor to the White House. And I thank you for being our guests today." He turned to Gifford Malone, whose eyes welled with tears. "God bless you, and God bless all of you."[4]

Although too frail to travel to Washington in person, Dumas Malone received a flurry of letters from dignitaries and notables upon news of his medal. James Bear, the curator of Monticello, assessed Malone's crowning achievement in a single line: "On the occasion of your latest signal honor, I salute you as our mutual friend surely would have—with all personal esteem."[5]

2   Reflections

It is a great subject and one in which both the subject and the author are worthy of each other.

—JULIAN BOYD[1]

Scholarship is and ought to be a lonely pursuit, but its results belong to mankind. When an author or any other creative person is recognized in this way, the society at large is not only honoring one of the very best members but is also acknowledging an abiding debt.

—ROUHOLLAH K. RMAZ[2]

The University of Virginia
Charlottesville, Virginia 1975

An old myth holds that the South is populated by eccentric socialites, con men, faded beauty queens, and a Civil War skeleton in every closet. The small college town of Charlottesville, nestled at the foot of Jefferson's beloved mansion, fulfills this stereotype without caricature or condescension.[3]

As book-laden students scurried down a brick sidewalk, a cool fall breeze wrinkled the fountain water near Alderman Library. Leaves floated off thick magnolia trees that Phi Beta Kappa students had planted years ago. Crystalline honeysuckle scented the Virginia air. Amid it all, Dumas Malone sat cloistered in his top floor study in the northeastern corner of Alderman Library, named after UVA's first president, Edwin Alderman. For more than twenty years, Malone wrote and researched in this roomy office among the fifth floor's "old stacks."

His striking view from faculty study number 524 overlooked the university chapel and Jefferson's famed Rotunda. Fading sunbeams streamed through the windows as he admired the Blue Ridge Mountains in the distance standing like a purple wall against the sunset. In another direction, Thomas Jefferson's Monticello—Italian for "little mountain"—looked serenely down on Malone. Albemarle County emerged as one of the most beautiful and historic of Virginia's provinces, its landscape rolling and mountainous. From its red soil had sprung some of the nations' greatest men: George Rogers Clark and Meriwether Lewis (of Lewis and Clark fame) and President James Monroe.

On this day Malone seemed lively, showing off his charm and zest for conversation even though he was eighty-one and nearly blind. He talked a blue streak and enjoyed an occasional hearty laugh. Malone clearly had not forgotten anything he had ever learned about American history. Any ungracious thought he might have had about the state of his health dissolved earlier that day on a drive to the top of Monticello.[4]

There, eight hundred feet above the town and campus, the eye reveled in one of the great vistas of the North American continent: to the east, rolling fields stretched out toward Richmond and the Tidewater country; to the west, the massive Blue Ridge Mountains marched across the horizon, proclaiming the nation's first western frontier. Malone savored the scene, and he captured it perfectly in Jeffersonian terms: "His eye like his mind sought the extended view."[5]

Nearly two centuries have passed since Thomas Jefferson first walked across an empty field in Charlottesville and staked off what would become "Jefferson's University" in 1819. As the institution's founder and principal visionary, Jefferson had selected the original grounds, designed to be his "Academical Village," which included a rectangular, terraced green space known as "the Lawn"; two parallel rows of buildings, the Pavilions, connected by colonnaded walkways; student rooms; and the Rotunda, the signature landmark of the university. A half-scale interpretation of the Pantheon in Rome, the Rotunda originally housed the library.

A small commercial area called the Corner developed adjacent to the university as the institution grew. Once literally just a corner where the main road to Charlottesville met the entrance to the university grounds, this district expanded to become five city blocks of around-the-clock activity.

For Malone, the Corner, specifically his beloved university cafeteria, was the seam of life that had always connected "town with gown." Charlottesville's first taverns, shops, and small businesses evolved around Court Square, an area frequented by Jefferson, Madison, and Monroe.

And if fate was the residue of luck, Professor Dumas Malone fell under the spell of this charming town of moss-hung oaks and shaded squares in 1923. "Age brings few gifts," Malone often said, as he adjusted thick glasses for his failing eyesight and sat in a swivel chair. Wearing a blue blazer and tamping his pipe, the historian strained to hear Steve Hochman's voice on a scuffed Sony tape recorder. Sitting across from Malone, Hochman, his youthful research assistant, scratched out a couple more sentences and read them aloud. Malone began to write, and his letters appeared large and round on a specialized magnifying device for the blind. His words flowed even though his fingers flared with arthritic pain. His hands had the long, tapered quality of a surgeon's, lightly tanned on the backs and corded with blue veins: "The miscegenation story, as elaborated after Jefferson's death, assigned to him the paternity of the children borne by Sally Hemings during his presidency, two of them in his second term. The latter charge can be disproved by testimony and information now available. To charge him with that degree of imprudence and insensitivity requires extraordinary credulity."

Malone paused a beat. His mind began to spin now but in a balanced way, like a gyroscope. Long vertical lines creased his face; his mouth was upturned at the corners, as though he had learned always to smile. His skin appeared paper thin with age, and he had nests of blue veins at his temples. He rubbed a patch of silvery stubble on his chin. Malone clicked off the tape recorder, rose from his desk, and brushed crumbs of fried chicken from his pressed khaki pants. He sipped on a cold glass of sweet tea and stared out the window to the colonnade. As student and teacher talked about Jefferson, Malone's drawl seemed as soft as velvet. He spoke quietly, yet forcefully.

Oak trees creaked outside as Hochman watched Malone rub his red-rimmed eyes, blink twice, and adjust both of his hearing aids. He knew that Malone's eyesight had failed from age-related macular degeneration and that he had been nearly blind for twenty years. It was a tragedy beyond imagination for a scribe who had dedicated his life to the visual: books and words.

Hochman surveyed the historian's study. Tall wooden bookcases swelled with finely bound biographies. A limited edition of the Fry and Jefferson map of Virginia hung on the wall. The map had been given to Malone at the retirement ceremony of Harry Clemons, chief librarian of the University of Virginia. The woodwork stood out on the chrome yellow of the walls, a brilliant pigment Jefferson had chosen for his own dining room at Monticello. The furniture seemed staid and heavy, the air musky. Books, purchased from book clubs that specialized in history and biography, filled Malone's shelves. His desk overflowed with typed, triple-spaced copy; three-ring binders; and yellow legal pads. A leaf of lined paper floated to the floor and landed next to Malone's shined oxblood loafers.

Malone's modest demeanor prevented him from showcasing his awards, among them the Pulitzer Prize, the John F. Kennedy Medal from the Massachusetts Historical Society, and the Wilbur L. Cross Medal from Yale. The gold coin, with the inscription "Joseph Pulitzer Medal" on one side and Benjamin Franklin's image on the other, was two and three-quarter inches in diameter and a quarter-inch thick. It shined with a twenty-four-carat gold plate and had been presented to Malone in a cherrywood box with brass hardware. Sitting on a bookcase shelf in his modest home, the historian's medal was surrounded by engraved plaques bestowed by the American Historical Association, the American Academy of Arts and Sciences, the American Antiquarian Society, the Southern Historical Association, the Massachusetts Historical Society, Phi Beta Kappa, Omicron Delta Kappa, the Century Club in New York, and the Cosmos Club in Washington, D.C.

Malone's thick glasses sat perched on the end of his nose as he and Hochman talked and edited until 4:30 in the afternoon. He wearied in the glow of sunset but felt renewed when he stared upward through the window to Monticello. The grass always seemed cooler up there in the evening and reminded him of his years in Mississippi, he told Hochman. His father would come home early, and they would play a game of pitch and catch in the backyard.

Malone often said that he could feel Jefferson looking down upon him. The mansion embodied the visible projection of its resident. Jefferson spent most of his life building and rebuilding his five-thousand-acre Palladian estate, ringed by the rolling mountains. Malone would later describe an absorbed Jefferson, tall and slender in a blue frock coat, standing at the east entrance, supervising his busy carpenters, the aroma of rich maple wood in the air. Jefferson would register the spring frost blanketing the peach orchard, his grapes ripening, pale rows of peas bursting upon Monticello's garden. The smell of the tobacco warehouse wafted in the air as Jefferson hummed a Scottish song while walking to his study.[6]

Holding Hochman's steady hand, Malone shuffled over to his desk. He displayed the confident manner of a perfectionist, a quality that fit his position as the preeminent historian in the country. He rested his Parker pen filled with blue ink among a mass of inchoate notes. His fatigue congealed into fond memories of youth. He would often regale Hochman with tales of Mississippi and Georgia, seventy summers ago, when, as a child, he longed for cold watermelon and sweet corn. He could see his mother, Lillian, through the screened porch door, frying eggs and cured ham slices in a heavy skillet. She lifted it by its handle without a hot pad. One of Malone's earliest recollections was the steady *thump thump* in the kitchen on Sunday mornings when Lillian would beat the dough for buttermilk biscuits. She spread the dough on a thick wooden board and belabored it with a wooden mallet shaped like a baseball bat, only shorter. The resulting warm biscuits melted delectably, served with strawberry jam and, for Malone's father, a strong cup of coffee.

Before she had fixed breakfast that morning, Lillian had returned from the small barn smelling of horse sweat. She had a pail of frothy milk in one hand and an armful of brown eggs held against her chest. She would iron clothes for seven children three hours a day in a house that reached 110 degrees in the summer.

A gentle knock sounded at Malone's office door—his wife, Elisabeth. "And then along came Elisabeth," Malone often murmured, "and saved my soul." She stepped into his office, her still bright eyes the color of blue glass. Her arms and the top of her neck were powdered with strawberry freckles. Malone's eyes almost glittered with tears, perfectly on cue. His adoration of this brittle, little woman warmed the room.

It was a Norman Rockwell scene of honeyed sentiment, Hochman recalled. There was something engagingly innocent about the way Malone held his wife with one hand and leaned on a maple walking cane with the other. As he placed his gray hat on his large head, they ambled outside together, each holding the other for support, fading smiles across their lips. The moon shone down on the scholar from Thomas Jefferson's mountaintop, beckoning like an old friend.

3   The Deep South

Most Americans haven't felt it or suffered from it. All the European peoples have suffered from history, and so have Southern people.

—DUMAS MALONE, 1981[1]

Dumas Malone was born eight years before the dawn of the twentieth century, in an age closer to Thomas Jefferson's than to ours. In 1892 there were only thirty-eight states. An American boy born that year could expect to live to be forty-six, a girl to be forty-eight. The U.S. population was approximately 75 million and the largest city was New York, with a population of 3.4 million. There were no airplanes and practically no automobiles. Radio, television, and the income tax all lay in the future. A dollar could buy lunch and dinner for two days, as witnessed by an advertisement for a Boston, Massachusetts, boarding house: "Turkey dinner, 20 cents, supper or breakfast 15 cents." In the Omaha, Nebraska, *World Herald*, sugar was listed at "4 cents a pound, 14 cents a dozen."[2]

Former president Grover Cleveland ran for reelection against the incumbent Benjamin Harrison. Cleveland defeated Harrison and thus became the only person in U.S. history to be elected to a second, nonconsecutive presidential term. In eight years Kodak would introduce the Brownie, the first camera for amateurs, and Theodore Roosevelt would write his old friend Henry Sprague, "I have always been fond of the West African proverb: 'Speak softly and carry a big stick; you will go far.'"[3]

On January 10, 1892, in Coldwater, Mississippi, south of Memphis, Dumas Malone was born, in the Old South in an age of gentle courtesies gone by. Coldwater was a tired old town when Malone knew it, and somehow he remembered it as being inordinately hot. Men's still collars wilted by nine in the morning in the summertime, and women bathed before noon and after their three o'clock naps. A day was twenty-four-hours long but seemed longer to Malone and his six brothers and sisters.

The second of seven children, Malone grew up in a wood-frame house on the edge of the black delta bottomland of northern Mississippi. He was the son of John Wesley Malone, a Methodist minister, and Lillian Kemp Malone, a schoolteacher with academic ambitions for all her children.[4]

Malone's roots imbedded themselves in the Deep South. His father had been born in August 1856 in Georgia and died in Cleveland, Tennessee, in 1930. His mother had been born in New Orleans, and she eventually retired there to live out her days until she died, at age ninety-two. Dumas's paternal grandparents hailed from North Carolina and Tennessee. His maternal grandparents came from Kentucky and Mississippi. His grandfather had fought in the Civil War for the Confederacy. "My father and mother endured its painful aftermath," Malone recalled, but they still named one of their daughters "Virginia."[5]

The Malone household was distinctly religious and highly tolerant. The independent thinking that prevailed was dramatically characterized by Lillian's advocacy of women's suffrage, an idea that was advanced for her time. Education played a key role in the Malone household. Lillian taught her children at home and gave Malone his appetite for books and knowledge.

"Perhaps it is only in childhood that books have any deep influence on our lives," Graham Greene once contended. Books initiated the Malone children into a larger world that included L. Frank Baum, Mark Twain, the Brothers Grimm, Hans Christian Andersen, and Greek and Roman mythology. Dumas's parents sent all seven of their children to college—no easy feat either today or in 1906. All three of Lillian's sons earned PhD's, and five of the seven Malone children worked in the field of education for most of their lives.[6]

"We were poor, but everybody was poor," Malone said. "The schools were not as good as they should have been." Although Malone had no personal share in the operation of the family farm, "I had grown up in an agricultural society and was not unfamiliar with its basic problems. As a young married man I had begun to be a gardener."[7]

Years later, in 1937, Malone would pen a speech on the Founding Fathers and the "riddle of greatness." It is a telling insight into his own family background and the formation of his personality. "If one were drawing up a formula for greatness," Malone wrote, referring to Thomas Jefferson's childhood, "he would begin with an unusual mother, whether or not distinguished in her own right. He would choose a father from any one of many occupations, but perhaps would prefer a professional man. He need pay little attention to the place of birth."[8]

The current town square of Coldwater, Mississippi, is located about two miles south of the Coldwater River. The original town began as the village of Elm Grove in 1856. At the time Malone lived there, the town was located in DeSoto County and was a mile square with the railroad depot at the center. When another Mississippi county was created in 1873 from land originally located in DeSoto, Marshall, and Tunica counties, Coldwater became a part of newly formed Tate County.[9] The town began to grow with an influx of settlers from Virginia, the Carolinas, Alabama, and other states who were seeking a better life for themselves and their families. There were 397 residents of Coldwater according to the 1890 census.

Other famous people born and raised in the Coldwater area include Dorris Bowdon Johnson, a screen actress of the 1930s and 1940s who played alongside such Hollywood legends as Henry Fonda. But the most famous native is the actor James Earl Jones, born on January 17, 1931. Jones, best known as the voice of Darth Vader in the *Star Wars* movies, is an American actor of film and stage. Jones was born in Arkabutla, Tate County, Mississippi.

Not long after Malone was born, the family moved from Coldwater to Oxford, Mississippi, where his father became president of the Woman's College of Oxford. When Malone reached age ten in 1902, his father became minister of a church in Brunswick, Georgia, on the Atlantic coast, and then, four years later, the family moved to Cuthbert, a small town in southwest Georgia, where his father was named president of Andrew College, a four-year school for women.

Malone had fond memories of the beautiful rolling hills of southwestern Georgia, only a short afternoon drive from the North Georgia mountains.

Cuthbert, Georgia, had been named for Col. John Alfred Cuthbert, an editor, congressman, and judge, and later in life, Dumas often referred to the town as "cut butt." The friendly, small city was incorporated on December 26, 1831. The Charter of Andrew College, granted in 1854 by the Georgia Legislature, was the second-oldest charter in the United States that gave an educational institution the right to confer degrees upon women. Originally named Andrew Female College, Andrew had operated as a women's four-year college for sixty-three years by the time John Malone became president. It had served as a Confederate hospital during the Civil War. In 1917, however, Andrew became a junior college, and in 1956 the institution became co-educational.

Malone described his mother as "a remarkable woman." Lillian was a pioneer suffragist at the time, and wherever she lived she advanced her ideas. Malone always thought his mother's advocacy was good for all his family because she had taught them not to be afraid to be a little different from other people.

Lillian was also a natural teacher, much more so than Malone's father. She used to make Malone and his siblings "do our lessons at home. We had to read aloud to her, and that was very important. We had to memorize things," he recalled.[10] "I was privately taught until I went to high school and our mother contributed very greatly to our education. She had been a teacher herself, and the story that's told in the family is that Mother wanted every one of her children to be a Ph.D. I'm sure her ambitions for us had a great effect on what we actually did."[11]

Malone's parents had grown up in the Reconstruction period, and their own economic opportunities were limited for that reason. Yet Lillian was determined that her children would have the opportunities that she did not.[12] "I knew what history had done to my father and mother's generation, how limited their opportunities were because of the Civil War and its aftermath," Malone wrote. "As I review the past from the vantage point of extreme old age I am reminded that there was little in my youthful experience to suggest that one day I would become an historian."[13]

In fact, the only history course Malone remembered taking in grade school or high school was one in ancient history. He learned about the Peloponnesian War under the guidance of his oldest brother, Kemp, and at some time "I became acquainted with the myths of Greece and Rome."[14] Malone recalled that once, when he was a boy, "I signed myself 'your scholar' in a letter to my teacher. I was told that my attainments did not warrant my use of that term as yet. Half a century later, still somewhat incredulous that I was now entitled to be called 'Doctor,' I thought of myself primarily as a teacher."[15]

Kemp emerged as the early intellectual star of the family. After graduating from Emory College in 1907, he went on to become a noted linguist at Johns Hopkins University and president of the Modern Language Association. Malone's other brother, Miles, taught at Andover College in Massachusetts for a quarter of a century. One of his four sisters taught at Sophie Newcomb College in New Orleans. Another married a professor from the University of Minnesota, ensuring that five of the Malone children were connected with higher education.[16]

In 1906, at age fourteen and still in short trousers, Malone traveled 150 miles from home to follow Kemp to Emory College, the forerunner of Emory University. The college was located at the Old College campus, and there were no dormitories for the three hundred or so students who enrolled that year. In later years Malone warmly remembered Emory as a "citadel of orthodoxy," yet "a modest home of humane learning." He always believed his undergraduate education played a major role in determining the kind of man he eventually became.

During the muggy Georgia summer of 1906, two students lived across the hall from each other at the Stuart Boarding House. They belonged to the same fraternity, Sigma Nu, and the tennis club. Tom Rivers came from Jonesboro, Georgia. Persuaded by Professor Ferdinand Duncan, a bachelor who ate at the same boardinghouse, Tom studied biology and chemistry in his junior and senior years. Had he not done so, he might have gone back to Jonesboro, where his father had a cotton warehouse business. Tom eventually went to Johns Hopkins Medical School and became one of the nation's medical pioneers, investigating such diseases as smallpox, encephalitis, and the quest for a polio vaccine.

Dumas Malone lived across the hall from Rivers. He took courses in Latin, which gave him knowledge of grammar that proved to be of immense use later. Courses in Greek literature and translation, taught by Professor Charles Peppler, also had a great influence on the young Malone. "If I am something of a classicist in spirit," Malone wrote, "that course is one of the reasons for it."[17]

Malone was not a particularly good student, he recalled later. "I was experimenting with life. I think it's a terrible mistake to go to college that young because you're not ready. It wasn't as bad as it sounds now because there were a good many people who went to college at 16. But even so, I wasn't ready. I could do the studies, but I wasn't mature and I wasn't ready for anything else."[18]

According to Malone, Emory

did not give me much history. Only one history course was offered at Emory. That was in modern European history. The man who taught it was Professor Edgar H. Johnson, an economist. He was one of the best teachers I ever had. I had the pleasure of telling him years later that I first became conscious that I was thinking . . . in his . . . elementary economics. Some of the things he said in his courses I remember until this day. He undoubtedly left an abiding impression on me.[19]

Although the small colleges in the prewar South did not have great scholars, they "maintained the classical and literary traditions very well," Malone recalled. "I look back on [Emory] with great respect. At my own institution, the authorities seemed more concerned to preserve learning and piety than to advance the frontiers of knowledge, but the little country college produced a good crop of scholars in those prewar years."[20]

Malone had no notable achievements as a classicist or a humanist, but he regarded himself as one in spirit. Some of this he obtained years later from his association with "Mr. Jefferson,"

but a lot of it came from Emory. I always felt at home in the ancient world, especially Greece. There was a professor of Greek at Emory, Professor Charles Peppler, we called him Pep. Pep was a friendly little man, and he was extremely grammatical too. He spent entirely too much time on that. . . . We were well aware of his foibles and what he was interested in and when we could get him off the track. But he gave a course that he called Greek Literature in English, and I absolutely devoured that course. It was all about the Greeks and their lives and mythology and so on, and it's one of the courses I remember to this day. I'm sure it had a great effect on me.[21]

Malone did not study any American history at Emory. Ironically, the only American history courses he took were later in graduate school. "But the classical atmosphere and the literary atmosphere were real at Emory, and it has affected me all my life."[22]

Because Malone was so young when he arrived at Emory, one of the most important aspects of his education involved meeting and learning to live with other students. He played center on his class football team and gained much experience from "just knocking up against the other boys."[23] There was a great emphasis on social relationships in those days, Malone recalled:

> I don't know exactly how to say this, but being liked by your fellows was extremely important. When I first went to Yale, I was struck by the different emphasis among students. The great thing at Yale was to achieve something, extracurricular or anywhere, make the *Yale News* or something. Being liked was important but not emphasized. I know it was terribly important for us at Emory. That was the only question: Is he a nice guy? Do you like him?[24]

Malone would find this of use in his later approach to biography.

> You know, that carries on into the life of Thomas Jefferson too. It was a very important consideration in trying to understand him, particularly in his relations with John Adams. The New Englander and the Southerner. The old New England tradition is one of plain speech . . . to make people like you, in a way, is a weakness. The way we were brought up in the South, though, it was very important to have people like you, and the worst thing in the world was to hurt somebody's feelings unnecessarily.[25]

Malone understood a great many things about Jefferson for this particular reason. For example, Jefferson hated to argue. John Adams did not hate it at all. "And what some of Jefferson's enemies used to call hypocrisy was really just his old Southern way of trying to be agreeable," Malone wrote. "I hope it still exists. It's so important. It can be a handicap, but it can also be a great asset."[26] That sentiment would carry on throughout

Malone's personal and professional life. He liked most people he met, and he especially came to like newspaper reporters. He once told an academic friend years later that "the most interesting people I knew in Washington were journalists."[27]

In 1982 Malone gave a speech in which he said honor societies such as Phi Beta Kappa did not exist at Emory when he attended. Emory was "a country college, with fewer than 300 students." He was elected to membership in Phi Beta Kappa as an alumnus in 1930. "That was lucky for me. I am sure they did not pay much attention to my old undergraduate record. I was too busy exploring life to do full justice to my studies."[28]

Halley's Comet caused a sensation in 1910. It completed its circuit every seventy-six years and would not be seen again until 1986. One night Malone and a few college friends watched the dazzling celestial phenomenon with its brilliant tail extending across the heavens. This was the same comet that had flashed alarmingly across the sky late in the year 1606, when the Jamestown settlers were preparing to embark from London for Virginia. Such an omen in that era was supposed to be ominous in the extreme.

Perhaps Halley's Comet was a portent of Malone's future brilliant career. But when he graduated as the youngest member of the class of 1910, he "was otherwise undistinguished."[29] In that same year Harvard graduated one of its most famous classes, which included the likes of T. S. Eliot, Walter Lippmann, John Reed, Heywood Broun, and Hamilton Fish. Eventually, Malone would surpass them all in a singular, towering achievement in history.

Malone spent the next several years teaching at small country schools in Georgia, including his father's college in Cuthbert. The 1912 catalog for Andrew College listed Malone as a mathematics and Bible instructor. The next year he taught Bible and history and served as secretary of the faculty. "My first position was that of teacher of the eighth grade in a small town school," he later wrote. "I had more disciplinary problems than I ever met with elsewhere, but I liked my work from the beginning. In fact, I had found my calling."[30]

In his spare time, Malone would spend a nickel and go to the newly invented "moving picture show." The films were silent and so were accompanied by a woman playing the piano. Another nickel would buy some peanuts or candy. Mary Pickford, Pearl White, House Peters, and Charlie Chaplin were among Malone's matinee idols.

In 1960, when he was invited back to the fiftieth reunion of his graduating class at Emory, Malone wrote a warm and personal note to the sponsor: "My mind often turns back to the old days in Oxford and the friends of my youth. I hardly need to tell you how sad it makes me to think that so many of them have gone." In the letter Malone gave a brief summary of his life as he saw it:

> This particular information may be of no interest to the class. On the more personal side, I have two children and one grandchild, a granddaughter. I hope that you will recall that I am the youngest member of the Class of 1910. I have bought a little house here where I should be glad to see any of my old friends who happen to come this way. I spend my summers in Cape Cod at West Falmouth, Massachusetts in an old house which has been in my wife's family for generations. . . . So far as I can judge, I am in very good health. My hair is white, but I still have a good deal of it, at any rate. Thanks to the diligence of my wife, who watches my diet very carefully, I am not particularly fat.[31]

Malone loved to teach, and it became obvious to him at a young age this was his true passion. He decided to focus his studies on the history of his native region and on the historic experiences of southerners. But before he could pursue this, the Great War interrupted his plans.

4   A Marine

You went to Parris Island as a boy—three months later,
you were a man.
                    —EDWARD A. LEAKE, FORMER MARINE, KOREA[1]

It is a fundamental responsibility for stronger people to
protect and defend those who cannot or will not defend
themselves. The best place to do that is the Marine Corps.
The Corps is always the first, and this is where I belong.
                    —MARINE CORP RECRUIT[2]

After graduating from Emory, Malone was uncertain of his future, but his family generally assumed that he would become a teacher or professor. Following his stint at Andrew College, he accepted a job at Randolph-Macon Woman's College in Lynchburg, Virginia, where he taught biblical literature for a year in 1914. This institution became the first women's college in the South to have standards comparable to those of an all-male college. Two of Malone's sisters graduated from Randolph-Macon years later. While he was there, Malone had total academic freedom and immensely enjoyed teaching, but he began to doubt whether he should further pursue knowledge in the field of religion.

Having taught for several years, Malone ventured north to Yale Divinity School to study theology. To a young southerner, Yale was liberating, religiously and in every other way. "In the free air of a great university," Malone wrote in his unfinished memoir, "I gained intellectual independence."[3] He earned his BD in 1916 and then thought seriously about continuing at Yale Divinity School for his doctorate.[4]

"I thought about working in the field of religion, but I ended up not being able to accept the whole body of the doctrines of the church," Malone explained. "It would have been impossible. I could have been a religious scholar, but the thing I finally concluded that I wanted to work at was the history of my own country. There's something in one of Jefferson's comments, where he says there are some things beyond human comprehension. In a way, I gave up struggling with the deepest mysteries of human life and turned to something I could handle. In history, you're dealing with concrete reality."[5]

Even though Malone could not accept strictly orthodox theology, his ethical standards did not change. He disliked "the immorality of this age. I think I could say that, like Mr. Jefferson, I've sought to guide my life by the teachings of Jesus," Malone wrote. "On the whole I agree that it's the greatest body of ethics that was ever promulgated. Mr. Jefferson thought the trouble with churches is that they weren't religious enough. They deviated from the teachings of Jesus, and they put in a whole lot that he never had. He wanted to go back to the original, and that in effect is what I did."[6]

Yet, his years at Yale had taught Malone to abhor the provincialism associated with the Deep South in the early twentieth century. Thus, even before World War I, he decided a career in theology was not for him—he wanted to go into history and would do it as a southerner. Malone saw history as an exercise in empathy. He felt that the South had a feeling about history because it "did something to them. They are aware of history. I taught Southern history . . . at Columbia . . . and somehow I always thought I could understand the problems of my own people better if I studied their history." In fact, he often confessed that "all southerners resent external criticism"—so who better to write history than one who could empathize with the South.[7]

Malone recalled early teaching experiences at Yale and Randolph-Macon: "There is always some imperfection, something wrong with something you do, or some lack of responsiveness on the part of the class. Always imperfect. You cast your bread upon the waters and you don't know what's coming back."[8]

He enjoyed teaching undergraduates immensely, more so than graduate students: "You have to know your stuff a lot better with graduate students.

They have other professors, and they know what they're saying, so you have to keep up. And yet undergraduates are more spontaneous and come out with what they really think." He went on to say, "You know the old saying: The professor came into the room and said, 'Good morning.' The undergraduates said, 'Good morning,' and the graduates wrote it in their notebooks. I don't think this ever happened to me, however, and my relations with my graduate students were very gratifying."[9]

Malone's lifelong passion for writing blossomed at Yale. "I knew I liked to write before I began my dissertation, but I became more aware of it at that time," Malone confirmed. "But writing has never ceased to be hard work. You can't have the unalloyed pleasure of just doing research. When you sit down to write, you just have to do it."[10]

World War I began in 1914 and quickened the budding historian's interest in public affairs. He later wrote, "I began to think that the hope of mankind lay in a wider knowledge and better understanding of human history."[11]

"Some dammed foolish thing in the Balkans," German chancellor Otto von Bismarck remarked on the incident that ignited World War I.[12] In August 1914 three field armies, sixteen army corps, thirty-seven divisions, 700,000 men wheeled through Belgium and marched on Paris. This tidal wave of men, horses, artillery, and carts cascaded down the dusty roads of northern France, sweeping implacably toward its goal of seizing the city and ending the war in the West, just as the kaiser's generals had planned.

The war upset Dumas Malone's academic plans but broadened his spiritual horizon. Leaving Yale in 1917, he enlisted in the Marine Corps, and after officer's training, he accepted a commission as a second lieutenant. Malone always emphasized that serving in the Marines altered a life he described as having previously been "sheltered." The war instilled within him a profound sense of history, and afterward he began to vigorously pursue the study of history. His decision to become a marine had answered his inner call.

Malone served in the Army YMCA at Camp Wheeler, Georgia, for a few weeks before enlisting with the Marines. "The vigorous outdoor life did me a lot of good," he recalled. He stayed at Camp Wheeler for nine days before he was assigned to a unit and shipped out. "Then I enlisted in the

Marine Corps," Malone reported, "and was shipped to Parris Island. I did not realize what I was getting into. In retrospect, I am glad that I made this decision."[13]

Malone became one of 4,500 recruits who struggled to survive the sweltering heat and further regimented training at the Marine Corps Recruit Depot, Parris Island, South Carolina. Referred to as Marine Boot Camp for decades, Parris Island was the first step in a three-month process that Malone had to endure before earning the title of marine. Whereas the other services provided recruits with shorter initial regimens or "basic military training," Malone underwent something more akin to a rite of passage. He soon realized that every marine was trained for combat (thus the motto "Every Marine a Rifleman") because the marines were often the first element of any major attack.[14]

The night he arrived at Parris Island, Malone rode into a spooky world full of biting gnats and even meaner drill instructors, who screamed so hard they lost their voices. Malone, along with five hundred other Marine recruits, took the train to a remote siding in the South Carolina low country at Yemassee. A tugboat and barge bore them to Parris Island, where they were herded into the quarantine station, a few rows of tents in the sand dunes. There Malone surrendered his civilian clothing and was issued utilities, pajamas, a cot, and blankets.[15]

From the time he was driven onto the base, Malone was told to keep his head down and eyes closed. The less the recruits knew about the base's layout, the less likely they were to try to escape. Malone pulled up in front of the recruit receiving building, unmistakable for the seventy-two pairs of yellow footprints painted on the asphalt outside. On those outlines they would stand in their first formation. It was 2:30 a.m. on Wednesday, and a staff sergeant was the drill instructor on duty. A barrel-chested marine with a thick Spanish accent and a flat-brimmed ranger hat perched on his crew cut, he looked as though he had come straight out of central casting. He bounded to Malone's bus to greet about forty recruits in T-shirts and jeans.[16]

"Let's go!" he screamed. "Get on the yellow footprints! Fast! Fast! Get on my yellow prints!" Instructed to keep his shoulders back and chest out, Malone listened intently to the drill instructor's speech. "You have taken a first step to become a member of the world's finest fighting force, the U.S. Marines," he shouted. He instructed Malone on military laws he must now obey; disrespect through words, gestures, or facial expressions would not be tolerated. "You will now become a team. You will train as a team. The word 'I' will no longer exist in your vocabulary. You will now refer to yourselves as 'this recruit.'"[17]

Just after 3 a.m., the drill instructor marched Malone and his unit into the building through the heavy silver hatches, which he said went only one-way—in. Then they were sent to a long wall with a row of phones, and each made the mandatory call home, following a script posted above the phones. It was a one-way conversation: "This is recruit [state your name]. I have arrived safely at Parris Island. Do not send any food or bulky items. I will contact you within 3 to 5 days via postcard with my address. Bye."[18]

Then it was into the barber chair, where a civilian sheared Malone's head like a sheep, down to the skin. His college degree from Emory seemed a distant memory. The genteel southern boy was tested for mental aptitude and physical condition, received a uniform, and had his first taste of military chow. In their first physical test, the men dropped their trousers for what the medical detachment called the "short physical inspection"—an examination of the genitals, a practice dating back to the Spanish-American War. To determine whether soldiers had contracted venereal disease, the examination was repeated whenever a soldier reported to a new post. Next, Malone was subjected to a lecture on sexual morality, which the doctor summed up with such witticisms as "Flies spread disease, so keep yours buttoned up."

The Marine Corps was also concerned about a soldier's feet. Shoes were fitted with care, sometimes under the supervision of an officer with an X-ray machine. Soldiers often tried shoes on while carrying two buckets of sand, to ensure the best fit. This was before mechanization, when the American military still moved on its feet. Then came the shots, the legendary injections that Marines referred to as the hook. These were the first in a series that Malone had to endure throughout basic training—they started with smallpox and typhoid inoculations.

The recruits' pajamas were sent home, and they went to bed Marine-style, wearing just underwear. Adaptation to this stark life was easier back in the early 1900s, as the Marines offered many things that civilian life did not. At least a third of the nation lived in homes that lacked central heat and running water. The barracks offered both. The military offered three meals a day, shelter, and clothing. Some of the recruits from the Deep South reported in bare feet. A Texas farm boy saw another advantage to life in the service: "I like the Army fine so far," he wrote home. "They let you sleep to 5:30."[19]

Six days after Malone checked in at Parris Island, he marched with others from quarantine to the supply depot, where he drew his uniform and equipment, shouldered his sea bag, and marched to his new camp by the maneuver grounds. That night he was issued a rifle, an M1903 Springfield. He spent hours cleaning and oiling the weapon. By daylight the next morning, Malone had finished breakfast, tried on his uniform, policed his camp, and reported to the parade ground. There, he and the other men formed companies.[20]

Malone spent twelve weeks without a single cigarette, a can of soda, or the sound of a radio. He trudged forty-two miles in two days while shouldering a full rucksack and Springfield rifle. It was a fifty-four-hour exercise that included just a few hours for sleep and four meals to sustain him. Once a week there was a sunset parade, and on Saturday morning the commanding general, Gen. Jack Myers, a Medal of Honor winner from the siege of Peking, conducted an inspection. Through the weeks of training, Malone learned one song, "The Long Last Mile." The words were drilled into his mind as he sang and jogged on marches:

> *Oh, they put me in the army and they handed me a pack,*
> *They took away my nice new clothes and dolled me up in kack;*
> *They marched me twenty miles a day to fit me for the war,*
> *I didn't mind the first nineteen but the last one made me sore.*

Malone's training at boot camp lasted for two months and was followed by two weeks on the rifle range, where an instructor stood over him with a swagger stick. On a different part of Parris Island, Malone worked on the Marines' core trade: shooting the Browning rifle. All Marine recruits, regardless of what job they ended up with, spent three weeks mastering the rifle. In contrast, the Army gave all soldiers only a week of rifle training, although those in the infantry also received advanced training.[21]

Malone lay on the ground and rehearsed shooting from the prone position. With each shot, he marked down where he thought the bullet would hit the target five hundred yards away; then he waited until a recruit behind a bunker circled the bullet hole and raised the target again. When he missed his mark, the drill instructor rapped a stick hard on his head. Malone then trained on the bayonet field, where big signs read, "Advance to Kill!"

At Parris Island, Malone met men from all over the country, not just from southwestern Mississippi or rural Georgia. When he was shipped out, the Marines split up boys from the same town, so that if something should happen to the ship, one town would not be emotionally devastated. This procedure was the result of the sinking of the *Lusitania*.[22]

Service rivalries aside, Marine boot camp was generally accepted as being harder than Air Force, Army, or Navy training. It was three weeks longer than the Army's training. Its physical standards were stiffer, and its drill instructors were legendary. "I was subjected to a considerable amount of unaccustomed discomfort if not of actual hardship," Malone later recalled with characteristic modesty. "The vigorous outdoor life did me a lot of good, however. I was no special object of the wrath of our irascible drill sergeant." Malone remembered his drillmaster to be excellent, and he had great respect for the training he received, "but Parris Island was a place that everybody was glad to get away from."[23]

Volumes about boot camp experiences at Parris Island are in the Marine Corps' archives and published books. Malone recalled that if you enlisted in the service west of the Mississippi River, you were sent to San Diego, California. Parris Island graduates sarcastically called San Diego boot camp graduates "Hollywood Marines," which often started fisticuffs.[24]

Malone wrote in his memoir,

> I felt like a square peg in a round hole or a round peg in a square hole, and when I had time to think, I wondered if I could not have found a way to serve my country more effectively. After the weather warmed up, I was assigned a task which I regarded as being in my particular competence: I was set to work drilling recruits. I was myself awkward at the Manual of Aras, but I was an experienced teacher. The hard-boiled sergeant who was in charge of this operation put the fear of God into the minds of the recruits but left virtually all of that drilling to me.

Malone never forgot the sergeant who continued to sleep in the barracks, even though he had a little tent in the camp with the recruits. "They visited me at night and told about themselves. It was a memorable experience, of which I wish I had kept a better record."[25]

At the end of it, Malone went to Officers Training Camp at Quantico, Virginia, from which he emerged a second lieutenant. "I was not good at anything except the written tests we took once a week, which I found very easy. We led a tough life, but I look back on it with real pleasure. It was a vigorous and healthy life," he observed.[26]

In fact, Malone felt he had gained a great deal of experience, especially in the matter of human relations. "I had always liked people, but I had lived a relatively sheltered and restricted life. I had not been associated with such a variety of persons as I met in the Marine Corps. I had never known anybody like the old-time sergeant, *Pop*, with whom I made friends in Officers' Training Camp. He was probably the most profane man in [the] platoon, and was certainly one of the most generous."[27]

In later years Malone did a good deal of boasting about having been in the Marine Corps. He believed that if he could survive the Marines, he "could get along with anybody . . . about anything."[28] Malone's military experience was both toughening and humanizing. Later, he often saw his "greatest achievement," his Pulitzer Prize notwithstanding, as having made second lieutenant in the Marines. Perhaps it explained his tenacity and endurance in studying "Mr. Jefferson" over the next forty years.

"Having lived the sheltered life of a Southern clergyman's son, it was a crazy thing to do," he remembered. "It was tough, being thrown into the middle of that, but I became awfully fond of those vile talking fellows. Wouldn't trade it for anything. Never got to France. But I've never felt any trouble getting along with any person ever since."[29] Malone's son, Gifford, proudly recalled seeing his father's Marine uniform hang in the attic, two silver bars adorning the crisp suit.

After twelve weeks of training, Malone graduated from Parris Island. He had matured beyond his years and was anxious, but ready to go to Europe and serve his country. But he never had the chance.

After a brief stint at the Philadelphia Naval Yard ("where I did guard duty during what I remember as a very cold winter"), in December 1918, Malone became a second lieutenant, from Company B Officers Training Camp, Marine Barracks, Quantico, Virginia. According to his military records, he was mustered out of the Marines in January 1919 while attached to the 187th Company, Fifteenth Regiment.[30]

"The war ended too soon for me to have much time as an officer," Malone said. "We led a tough life, but I look back on it with real pleasure." He was on duty with the Fifteenth Regiment at Quantico when he was discharged. He had no job to return to, but his desire to acquire knowledge had increased rather than diminished during those months he had been deprived of reading.[31]

In the end, the Marines provided Malone with a searing set of personal experiences that shaped his basic outlook on the world. This was a good time to go back to school, he thought. "As soon as I got my discharge, I returned to Yale, to seek a doctor's degree in history. At that time, Thomas Jefferson was little more than a name to me, and he had no influence on my thinking in this particular matter." Instead of going to war, Malone returned to his true interest: academics. "The First World War may not have caused me to become a historian but it certainly provided the climate in which I became one."[32]

5   Brothers

I have just learned that my older brother Kemp is to be at
your university this year as a visiting professor of English.
He retired from Hopkins four or five years ago. . . .
He is much more learned than I.
> —DUMAS MALONE, 1963[1]

The relationship between Dumas and Kemp Malone, his oldest brother, was not always close, and in fact, in adult years they saw each other infrequently, recalled Dumas's son, Gifford Malone.

Born on March 14, 1889, in Minter, Mississippi, Kemp Malone was three years older than Dumas but died much earlier, in 1971 in Eastport, Maine. Author, editor, educator, and philologist, Kemp was a professor of English literature at Johns Hopkins University from 1926 to 1956. He wrote a number of scholarly books focusing on English language and literature, including *The Literary History of Hamlet* and *Chapters on Chaucer*. He was also a cofounder of the linguistics journal *American Speech* and a president of the Modern Language Association of America and the Linguistic Society of America.

Kemp received his BA from Emory University in 1907, three years before his younger brother. When he graduated from Emory at the age of eighteen, Kemp sometimes signed himself *R. K. Malone*. His full name, Raiford Kemp Malone, appeared only twice. Once was opposite his formal graduation portrait in the yearbook, published by the Pan Hellenic Council of Emory. The second were his initials below a Tennyson poem that he had contributed to that volume. Raiford was also the maiden name of Kemp's grandmother and a local surname of English origin, meaning "the Ford in the stream."[2]

After four years as a high school teacher, Kemp resumed graduate studies in Germany and Denmark before taking an appointment at Cornell in 1960. War service as a captain in the Army from 1917 to 1919 followed a year in Iceland, and another at Princeton before he moved to Minnesota in 1921. Called to Johns Hopkins in 1926, Kemp occupied the chair of the English Department there with distinction for thirty-two years. On his retirement in 1956, he became director of the Georgetown University language program, which took him to Ankara. He was a visiting professor at New York University in 1961 and Catholic University in 1966.

A career so brilliant could not fail to bring Kemp many honors. He was decorated by the Danish and Icelandic governments; he became a member of the Royal Danish Academy, a Guggenheim fellow, and a leading figure in many distinguished academic associations. After Kemp married Inez Chatain in 1927 in Richmond, Virginia, the couple became known for their annual Christmas cards, which they would send with graceful original poems.

The Malone brothers shared many traits and a subtle professional rivalry. Like his brother's, Kemp's scholarly activity was unremitting. At the time of his death, he was at work on the history of the English language. Unfortunately, he had written only a fifth of it by that time. It would be a mistake, however, to think that Kemp's life was all work and no play. He was a strong swimmer, and in his earlier days, he engaged in boxing. He enjoyed tennis and bridge, both of which he played well. He wrote unpretentious poetry, not just for the annual Christmas card. Kemp was an avid reader of mystery stories and science fiction, but above all, he loved music. During much of his life, Kemp played the violin and was accompanied by Inez on the piano. They had a box at the Lyric Theatre and attended many concerts there. A philologist seldom becomes rich in worldly goods, but if a full and happy life crowned by numerous professional awards was a reasonable goal, Kemp Malone attained it.[3]

In fact, Kemp Malone scholarships are still awarded at Emory University. Eventually, Kemp became known as the most distinguished American scholar focusing on Old English language and literature of his generation, and one of Emory's libraries is named after him—the Kemp Malone Library.

"My father certainly respected Kemp's academic achievements," Gifford Malone recalled.[4] It seems that even though the brothers were not emotionally close, Dumas always acknowledged Kemp's towering intellect. "You will understand of course that I have not such learning as Kemp had. As you might suppose, he was impressively learned, even in boyhood, and I found him quite overwhelming at times. However, he stimulated me no little, and I often wonder if, but for him, I would have been a scholar at all."[5] Gifford added, "As to any brotherly rivalry, I certainly never had any hint that in growing up my father regarded [Kemp] in that way. In fact, in talking about his boyhood my father did not talk much about Kemp."[6]

Gifford, who was married in 1958 and had a distinguished career in the Foreign Service and State Department, recalled that in the early years of the Malone family, Kemp was regarded as the born scholar, "born a PhD." But in adulthood the scholarly interests of Dumas and Kemp were very different. "For my father, his broad interest [was] in history and the importance of understanding history in order to understand society. Kemp's interest [was] in languages, especially old languages, Anglo-Saxon, early English and Icelandic. [This] was not something that my father could have conceived of devoting himself to," Gifford said.[7]

Gifford did not recall whether Kemp and Inez ever came to visit the Malones in Charlottesville. The only time he remembered seeing Kemp was once in New York, when Gifford was a college student and Kemp came to the family's apartment for dinner. "No doubt there were times when my parents did see him, but it was certainly infrequent," Gifford observed.

> I do recall once being invited, together with my wife, to have lunch with Kemp and Inez in Baltimore, not long after I had returned from our assignment in Moscow. We were living in Bethesda, probably 1967. We had a very pleasant time with them. I had the feeling that it was not only the fact that I was his nephew but that I had become proficient in the Russian language that aroused his interest. However . . . it was clear that he and my father did not often meet.[8]

Kemp died in Eastport, Maine, where he and Inez had a place and always spent the summer. The cause of his death was a massive stroke. He left no children. "Margaret and I were living in Poland at the time," Gifford remembered, "and I remember writing to Inez after I learned of [Kemp's] death. I don't recall my parents ever telling me that they attended his funeral, which was in Eastport. That, of course, would have been a major trip for them from Charlottesville."[9]

Kemp's influence on Dumas was profound in one respect: Malone's intense love of reading was directly related to his older brother's influence. "I followed the course of the Peloponnesian war under the guidance of my elder brother Kemp, who was a voracious reader," Malone wrote. "My brother, Kemp, set the pace for us in intellectual matters, and was on the way to taking a Ph.D. degree in English at the University of Chicago."[10]

Kemp apparently did not enjoy people as much as Dumas did and was sometimes dependent on his little brother in social matters. "But I supposed I would always be second to him in learning as I was in age," Malone wrote.[11]

Gifford's assessment of the brothers' relationship seems to be accurate as Kemp is mentioned only twice in Dumas's unfinished memoir. Moreover, in Kemp's will, probated by the law firm of Piper and Marbury on October 22, 1971, he left nothing to his brother Dumas but left his entire estate to his wife, Inez. Moreover, if Inez did not survive him by sixty days, he would "leave his estate to Eastport Memorial Hospital, certain friends and the balance of his estate to Emory University."[12]

In a letter to the editor of the *Baltimore Sun* on October 26, 1971, after Kemp's death, Charles Davis, the Malones' mailman, wrote,

> I sincerely wish to express my heartfelt condolences in this time of deep sorrow. These are not idle words, for in the 20 years since I began work in the post office, I have come to respect and admire the Malones. Many of my fellow workers and neighbors in Eastport share my feelings. The phrase gentleman scholar must've been coined with Kemp Malone in mind. . . . It epitomizes this great, kind and humane man perfectly. God will be most happy to welcome him in heaven this remarkable, humble man who contributed so much to the education of mankind.[13]

In 1975 Emory University received the majority of Kemp's vast library. In a letter to Kemp's widow, H. Prentice Miller, the president of the Alumni Association, wrote, "My dear Inez, as I'm sure that you've already heard that Kemp's books and other possessions arrived in perfect order on Monday. Again, we at Emory will be forever grateful to you for this magnificent and incomparable gift to Emory."[14]

In a letter to Dumas Malone, Judson C. Ward Jr., executive president of Emory University, described the day that Kemp's books were received and the library was named for him:

> Saturday was a beautiful day here at Emory. Despite the unusually cold winter, spring is on schedule and dogwood and azaleas and redbud and flowering fruit trees are decked out in all their glory. As you know, we've been working with Mrs. Kemp Malone for the past three years to bring your brother's library here. On Saturday morning we had a ceremony in which the president and the department of English acknowledged the gift and tried to thank Mrs. Malone for it. She made a delightful little speech which charmed the crowd of 75 or more, who assembled in the rare book room of the Woodruff Memorial Library for the opening formalities. All in all it was a delightful affair with many members of the family present and also . . . the chairman of English from Virginia and Vanderbilt.[15]

Malone wrote back commenting, "It was certainly good of you to send me such a full account of the dedication of the Kemp Malone Library. Reading your letter was the next best thing to being there. I wish I could've attended, but I did not learn about it in time to make the necessary plans and would've had great difficulty in coming anyway. Getting around has become something of an ordeal now that I have so much trouble with my eyes."[16]

Malone also corresponded with Inez:

> I am deeply disappointed at my inability to attend the dedication of Kemp's library on Saturday. I shall greatly miss seeing all of you. If I had known longer I might have been able to arrange it, though it would have been difficult in any case. I am recovered from the attack of pneumonia I had last winter but my eyesight is so poor that in recent years I've never traveled alone. Pam has had a tough winter, and has a badly swollen hand as a result of arthritis. She could not well make the trip and Elisabeth is loaded with commitments at this season.[17]

"I hope the library will be an inspiration to young scholars," instructed Mrs. Malone as she handed copies of her husband's first published work—and his last—to President Sanford Soverhill Atwood. Professor Malone's career proved Emory was producing excellence when the class of 1907 came along, Atwood noted, and his life was an inspiration to scholars. He said he felt great libraries would be built in the future by gifts such as that from the Malones.[18]

Kemp was eighty-two years old when he died and was buried in Baltimore at the old St. Paul's Episcopal Church at Saratoga and Charles streets. At the time of his death, Kemp was working on the history of the English language for Random House and was preparing to fly home from Maine at the end of the summer. Inez recalled that Kemp had a slight stroke and fainting spell. "We got into the hospital and it was followed by another [stroke]."[19]

Kemp authored more than five hundred scholarly works and was an unceasing student who had an enthusiasm for the English language. The eldest of the three sons and four daughters of a college Latin professor, Kemp had a bookish environment all his life. In fact, he had never lived out of it.

6   Yale

One of the saddest things about the academic life is the very fleeting contact between teacher and pupil. As you know, I am no longer teaching. The loss to the world is to be regretted!

—DUMAS MALONE, WRITING TO
A FORMER STUDENT, 1963[1]

On sight, I liked Professor Malone and judged him to be a kindly man. At the end of the first session of the class, I judged him to be a good teacher.
—FORMER STUDENT OF MALONE'S, 1958[2]

Dumas Malone enrolled in Yale to pursue his PhD in history after his discharge from the Marines in 1919. He could not possibly have known that fifty-two years later, he would be honored with the Yale's highest award for scholarship, the Wilbur L. Cross Medal, for his "varied career [as] a great humanist, as editor, teacher and scholar. . . . Your scholarship has now made you the instructor of all Americans who would learn of the values and virtues, the failures and successes of the founding fathers."[3]

When Malone first arrived, Yale's central campus covered 310 acres stretching from the School of Nursing in downtown New Haven to residential neighborhoods around the Divinity School. Yale's 260 buildings included contributions from architects of every period in its history, ranged from New England Colonial to High Victorian Gothic. Yale's buildings, towers and arches composed what one architect called "the most beautiful urban campus in America."[4]

It was here that Dumas Malone's academic and teaching career blossomed. He saw firsthand how Yale college transformed itself by the establishment of residential colleges. Taking medieval English universities such as Oxford as its model, Yale divided the undergraduate population into twelve separate communities, enabling the university to offer its students both the intimacy of a small college and the resources of a major university. Each college surrounded a courtyard, providing a collegial community where residents live, eat, and socialize. Every college also had a master and dean, as well as resident faculty members known as fellows.[5]

Malone entered Yale as a graduate student in history. His tuition was three hundred dollars a year. Room and board added another five hundred dollars a year. (Sixty years later, the total came to $34,350.) When he had writing to do, Malone filled his fountain pen from an inkwell. Telephone calls cost a nickel. If he had a letter to mail, he used a two-cent stamp. Special delivery cost ten cents. When he was sick, a doctor would make a house call but could not prescribe penicillin, which hadn't been discovered. Newspapers cost two cents and often came twice a day. The Sunday edition of the *New York Times* cost ten cents.[6]

In his early days, Malone was most eager to explore the field of religion. It was with a view to doing this that he attended the Yale Divinity School. "This was the first time I ever left the deep South for an extended period," Malone recalled. "My stay at Yale was a liberating and enriching experience."[7]

In the society and family in which Malone had grown up, religion was predominantly evangelical and theology was fundamental. "There was a good deal of anti-intellectualism," he wrote. Christian doctrine and the sacred scriptures were supposed to be accepted on faith with no regard for the discoveries of modern science and the dictates of human reason. At Yale, however, Malone was able to study these concepts with an open and critical mind. In the free air of a great university, Malone "attained intellectual independence."[8]

At this stage the future historian did not anticipate that his exploration of religion would peak his interest in history. He later admitted, "I did take some steps in that direction. My approach to the study of religious institutions and doctrines was essentially historical and the courses in church history were particularly illuminating."[9]

Malone, by no means, became anticlerical. In fact, he took his Holy Confirmation at the Trinity Church in New Haven on April 2, 1922. While in Washington, during his later years at the *Dictionary of American Biography*, he worshipped at Georgetown's Presbyterian Church. He wrote the pastor, "Just a line to tell you what a delight it was to attend services at your church on Sunday. . . . Elisabeth's comment on the service was that she had rarely attended one that was marked with so much vitality. It is obvious you are doing wonderful work in your parish."[10]

But Malone did draw a line in his scholarship between personal and organized religion. While at Yale, he first became aware of the historical opposition of the Christian church to advances in science thesis and knowledge.

Malone performed his teaching assignment tasks well enough to be appointed, and then reappointed, an instructor of history in 1919. He was assigned to a general course in American history required for sophomores and designated as History B-2. Malone recalled,

> I began teaching American history as an instructor at Yale the year after the First World War. A professor had resigned in the middle of the summer, [so] they had to bring someone in and my friend Ralph Gabriel suggested me. I would teach the antebellum South. In the case of the Yale students, I had to try to get them to understand more about it. I told them, "I am Southern." I needed to show them what was good about it. Down here, it was entirely different. I loved to teach, and I thought I was going to be an undergraduate teacher all my life.[11]

At the time, Malone's friend Dr. Ralph Gabriel was the Sterling Professor of History at Yale and had developed a pioneering course in American thought and civilization. A native of Reading, New York, he became a member of the university's faculty in 1915 and stayed at Yale until he retired in 1958. The course that gained Gabriel prominence, which he initiated in 1931, stressed the systematic study of the history of the viewpoints of American writers, scholars, statesmen, and reformers.

Gabriel was in charge of the course Malone was initially assigned, and Malone credited him with keeping the novice professor's head above water.

It was about all I could do to keep ahead of the students. We had specific assignments then, much more than now. We gave a little time to the colonial period, but we really got started with the American Revolution. We assigned the account of the Revolution in W. E. H. Lecky's *History of England in the Eighteenth Century*, a British work. It was an interesting experience, using that book. It was just after the war, and the British had been our allies. It was a wonderful experience for a young American to discuss the causes of the Revolution and to try to be fair to the British.[12]

One of the other books assigned in the course Malone taught was Henry Cabot Lodge's biography of Alexander Hamilton. Malone recalled, "The students generally reacted against the extreme Federalism of this author without any prodding from me."[13]

Malone did most of his graduate work while he was teaching. He earned his master's degree in 1921 and his doctorate in 1923, both in history. He sought a PhD because he had to have a union card to teach in college. At this point, though, he did not think much about being a professional scholar. He wrote,

I am sure I didn't know much about research, but I found, to my great surprise, that historical research was a great deal of fun. I never got over that feeling. I think historical research is one of the most interesting activities men have ever found. I think when I did research on my dissertation I must have done a lot of analyzing as I went along because I wrote it very fast, in about three months. Now it would take three or four years.[14]

Malone looked back on those days in the manuscript room of the Library of Congress where he could read both a volume of Jefferson's papers and a corresponding volume of Madison's papers. Malone often confirmed that he had lived through great events with great men. He looked back on those hours in the Libraries at Yale, the University of Virginia, and the Library of Congress as "delightful." Later he explained,

You see, I could just explore, and it may be that I hadn't been there before. It was a great experience. I knew I liked to write before I began my dissertation, but I became more aware of it at that time. But writing has never ceased to be hard work. You can't have the unalloyed pleasure of just doing research. When you sit down to write, you just have to do it. I think when you get to a point, you don't get much better in writing. But there never comes a time when you don't learn things you ought and ought not to do. Little fine points. I go back and look at early writings and find things I wouldn't say now.[15]

At Yale, Malone found genuine intellectual freedom. It may have been during this period that he realized that he could maintain freedom of mind more easily in a university setting than anywhere else. Malone studied much harder than he had as an undergraduate and became more confident in his ability to make his way in the world of learning. "I took several courses in Yale College, including one in the history of philosophy. But I was relatively indifferent to formal philosophy, as I was to systematic theology," he declared. "The courses in church history were interesting though disillusioning. My Biblical studies were richly rewarding. I wrote a thesis on the controversy between Jesus and the Pharisees. Perhaps it can be regarded as my first serious historical study."[16]

The teachings of Jesus made an indelible impression on the young Malone, but in the end, he decided to devote his professional life to the study and teaching of history, rather than religion. Malone's own religious views were not unlike Jefferson's. Malone had gradually arrived at the conclusion that divinity, "like eternity and infinity, was beyond the reach of my mind. I could not fathom the nature of God or the meaning of the universe. I had to settle for humanity. So I turned to history, which deals with people and their affairs, which is the record of human experience. I've had a wonderful time working in this rich human field and have never regretted having chosen it," he wrote.[17]

Under Professor Allen Johnson's tutelage, Malone wrote a doctoral dissertation titled "The Public Life of Thomas Cooper, 1783–1839," which won the John Addison Porter Prize in 1923.[18] The strong points of Malone's future work were all foreshadowed in this dissertation, which was published as his first book in 1926. Cooper, "an exceedingly interesting person," a professor of chemistry, and the president of South Carolina College, had been a supporter of Thomas Jefferson's and a longtime correspondent with him on scholarly and educational subjects. "The first time I ever looked into the Jefferson papers in the Library of Congress was when I was seeking to uncover his [letters] with Cooper," Malone wrote.[19]

Malone concentrated on Cooper's public life as a supporter of the Jeffersonian opposition to the Federalists because that was the area for which the records existed. He found that many of the records concerning Cooper's childhood and early life had been destroyed by fire during the Civil War. In both this work and his later Jefferson biography, he avoided describing events and people about which he had no documentary evidence because he felt attempting to do so would be wrong. Malone used this approach throughout his career. He always worked exhaustively with recorded information and refused to speculate without concrete data.[20]

The Public Life of Thomas Cooper, 1783–1839, bore evidence of Malone's background and interests. Cooper was involved in "many important political, economic and intellectual movements," and Malone skillfully described his subject's actions. The work was an impartial appraisal of Cooper's life and contributions to humanity. Malone did not criticize Cooper for his liberal religious attitudes or controversial political ideas but instead emphasized his close association with education.

Besides presenting a balanced appraisal of his subject's public life, Malone utilized his most important contribution to the art of biography: he depicted the subject within his own time period and did not judge him by present-day standards or beliefs. Throughout all Malone's works this approach stood out, but he was unable to employ it on his most challenging subject, Thomas Jefferson, until much later.[21]

By all accounts, Malone seemed content and happy at Yale, but "I expected to return to the South in due course and to spend the rest of my life there teaching history to young southerners and hoping they would heed its lessons." In December 1922 a fateful breakfast meeting took place in the mezzanine of the Hotel Taft in New Haven. The stately University of Virginia president, Edwin Alderman, sought to steer Malone back "home." He offered Dumas Malone an "unusual opportunity" that would propel him into "one of the happiest periods of my personal and professional life at Mr. Jefferson's University."[22]

7 Along the Lawn

*I loved the Academical Village and the beautiful
countryside of Albemarle. . . . I had never ceased hoping
that one day I would be able to return to . . . my
academic home.*

—Dumas Malone[1]

*I would venture to guess if a person came to the University
of Virginia for four years, lived on the Lawn, stayed in
the library, made frequent visits to Monticello . . . read
these men . . . and sat on the steps of the rotunda and
saw the golden sunlight hit the lawn, he or she would be
educated.*

—Professor Joseph L. Vaughan, UVA[2]

Edwin Anderson Alderman's and Dumas Malone's lives intersected at the American Historical Association in New Haven, Connecticut, in December 1922. Malone was interviewing for a new position at the University of Virginia. These two southern gentlemen and scholars, although of different generations, charmed each other. Alderman had a marvelous sense of humor, Malone recalled, and "I liked him from the start." Malone took up his duties as associate professor of history the succeeding fall. "I fell in love with Jefferson's 'Academical Village' at first sight and was very much at home in his country from the beginning," Malone recalled in his memoir.[3]

Alderman interviewed Malone in the mezzanine of the Hotel Taft, diagonally across the street from the building (now destroyed) where Malone had taught his Yale history classes. About the occasion, Malone wrote, "I was much impressed by that stately Southern gentlemen and most interested in the position he wanted to fill." Malone recalled that he was overawed by Alderman, but "he liked me well enough to invite me to visit Mr. Jefferson's University that spring and to offer me a post on its faculty." President Alderman was a major influence on Malone, and he thought so highly of Alderman that he wrote a highly praised biography of the university's first president years later.[4]

Malone remembered Alderman as a "fascinating man." He was a great orator, not in the flamboyant style but almost conversational. Malone recalled that Alderman delivered a memorial address on Woodrow Wilson, and he obtained a ticket to the event for Malone. Everyone was there, he recorded, including the president and some members of Congress.[5]

Six months before Thomas Jefferson died on July 4, 1826, a young man enrolled in the former president's newly formed "Academical Village." His name was Edgar Allan Poe.

Located near the village of Charlottesville, sixty miles from Richmond, the school lay in a verdant basin between the Southwest Mountains and the Blue Ridge. The university had opened only the year before, in 1825, the fulfillment of forty years' thought and planning by its eighty-three-year-old rector, Thomas Jefferson.

Jefferson once wrote that "nothing more than education advances the prosperity, the power, and the happiness of a nation," and his university was often said to be the most beautiful institution of higher learning in America.[6] The architectural genius of Thomas Jefferson flowered in this last work of his life. He drew inspiration from Greek and Roman prototypes and from the work of the great Italian architect Palladino. The central core of the buildings—the Rotunda, Lawn, and ranges—stand today almost exactly as they did in Jefferson's time.

The Rotunda, modeled after the Roman Pantheon, is at the head of the rectangular Lawn, a lovely stretch of green bordered by trees. Five two-story pavilions, no two of them alike and each illustrating a famous classical structure, stand on each side of the Lawn. The pavilions contain lodgings for professors above and classrooms beneath. They are linked together by long, low rows of small, one-story rooms for students. White columns comple-ment the redbrick buildings. Paralleling these structures, but separated from them by gardens, are the East Range and the West Range, which provide additional quarters for students. Their counterparts are the East Lawn and the West Lawn. In modern terminology, it is "the Grounds," never the cam-pus, and the "G" is always capitalized.[7]

By Jefferson's plan, the faculty in 1826 consisted of eight professors, each heading a school. Edgar Allan Poe enrolled in the School of Ancient Languages, taught by Cambridge Master of Arts George Long, and the School of Modern Languages, taught by the German George Blaettermann, a handsome, curly haired man, careless in dress and appearance. Poe joined the Jefferson Society, a debating club, and acted for a while as its secretary. It was said that he "grew noted as a debater." Unfortunately, Poe lasted only a year at the university before he returned to Richmond.[8]

In 1923, when Malone arrived, Charlottesville had a population of about six thousand. Mud, dust, and wooden planks made up the streets. To get around, one would either take the jangling trolley car from downtown that terminated opposite the Rotunda or walk. Later, the trolley extended to a point beyond Rugby Road. In those days, walking for one's errands and excursions was typical. Some still used a surrey, pulled by a horse.

The University of Virginia in the 1920s was far different from what it is now or was even in the 1960s or 1970s. Nearly a century ago, there were fewer students and faculty, and they were more homogenous and more inti-mate. The boys were well groomed and wore coats and ties. Very few of the students were married, and the vast majority would not consider marriage until after graduation. Only a handful of undergraduates had automobiles, and the virtually all-male student body did not go away on weekends. In fact, according to a December 1963 issue of *The Cavalier Daily*, women were not allowed to walk on the Lawn until the 1920s. If he saw a woman, a male student would cry out, "Quail on the Lawn!"[9]

In 1923 Dumas Malone was encouraged by several scholars to enter aca-demia at the University of Virginia. Professor William Dodd at the University of Chicago wrote to Malone, "I'm glad you're going to Virginia. There's no better place in the country to do a great work in history. Virginia as a state is now taking a new turn in its attitude towards history and the University is the place for the leaders of the new movement to be. Do your very best, it is a great prospect."[10]

For more than twenty-five years thereafter, Malone had his office cloistered on the top floor at the Alderman Library. The library, a Works
Progress Administration project, was completed in 1938, and an addition
was built in the 1970s to contain the growing collections. In his office, hundreds of students visited the historian. When he first started teaching, professors and students tipped their hats to one another on the sidewalk, and
the students were deferential at all times. They wore white shirts and black
ties, a stylistic edict that came down from Malone's alma mater, Yale. It was
a truly different era.

"The university was a relatively small place when I first knew it," Malone
admitted. In fact, university dances in Malone's time and for many years
thereafter were held in the gymnasium and were "pledged." No student
could attend who had had a drink of anything alcoholic since noon of that
day. This pledge was observed 100 percent. If a student failed to obey the
pledge, it was an honor code violation, and the student would be subject
to permanent expulsion.

Richard Heath Dabney, father of Pulitzer Prize–winning journalist
Virginius Dabney, was the entire UVA history department until Malone
joined it.[11] Malone recalled that Dabney was a jovial man with a fine sense
of humor.[12] Standing five feet ten inches tall, Dabney was an imposing 170
pounds and "tough as a pine knot." His son Virginius recalled that when
Heath was fifty-six and Virginius was sixteen, they used to sweep snow from
the ice on the pond across from Rugby Road. Virginius thought he was in
good shape compared to his father, but Heath "just about ran me into the
ground as he brushed the snow from the glittering surface at a dizzy pace.
I ended with my tongue hanging out and he was not even out of breath,"
Dabney recalled.[13]

"The Dabneys were wonderful to me," Malone remembered. "Mrs.
Dabney [Lily Heath Dabney] was a grande dame, and she took me under
her wing as a young professor. She was my social arbiter, and I didn't dare
do anything she would disapprove of."[14]

Richard Heath Dabney, throughout his eighty-seven years of life, exhib-
ited the salient characteristics of the old-fashioned Virginian: chivalry, courtesy, and adherence to the principle of honor, which was paramount above

all. A man of personal charm, he had a profound influence on the young Malone. Dabney loved outdoor sports, Malone recalled, and was a good tennis and golf player. In addition, he was chess champion of the University of Virginia faculty. Dabney's musical talent was also considerable, and he wrote incisive prose and witty verse. One of Dabney's most dominant traits was his candor. Richard Heath would not remain silent when he felt that an overriding principle was at stake. On more than one occasion, he risked dismissal from the faculty because of his outspokenness.[15]

Dabney had been awarded his MA at the University of Virginia in 1881. At that time, the university's master's program was among the toughest anywhere. It required that the applicant take the highest class in each subject, with no electives. While at UVA, Dabney became an intimate friend of his fellow student, Woodrow Wilson, and got Wilson into his fraternity, Phi Kappa Psi. In a biography of Wilson years later, the author described Richard Heath Dabney as Wilson's best friend at the university. The two men remained on cordial terms, but Dabney saw little of Wilson after he entered the White House.

In fact, when Dabney thought he was about to be fired from Indiana University, he informed Woodrow Wilson of his apprehension. Wilson promptly wrote the University of Virginia, urging the university to prepare a place for Dabney to land, if the occasion should arise. It did not, but Dabney took an offered position on the faculty at Charlottesville in 1889, and his ambition became realized. He spent most of his life on the faculty, retiring at age seventy-eight.[16]

Malone remembered Dabney as an interesting and stimulating lecturer. He was also a no-nonsense taskmaster, but still kind, considerate, and understanding with a student who was willing to work. He never showed favoritism or passed a student who had not made the necessary grade. Once, a football star failed one of Dabney's history examinations and came to see his professor in a belligerent mood. When Dabney told him that he could not do anything about his grade, the gridiron hero threatened to "take it to the Dean." "Take it to the Dean and be hanged!" exclaimed Dabney. And that was the end of it.

Until Malone arrived, Dabney had a tremendous workload at the university; he had taught all the courses in history from 1889 to 1923. He had also taught all the economics courses for nine years (1897–1906) and served as dean of the graduate school for eighteen years. When Dabney reached the mandatory faculty retirement age of seventy, he duly submitted his resignation to President Alderman, who replied that he had no plan to accept it. So, Dabney continued to teach until he was seventy-eight.

Malone's fondness for the Dabneys was apparent. Years later, on Lily Dabney's ninety-fifth birthday, Malone and his wife, Elisabeth, gave her a party in their home. Malone offered the following toast to Mrs. Dabney, who had nurtured him when he was a young college professor:

> I claim the privilege of proposing a toast to our guest of honor. I do not emphasize the fact that this is her birthday, for in her case birthdays don't count. She has a spirit of eternal youth, and her joy in life has not diminished perceptibly with the passing years. She is the personal embodiment of the best traditions of this ancient Commonwealth. We salute her as a great lady and take this occasion to remind her that she is very dear to all of us. Let us drink to Mrs. Dabney.[17]

In Malone's second year of teaching, F. Stringfellow Barr, generally known as Winkie, added much color to a department that now numbered five. Because of its historic associations, the University of Virginia became a distinguished center of historical scholarship during Malone's tenure. Yet during his early years, Malone wrote, "A historian was greatly handicapped by the inadequacy of the library. That was handsomely overcome at a later time as I found when I came back to work on Thomas Jefferson." Malone credited Harry Clemons, with whom he worked on the Library Committee, for the library's major development. Malone paid grateful tribute to Clemons in the foreword of the history of the university library that he wrote years later.[18]

In 1975 Malone recalled,

> I first practiced the teacher's trade in a wing of the Rotunda that had been used for storing rifles during the First World War and had not been redecorated. I called the dismal place the "black hole of Calcutta." . . . President Alderman came strolling by . . . one day, tapping his cane on the concrete walk as he was wont to do. He took one look at the room and ordered it painted—it was soon thereafter in glaring white.[19]

In the mid-1920s, while teaching, Malone began to develop an interest in Jefferson. He was attracted by the idea of approaching history through biography, and under the circumstances, Jefferson seemed like the most challenging biographical subject available. In fact, Malone went to France on a fellowship in 1927 to examine Jefferson's life in that country, and he published his first article about Jefferson in the *Virginia Quarterly Review* in January 1931. By then, however, Allen Johnson, his old dissertation director at Yale, had wooed Malone to Washington, D.C., to work on the *Dictionary of American Biography*. And although Malone didn't know it at the time, a dozen years would pass before he returned in earnest to his study of the nation's third president.

Life along the Lawn in the 1920s was different from what it is now at the twenty-first century's UVA. In 1908, with the inauguration of Edwin Alderman, the university began to change, at first in small ways and later in larger ones. During Alderman's tenure, academic robes came into fashion at the university. Malone suggested that "the various doctors' hoods were described in local accounts in much the way that ladies dresses are in society columns."[20]

As president of the University of North Carolina, of Tulane, and of the University of Virginia, Alderman continued to proselytize for universal education. At the University of Virginia, one of his first achievements was the founding of the Curry Memorial School of Education, and ten years later, the building of Peabody Hall to house the school.[21]

Alderman also worked to extend higher education to women. He believed the state's failure to educate the "forgotten woman" was a gross failure of democracy. Under Alderman's leadership, women were first admitted to the university as degree candidates in 1920. By 1924, sixty-one women had enrolled at the university: two in law, seven in medicine, fourteen in graduate arts and sciences, thirty-six in education, and two in the college.[22]

Although he never enrolled in a doctoral program, Alderman was always addressed as "Dr. Alderman." He had earned enough honorary doctorates (nearly a dozen) to merit the title. But while he was an ardent bibliophile, he did not fully appreciate the value of what Malone had called "minute research." Under his leadership, although the professional graduate schools flourished, enrollment "in the College of Arts and Sciences hovered in the thirties," as Malone recalled.[23]

Because of President Alderman's charisma, energy, and managerial talents, Malone recounted, the faculty, student body, and endowment grew during his tenure. Shortly after his appointment in 1904, the American Association of Universities elected the University of Virginia to full membership; it was the only southern university so distinguished. Alumni also had tremendous confidence in Alderman. Their gifts built the Steele Wing addition to the Old Medical School; McKim, Clark, and Cobb Halls; the Monroe Hill dormitories; and Scott Stadium.

Virginius Dabney recalled that when he was a student at the University of Virginia, he used to see Alderman strolling to and from his office. Dabney wrote in his memoir that Alderman was a person of immense dignity. After the passing of Woodrow Wilson, he was probably the most eminent southerner of his era, a polished orator, and a personality of great potency and considerable charm. Alderman found it difficult to unbend, and in the words of Malone, he frequently appeared "unduly conscious of his presidential state." Malone went on to relate that "the younger members of the faculty who might have been called by their first names with entire propriety were sonorously addressed as 'Doctor,' and a recent bride could hardly conceal her astonishment but when greeted with good morning Madam. These pomposity's were visible to all."[24]

Once, Dabney recalled, the faculty discussed bringing a distinguished speaker to the university. Alderman suggested that Lord Kelvin be invited. "But Lord Kelvin is dead," physics professor Llewellyn Hoxton interjected. "Oh yes, in a general way," Alderman replied unblinkingly and in his most resonant tone.[25]

Malone began teaching full-time at UVA in the fall of 1923. This was a fateful step in both his personal and professional lives. He was at home in Jefferson's country from the beginning. During his first two years at the university, Malone lived in the Colonnade Club on the Lawn—the first of the pavilions to be erected. He often walked over to the popular university cafeteria at the Corner for lunch, or "supper," and there he enjoyed true southern cooking—fried chicken, warm biscuits, and vegetables. He especially liked the homemade cornbread—with white, not yellow, cornmeal—and ice cream for dessert, or as Malone termed it, his "cream." Malone would often eat and watch some of his students repair to the neighboring Johnny LaRowe's pool room after classes.

Numerous faculty members, all dressed in coats and ties, would also meet Malone for lunch. Apparently Malone wore neither shirt sleeves nor shorts, even in the hot summers. His clothing was conservative and "academic." Although no alcohol was served at the cafeteria, Malone did drink moderately. His son, Gifford, recalled his father having an old-fashioned at times before dinner at the family house. Whiskey was Malone's alcohol of choice, and he was never attracted to exotic cocktails. As he grew older, he limited himself to one cocktail before dinner and eventually shifted to having one glass of beer. Malone, unlike Jefferson, never drank wine.

Much later in life, the historian suffered a severe fall on the icy sidewalk on one of his journeys to the university cafeteria and broke several ribs. Steve Hochman remembered that Malone was really never physically the same after that incident, and he walked with either a cane or with assistance over to the cafeteria for his "warm biscuits."

While on the Grounds, Malone became aware of Thomas Jefferson as an architect, a patron of learning, and a human being. In his first year at UVA, Malone wrote an outline of Jefferson's life, which was published in the Extension Series in March 1924. This maiden production of Malone's "was certainly no contribution to scholarship: in fact it contained errors that I afterwards found embarrassing. But it represented my first effort to view this prodigious life as a whole and marked no inconsiderable increase in my own knowledge of it."[26]

During that first year Malone spent nearly all his time trying to keep a jump ahead of his classes. After teaching a class in the basement of the Rotunda, he went back to his office on most days from nine to five. Dressed in either a suit or a tweed sport coat and dress pants, Malone would address students who themselves wore coats and ties to classes.

At this point, Malone was not seriously considering any scholarly undertaking until after he had finished with his Thomas Cooper book. He had written the dissertation in haste, and it needed much rewriting before being ready for publication. Malone worked on it the entire summer of 1924 and during what little spare time he had the next academic year. By the spring of 1925 it was in the hands of the Yale University Press, "where I was to find a place in the Yale Historical publications."[27]

After that, Malone's interest gradually turned to his life's masterwork: the biography of Jefferson. "Besides the particular reasons why my mind should have turned to Jefferson at this time, there was a more general one," he wrote. "The sesquicentennial of the Declaration of Independence was celebrated in 1926, and interest in him was greatly quickened."[28]

Malone consulted several historians about his proposed biography and was not encouraged. The first person he approached was Allen Johnson, who had done more for Malone professionally than anybody else to that point. Malone's former professor at Yale was just beginning his fruitful service as editor of the *Dictionary of American Biography*. Malone had asked his advice while he was teaching in the Harvard Summer School. Johnson had received, and presumably had read, a copy of Malone's book on Cooper by that time.[29]

Johnson's reply to Malone was distinctly discouraging:

August 2, 1926
Dear Dumas:

You have asked me to assume a grave responsibility in advising you about a life of Thomas Jefferson. I am saying that the future biographer of Jefferson must not consider him merely as a politician or statesman, but deal with him in many ways as the most versatile American of his time, Benjamin Franklin not excepted. The biographer of Jefferson must interest himself in science, in ethics, in architecture, in horticulture, and in those many other interests which Jefferson professed. Unless you are ready to study Jefferson from these varied points of view, I could not advise you to undertake his life. In other words, the biographer must be as many-sided as Jefferson himself. As to your capability I can only say that I suspect you are not well versed in the sciences. And that will certainly be a handicap . . .

Cordially yours,
Allen Johnson[30]

Malone later wrote that, "This candid letter did not discourage me, but it did give me pause." In fact, if he had to date his decision "to set out on a long journey through my story with Mr. Jefferson, I would pick the late summer of 1926." At that time, Malone sought the advice of another elder statesman, Nathaniel W. Stephenson, who had been a visiting professor at

Yale when Malone was there. A bewhiskered gentleman of the old school and a mellow scholar, Stephenson "was a man of admirable literary taste." Summing up his own view of what was needed, he advised, "To give us Jefferson in his entirety, animated by his real motive, with all his limitations confessed and yet with a full appreciation of his transcendent genius is, to my mind, one of the greatest services that anybody could do at the moment [in] American history." Deploring partisanship in historical biography, Stephenson advocated to Malone "portraiture pure and simple." In his memoir, Malone wrote, "I tried to do what Allen Johnson and Nathaniel Stephenson told me the biographer of Jefferson ought to do. I have sought to view the whole of this many sided man. I have consistently sought to portray him in the setting of his own time and circumstances—not in ours."[31]

By the following spring, Malone had concluded that in preparation for this undertaking he would travel to France. Jefferson had spent five years there, consorting with savants, collecting books, viewing noble architecture, observing the ways of diplomats and courtiers, and breathing the air of revolution. By associating with him at this focal point, Malone could hope to catch something of Jefferson's spirit and the spirit of that turbulent age by the process of osmosis.

In the spring of 1927 he returned to Yale briefly as a visiting professor, attempting to fill the shoes of his old friend, Ralph Gabriel, who was on leave. In the summer of 1927 he departed from New Haven for France. "I was so fortunate as to be granted a traveling fellowship that enabled me to spend somewhat more than half a year in France." He had to be back in Virginia by February 1, 1928, to resume his teaching position.

He and Elisabeth spent most of that summer in France, seeking to improve themselves in the language and culture. In Paris they lodged somewhat uncomfortably in a subleased apartment located on the Rue de Suresnes near La Madeleine. Only one of its fireplaces worked, and their bathing facilities consisted of a tub that had to be filled with water from a kettle and that was kept under their bed. But it was conveniently located and afforded the Malones with "opportunities of entertainment and gustatory enjoyment" of which they availed themselves.[32]

Despite the minor inconveniences during those months in Paris, "it was a joy to be alive and my experience as a whole had great educational value," Malone recalled.[33] The tangible results of his research, however, were somewhat disappointing to him. At this stage, he could undoubtedly have accomplished more at the Library of Congress than at the Bibliotèque Nationale. But it was at this time that Malone's love affair with the eighteenth century began to blossom, and he imbibed some of the spirit of both prerevolutionary and revolutionary France.

Malone did not follow Jefferson everywhere in Paris, but he visited many of the places and buildings that he saw, including the Maison Carrée at Nîmes. Jefferson's own papers were the best source of information about his life in France, as they were of every other phase of his career. Malone had done little more than sample these as yet. The chief value of his stay in France did not lie in the notes he took, but in the familiarity he gained with the larger world in which Jefferson's spirit lived. "I still had much to learn about that world, but at least I had made a beginning," he said. "I'm sure I couldn't have written up the French so well, if I hadn't been there. I think it is very important to go where one's subject went."[34]

Malone concluded that Jefferson's five years in France were among the happiest period in his private life: "The French period was almost certainly the part of his public service which he most enjoyed. He said that, when in France, he was able to serve the American Republic while keeping out of sight." Malone revealed that there was a degree of eighteenth-century formality in all Jefferson's letters, but in those of his Paris years, "to Maria Cosway, Angelica Church, and Madame de Corny, there is grace, lightness of touch and play of fancy which would have been wasted on crude men but befitted and delighted these lovely ladies."[35]

While the Malones were abroad, the cottage they had rented in Charlottesville was sold, and they decided to build a house of their own. In the spring after his return, "my mind was so full of the house we were planning and building that there was little room for Mr. Jefferson. It was all I could do to keep up with my classes."

Malone pledged to devote considerable more time to Jefferson in the fall, after they moved into their new house, and in fact, he did so. The University of Virginia had received a handsome bequest from a member of the du Pont family, and President Alderman thought that this would be an appropriate time to publish an edition of the correspondence of Pierre

Samuel du Pont de Nemours and Jefferson. When he asked Malone to edit the collection, the professor "could not refuse."[36]

Malone's teaching load was reduced, and he was ably assisted by Professor Linwood Lehman of the French Department, who translated du Pont's letters. The academic year 1928–29 was largely devoted to this project, and an attractive little volume appeared in 1930. Malone reasoned he was doing something small before attempting a major work but was disappointed at the outcome. "This book appears to have done little or nothing to advance my standing as a scholar. It was blanketed by a somewhat fuller collection edited by Professor Gilbert Chinard, whose reputation far exceeded mine," Malone recalled.[37]

Malone loved to teach. During his first year at UVA, he taught general European history and American history. He taught the European history class for only one year because the university decided to hire another professor to teach it. "I have always regretted that," he wrote.

> Some scholars today never teach general European history. When we gave it, we started with the fall of Rome. Years later, they started with the Renaissance, and they tell me now the course begins with the end of the Thirty Years' War. I suspect that the way things go now in universities a man might go his entire career and never teach general European or American history. All scholarship is now so specialized. I taught general American history ten years, and that is where I learned most of it.[38]

Six years at Virginia led Malone to a proverbial fork in the road and one of the hardest decisions he had to make in his life. In the spring of 1929 Malone's professional mentor, Allen Johnson, created a crisis in the Malone household by coming down from Washington and inviting Malone to share the editorship of the *Dictionary of American Biography* with him. Sponsored by the American Council of Learned Societies, the dictionary was one of the most ambitious and prestigious endeavors of the generation. Malone's old teacher, who was generally called Dr. Johnson in Washington, but whom Malone always called Mr. Johnson, had resigned his professorship at Yale and assumed the editorship in 1926. He had published two of the projected twenty volumes but had been deeply grieved by the death of his wife, which occurred before Malone left Yale. Malone recalled that Johnson was not a robust man and that he had told him how he did not think he would ever be able to finish the enterprise. Johnson wanted a partner who could be his eventual successor.

"Of course I was flattered," Malone remembered. "I was flattered by his offer of this post to me and considering my age and relative inexperience." It was a generous proposal, but numerous uncertainties in the situation entered Malone's mind. "I realized that I was faced with the necessity of making a fateful decision."[39]

Malone took his time deciding whether to accept or reject the offer. He consulted professional friends whose judgment he particularly valued. He did not want to give up his teaching position, which he loved, and sever his relations with an academic institution "to which I had become greatly attached." He wondered what would happen to his academic career once the editorship assignment was over. He consulted his friend Arthur M. Schlesinger Sr. of Harvard who advised him to accept the position. The *Dictionary of American Biography* would "be a monument to those connected with it," Schlesinger advised, and the best positions in the country would be open to Malone after his tenure.[40]

Finally, Malone consulted President Alderman about the generous offer from Johnson. Alderman told Malone that his departure from the university was probably inevitable. "He said something more which I believe I never reported to anyone except my wife. 'It is too bad, for you were born to live here.'"[41]

With both hesitation and excitement, Malone accepted the position shortly after the meeting with Johnson. "Given these circumstances," he later wrote, "my decision to leave may have been virtually inevitable but as I look backward, it seems the most painful decision I ever made. Elisabeth literally shed tears on leaving Mr. Jefferson's country."[42]

8   Elisabeth

You have in effect been married to two men, Dumas Malone and Thomas Jefferson, for all the decades that your husband's great work has been in progress.

—THE SEVEN SOCIETY, IN A TOAST TO
ELISABETH GIFFORD MALONE[1]

I hope you all realize how large a share of the credit she deserves for everything I do.

—DUMAS MALONE, ABOUT HIS WIFE, ELISABETH[2]

On October 17, 1925, Dumas Malone's placid life changed for good. He married the love of his life, Elisabeth Gifford, a born and bred New Englander, to whom he dedicated his writings: "My solicitous wife has kept me going despite the ravages of time. I trust she is not weary in well-doing nor tired of being thanked."

When she met Dumas, Elisabeth Gifford was visiting family friends, the Hudnut family, in Charlottesville. Hudnut, a professor of architecture at the University of Virginia, lived in a house on the Lawn, which suggested that he was a well-established member of the faculty. Dumas met Elisabeth at the Hudnuts' house during a cocktail party. He was immediately attracted to the New England beauty of medium height and slender build. Her face was framed by light brown hair (which was blonde when she was a child), and she had crystal blue eyes. Her son, Gifford, described his mother as someone who meticulously watched her weight and "took care of herself. She was well dressed, but conservatively, never ostentatiously."[3]

"The most important thing I did," Malone once wrote, " . . . was to get married to Elisabeth Gifford, whom I induced to come to Virginia from Massachusetts."[4]

Elisabeth was born on May 16, 1898, in Fall River, Massachusetts. She was the daughter of Benjamin S. C. and Mary Gifford. On her birth certificate her name is spelled "Elizabeth," and her father's occupation is listed as "merchant." The Giffords lived at 338 Locust Street in Fall River when their daughter was born. Elisabeth's mother was born in Worcester, Massachusetts; her father, in Fall River.

The Malones' marriage, by all accounts, was loving, strong, and enduring. There are numerous references in Malone's papers to Elisabeth and his concern for her health and welfare. She lived with chronic insomnia for many years. The Malones traveled on the *Queen Mary* from London to New York, and when they returned home, Malone made a special request of Dr. John Henderson, whom they had met while overseas. Malone wrote to Henderson telling him Elisabeth was "always a very poor sleeper" and asking for the name of a sleeping pill the doctor had ordered for her, later identified as Moganon. "It has worked beautifully for her, but unfortunately it is not obtainable in the United States. She does not use them except when she has slept badly for a good many nights, and they are a lifesaver."[5]

In another letter, Malone explained to attorney Paul Barringer, "My European trip was a great success and we had a wonderful visit with my son and his little family. However Elisabeth had a bad time with her ailing knee toward the end of the trip and has not fully recovered. I hope I shall see you sometime in New York or here."[6] After Malone was invited to speak at the University of Florida, he told his sponsor, "There are certain practical considerations, however. I don't really want to make a trip . . . without taking my wife."[7]

Malone and Elisabeth were well traveled and became even more so when their son entered the Foreign Service. The happy couple traveled throughout their lifetime to Italy, England, France, Germany, Spain, Poland, and Austria. At the end of one summer, the family members all met in Switzerland, at a small village in the Alps. At the time Gifford was working as a volunteer in France for the American Friends Service Committee. But one of the Malones' most memorable travels was the cruise aboard the original *Queen Mary*, a trip they took for both business and pleasure.

Malone recognized his dutiful and patient Elisabeth in many interviews:

> I'm glad of this opportunity, however, to pay tribute to my wife and to the wives of all writers. I think it must be a great strain on the woman to have a husband who writes, especially when he works at home, as most of them do. You have a man around the house, as much as a writer is, and to have him living in another world means a housewife has to put up with an awful lot. You will note that in the acknowledgments in practically all books something about the author's wife. This is entirely proper. They deserved to have the books dedicated to them as my wife certainly does.[8]

In fact, Malone relied heavily on Elisabeth not only for emotional support but also to read and constructively critique selected chapters of his Jefferson book, especially the ones dealing with Monticello.

All her married life, Elisabeth Gifford Malone was not only a meticulous editor of Malone's works, but she also had her husband's knack for precise detail. In a letter to the head of the Domestic Science Department in Falmouth, Massachusetts, one summer, Elisabeth instructed,

> I am writing to ask whether you have any girls you can recommend who want and are trained for jobs, doing cleaning and housework—not cooking—this summer. I want a reliable girl on an hourly basis several times a weak [*sic*]. I have a friend on Chappaquoit who had one of your girls last summer and found her most satisfactory. I live in an old farm house on the old main road for four months every summer. . . . The main thing is to keep the place tidy and press out a few summer clothes. . . . I would hope to get someone from that locality who could come on her bike, as I do not wish the problem of transportation.[9]

It seemed Malone echoed his wife's meticulousness, especially when it came to their beloved house on Cape Cod. Writing to their handyman, John Wyatt, Malone requested that "as for the flower beds Mrs. Malone asked me to remind you that she wants you to fertilize the one next to the living room on the front side of the house. We never have much luck in getting anything to grow there. She also asks that you be very careful in the herb beds, since it is so easy to confuse an herb with a weed."[10]

Elisabeth's father, Benjamin Gifford, had deep roots in Cape Cod, where his direct ancestor, William Gifford, settled in the 1680s. Quaker William Gifford and his family, together with a few other Quaker families, were the first settlers in the area that later became West Falmouth, having moved from the town of Sandwich, where they were poorly treated by the town's Puritans. Gifford was born a Quaker, and in his old age he still used the familiar "thee" and "thou." However, at some point early in his life, he abandoned the Quaker religion because he found it too severe and became a Congregationalist. Elisabeth, however, turned toward a more ceremonial religion and became an Episcopalian.

Cape Cod was an important part of Elisabeth's life from early childhood until her death. Her son remembered his mother as a good ice-skater, a skill she probably picked up during her winters there. Elisabeth enjoyed skating immensely when she was young and living in Fall River. But it was during the family's seven years in Massachusetts, in Lincoln, and then in Belmont, that her son remembered her skating on many occasions. She loved the sport.

"I can still remember at age six or seven my mother buying me skates and taking me and my sister out to a small pond for our first attempts at this new sport." The many ponds and lakes in Lincoln normally froze by the end of December and remained that way until March. "I can recall many occasions," Gifford said, "when we would go skating there, and my mother practicing figure skating turns, while the rest of us learned the basics. Even my father sometimes joined us. He was not very good, but enjoyed being with us there." When the family moved to Belmont, the children learned to skate on a local pond, and later at the Belmont Hill School, Gifford began playing ice hockey. "We also were members of the Cambridge Skating Club, which had an outdoor rink, and where, together with my mother, we would skate. My father's occasional skating . . . occurred only when we lived in Lincoln." The family also enjoyed the Boston Skating Club, which had an indoor rink, open to the public on Saturdays. "As far as I can remember," Gifford observed, "my mother did not do any skating after we moved from Belmont."[11]

Elisabeth's father had built a house in West Falmouth for his family, on property that adjoined land held by an old Quaker aunt, who had lived there in a house dating back to the 1780s. When Benjamin Gifford eventually retired in his late seventies, the old summer house became his year-round residence, although it appears that he spent much time there throughout his life.

When Elisabeth and Dumas were married in October 1925, they chose Cape Cod rather than Fall River as the site of their modest nuptials. They were married in Falmouth, four miles from West Falmouth, in a church that overlooked the village green. Starting in 1930, the year Gifford was born, and probably earlier, Dumas and Elisabeth spent their summers in West Falmouth. Even when they occasionally vacationed elsewhere, when Malone later taught in Ann Arbor or when the family spent the summer in Maine, they always enjoyed a little time at the Cape. After the death of Elisabeth's father in 1941 and that of her mother not long afterward, the house became hers and was the family's summer home thereafter. In his later years, Malone did much of his writing on Jefferson there.

Elisabeth was the youngest of three children. Her sister, Edith, died in childhood, and her brother, Paul Gifford, eight years older, graduated from Harvard. Her father was a prosperous businessman in the wholesale grocery trade. He and his family occupied what was, for its time, a fine house in one of the best neighborhoods in Fall River. In the 1920s Benjamin fell on hard times as his business suffered from the proliferation of grocery chains such as A&P. By the time he took up year-round residence in West Falmouth, he depended on a small annuity.

Elisabeth attended schools in Fall River and sometime in her teens was sent off to a finishing school for girls, Rosemary Hall, in Greenwich, Connecticut. Records do not reflect how long she remained there, only that she did not attend college. According to her son, "she had no thoughts of attending college—which was not unusual for women of her generation."[12] But Elisabeth had a bright, inquisitive mind and was extremely well read. Her father, who also never attended college, had an impressive library of English and American literature and was noted for his knowledge of poetry. Throughout her life Elisabeth read books—novels, biographies, history, and other works. Current events and politics held her interest. An avid reader of the daily newspapers, she usually also watched the evening news with Dumas, when television became available. Fond of music, Elisabeth played the piano, which she enjoyed for many years.

Records do not shed much light on Elisabeth's life as a young adult before her marriage to Malone in 1925. Fall River was her home until that time, and even though she was away for various periods, she seems to have had an active life there. In 1923 she cofounded the Fall River Junior League. Gifford explained,

> We know from an old photo that Elisabeth ran a tearoom in New Hampshire in the summer of 1922, perhaps together with one or two friends. We know from a collection of photos and from what she told us that she made a fairly extended trip to Europe in 1924, visiting a number of countries. We also know that she lived in New York City for a period of time, and that she was engaged in lobbying activity at the state level in Albany. We don't know what the issues were, but we can assume they were liberal issues, in the context of that time.[13]

The circles in which Elisabeth grew up were conservative and solidly Republican, as was her immediate family. Yet, rather early in her life, perhaps in her teens, Elisabeth developed a liberal political outlook, and with a few exceptions later in her life, she supported Democratic candidates. She and Dumas were both strong supporters of Franklin Roosevelt, which put Elisabeth at odds with her New England family and relatives. Gifford remembered one story about his father's conversation with their family dentist in Boston. The dentist, Dr. Brown, was married to a cousin of Elisabeth's and was himself a southerner. In response to Malone's question about how he managed to get along with New Englanders so well, Dr. Brown retorted, "You just go nine-tenths of their way."

In the years before her marriage, Elisabeth took art courses in Boston. Until fairly late in life one of her happiest pastimes was painting watercolors of familiar scenes in West Falmouth and some of the places she visited in her travels. She received much pleasure from the art museums in Boston and later in New York and encouraged her children to visit them as well. She enjoyed the theater, Gifford related, and as "a child living outside Boston, I can remember being taken to Gilbert and Sullivan performances and an occasional concert as well as a ballet. Later, after the family moved to New York, first in the suburb of Bronxville and then in Manhattan, she saw to it that all of us took advantage of this opportunity to attend the latest Broadway plays and musicals, as well as concerts by the New York Philharmonic."[14] Dumas was not a frequent museum visitor, but he enjoyed the theater and the concerts. Elisabeth took the lead in all this, and he was happy to have her come up with the ideas and make the arrangements.

Elisabeth always kept in touch with their many friends—many of them dear friends dating back to their early years in Charlottesville in the 1920s. She not only kept in touch, she managed Dumas's social life, arranging dinners and get-togethers with friends and colleagues. The scholarly professor appreciated this greatly. "I can recall his telling me more than once," Gifford confided, "how much he relied on her for all of that."[15]

The Malones enjoyed entertaining people, and they continued to have guests at their house well into their old age. Kay Sargeant, Malone's personal secretary for fourteen years, recalled many cocktail parties to which she was invited. Elisabeth was a perfect host, Sargeant remembered, just a "delight."[16] The parties, however, were never on a lavish scale and in their last years they consisted mostly of having people over for drinks.

Throughout his life Dumas greatly benefited from Elisabeth's strong and refined interest in food. "She was an excellent cook," Gifford said. "During the period they spent in France in the 1920s they rented for a time an apartment in Paris, and she attended the Cordon Bleu cooking school, which helped her to develop her skills and expand her culinary knowledge." Dumas was the beneficiary of these talents; he always knew that he would have a good meal—something he often spoke about with his children. While Elisabeth was always conscious of nutrition and health, hot hors d'oeuvres with an evening cocktail, cheese soufflés, or hot powder biscuits were more the rule than the exception. "She was a care-taker in the best sense of the term," Gifford observed.[17]

In the early part of World War II, when the Malones were living in Belmont, Massachusetts, Elisabeth worked in a small store in Cambridge, just off Harvard Square, called the Window Shop. This shop was a combination of a small restaurant and what could be termed a take-out shop. The store helped refugees from Europe who had relocated to the area by providing employment and other assistance. Elisabeth's cooking experience came in handy in her work there, as she helped create the menu and develop appropriate recipes. "I can still recall an excellent fish chowder which she and a friend created for the shop," noted Gifford fondly.

Elisabeth's wartime experience also included serving as the air raid warden for the neighborhood in Belmont. The entire family participated in the air raid drills that were held from time to time.

Elisabeth and Dumas had many different residences during their long life together, starting in Charlottesville and eventually returning there. "Our mother was strongly supported by my father, who often commented on Elisabeth's 'good taste.' She always did what she could to improve these residences and make them as nice as she could for family and visitors," Gifford explained. When they eventually purchased a house in Belmont, Elisabeth installed in the living room a row of three large floor-to-ceiling windows looking out into the garden. In those days that was a modern style, Gifford said. None of the other houses in the neighborhood had anything like it.

Throughout these years of moving from one spot to another, the place on Cape Cod was a constant, a second home to which the family always returned. There Elisabeth kept an herb garden, as she had in most of the other places where they had lived. She and Dumas put in new plants and shrubbery, which in his later years, he enjoyed caring for, as a respite from writing.

In West Falmouth Elisabeth also played a key role in a local government issue that affected the community in an important way. In the early 1950s the state began construction of a new highway from the Cape Cod Canal to Falmouth. The original plan called for the significant expansion and redesign of a road running straight through West Falmouth. This major artery would pass directly in front of the town's small post office, its general store, its library, and the numerous old houses, including the Malones' home, that lined the existing road. Elisabeth took the initiative in organizing citizen opposition to the new project, circulating petitions and contacting state representatives. After much work, the new road was ultimately built a mile away from its originally planned location, passing through countryside rather than the village. Some of the documents from this successful effort are still in Elisabeth's old desk at the Cape, including the signed petitions and copies of letters to elected representatives.

Like her husband, Elisabeth was energetic, outgoing, independent-minded, and deeply involved with her family, but at the same time, she was very much interested in what was going on locally and in the world in general. She remained in touch with friends until the last years of her life. She always seemed to find pleasure in the various places she lived and made the most of wherever she was. Some places, such as Boston and New York, offered more than others, but by all accounts she enjoyed her days in Washington as well. Still, Elisabeth, like her husband, always had a special affection for Charlottesville, which seemed the perfect place for the Malones in their later years. Throughout her married life, she was totally devoted to her husband and her family. "And, as he said to my sister one summer," Gifford confessed, "when he was obliged to spend a week in Charlottesville while Elisabeth was in West Falmouth, 'life always seems a little drab without your mother.'"[18]

The last years of Elisabeth's life were difficult. She outlived her beloved husband by six years but suffered steadily declining health and eventually required constant care. She continued to live in the Lewis Mountain Road house in Charlottesville until her death at age ninety-four.

After the publication of the final volume of *Jefferson and His Time,* Dumas Malone was honored at a special dinner in the Rotunda at the University of Virginia. Among the words of praise was an award in recognition of his achievements from the Seven Society, the most famous of UVA's secret societies. The citation included the following words, directed to Elisabeth: "Your loyalty, patience and charm have contributed tremendously to the accomplishment of this notable achievement."[19]

9   The *Dictionary*

*Teaching, writing, and editing—I think I was happier
teaching and writing. I like editing, but if you do too
much, it cramps your style.*

—DUMAS MALONE (1985)[1]

It was a glorious night in January 1931. The crisp air announced the
arrival of winter in the nation's capital. The moon glowed against a black
sky as Professor Allen Johnson, the editor of the *Dictionary of American
Biography*, strolled home.

Against a green light, Johnson entered the intersection of Rhode Island
and Connecticut avenues. In the space of seconds, he heard screeching tires
and saw high-intensity headlights. The oncoming car veered at the last second. Johnson tried to get out of the way, but his actions were slowed by
some unseen force. The car speared Johnson, and bystanders watched in
horror as he disappeared under the hood with a battering thud. The air
filled with screams, brakes, and honking horns. A crowd gathered around
Johnson's crumpled body.

The report the following morning in the *Washington Post* read,

Dr. Allen Johnson, author and editor and former Professor of History at
Yale, died here last night soon after being hit by an automobile as he was
trying to cross the street on foot against traffic. Samuel Cherkosky, the
driver of the automobile which hit Dr. Johnson, at Connecticut and Rhode
Island took him at once to the Emergency Hospital, where he succumbed

within an hour of the accident. Doctors found he had suffered a fractured leg and arm, but ascribed his death to shock. Cherkosky was later questioned by police.[2]

Allen Johnson, age sixty-one, was pronounced dead hours later. His assistant editor, Dumas Malone, would not learn of his death until the next day. "Allen Johnson was one of my greatest professional friends and patrons," Malone declared. "He wanted to work with me on the DAB because he knew he could never finish it alone. We worked together for a year and a half, and then he was killed in an automobile accident."[3]

Before breakfast on January 19, 1931, Malone received a telephone call from Harris Starr, who asked him if he had seen the morning edition of the *Washington Post*. "I told him that I had not," Malone said, "and he gave me the shocking news that Allen Johnson had been killed in an accident the previous evening."[4] Starr had wanted to make sure that Malone heard the news before he arrived at the office. The accident had occurred, Malone learned, at a street crossing near the Mayflower Hotel on Connecticut Avenue. Malone later did not remember any story in the *Washington Post*, but Johnson's death was front-page news in the *New York Times*, which featured an old photograph of the former Yale professor.

Johnson's son, Allen Jr., arrived from New England promptly. He had been a student of Malone's at Yale and asked Malone to accompany him to the funeral home to identify his father's body. Malone also attended the inquest and was a pallbearer at Johnson's funeral in Brunswick, Maine, where his wife had been buried some years before. Johnson had once told Malone that he left Bowdoin College because his wife could not stand the severe winters there.

Johnson had left things in perfect order for his successor at the dictionary and thus had facilitated Malone's assumption of full responsibly. But Malone later admitted, "It took me a long time to get over the shock of his tragic departure. In fact I dreamed about the events for weeks thereafter."[5]

The Committee of Management elected Malone as sole editor of the dictionary, and within weeks he became an ex officio member of that body. The chairman was the dean of American historians, J. Franklin Jamison. Other members chosen by the American Council of Learned Societies were Charles Warren, the noted legal historian; Professor Fredrick L. Paxton, then of the University of Wisconsin and later of the University of California at Berkeley; and Carl Van Doren, a well-known critic and literary historian. The *New York Times* was represented by John H. Finley, its associate editor, and Mrs. Iphigene Ochs Schulzburger, daughter of Adolph S. Ochs. A half century later, Mrs. Schulzburger told Malone that she stood in some awe of the learned gentlemen on this committee. "At the age of thirty-nine, so did I," Malone said.[6]

Allen Johnson was not only Malone's professor at Yale, but he became one of his most influential mentors. In fact, the first person Malone approached when he began to think of his biography of Jefferson was Johnson, "who had done more for me professionally than anybody else."[7] Johnson was born on January 29, 1870, in Lowell, Massachusetts, the son of Moses Allen Johnson, manager of the Lowell Felting Mills, and Elmira J. Shattuck. Johnson graduated as high school valedictorian in 1888, then received his BA in 1892 from Amherst College. Johnson impressed both faculty and students with his meticulous scholarship, and he was considered more mature than most college students. He enjoyed dressing up and displayed impeccable manners in his dealings with others.[8]

Following graduation, Johnson became an instructor in history and English at the Lawrenceville School in Lawrenceville, New Jersey. In 1894 he was awarded the Roswell Dwight Hitchcock Fellowship at Amherst College, and earned his MA in 1895. Moving to Bowdoin College in 1905, he accepted a position as assistant professor of history and political science. He quickly rose to national prominence as a historian while at Bowdoin, writing a biography of Stephen A. Douglas. As one of the first university teachers to introduce small, informal undergraduate "discussion sections" to classroom lectures, Johnson received nationwide attention for his teaching innovations.[9]

In 1910 Yale University offered Johnson the Larned Chair of American History. He remained at Yale until 1926 and, during those sixteen years, prepared two college textbooks, *Readings in American Constitutional History* (1912) and *Readings in Recent American Constitutional History, 1876–1926* (1927). After teaching a course on historical methods, he published *The Historian and Historical Evidence* (1926), which offered practical advice and guidance to American students, whom Johnson considered impatient with the subtleties of professional methods and often careless in their scholarship. In 1925, because of his success with the Chronicles of America series and his reputation as a fair-minded biographer, the American Council of Learned Societies invited Johnson to edit its proposed *Dictionary of American Biography*.

Johnson then moved to Washington, D.C., where he spent the final years of his life. His accomplishments as editor of "the *Dictionary*," as he called the *DAB*, received international acclaim from scholars and learned societies, which recognized the immense effort involved in assembling a twenty-volume work that included thirteen thousand biographies written by more than eleven hundred authors. Breaking with the past practice of giving biographical prominence exclusively to soldiers, statesmen, and clergymen, Johnson also devoted a large proportion of the work to individuals who had made significant contributions in science, art, and industry. Six volumes of the dictionary were published under his editorship (one posthumously), but the impact of Johnson's editorial decisions and his choice of contributors were evident throughout the entire collection.

In its written eulogy of Johnson, the commitee of the dictionary said,

> It is a national calamity that Dr. Allen Johnson, who began four years ago the editing of the Dictionary of American Biography should be suddenly cut off by death in the midst of this monumental work. The lives of many who would otherwise have stepped into oblivion will be prolonged in the memory of this country by the earlier volumes edited under his direction. And thousands of other lives already known to history will have more faithful remembrance through generations to come because of his discerning, competent, valiant service to the nation in this undertaking of the Learned Societies of America. . . . No one else in the country could have done the work so well.[10]

At the time of Johnson's death, Malone had been his assistant editor for more than a year and a half and was considering leaving his work on the dictionary. For a man who aspired to write great biographies, not edit reference books about them, "this was a very confining job," Malone wrote. "It wasn't what I'd intended to do, being shut up in an office all the time and telling other people what to write and not doing it myself, but I had to finish it. There was no way out, so I stuck on for five more years and finished it."[11]

On Malone's nomination to the position of editor in chief of the dictionary, the *New York Times* published the following:

> Dr. Malone has been active in compiling the literary histories of 13,000 or more Americans since July, 1929, when he resigned a professorship of history at the University of Virginia to join Dr. Johnson. He has been a visiting professor of history at Yale, a holder of the Sterling fellowship for travel and study, a winner of the John Addison Porter prize for a historical essay, and incumbent of the Richard Alumni Professorship of History with the duty of directing compilation of a "Bibliography of Virginia History Since 1865." During World War I he enlisted as a private in the Marine Corps and rose to the rank of Second Lieutenant. He is married and lives in Alexandria, Virginia.[12]

Malone was obviously happier when he was teaching and writing than when he was editing. He enjoyed editing but felt "it cramps your style. My years on the Dictionary of American Biography were invaluable to me as a writer because of what they taught me about precision and clarity." But after a time, Malone grew weary of handling other people's work, and he became "too fussy."[13]

He once said that when he left the *DAB*, he would never edit again. But that did not happen. Although he did not formally edit at the Harvard University Press later in his career, when teaching at Columbia, he did edit the *Political Science Quarterly* for five years. He had an innate sense that he wanted to improve the writing of scholars. "We really had the lowdown on them on the DAB," Malone contended. "We knew who was good. We knew them both as scholars and writers. There was nearly always something wrong with every sketch, though it was often very trivial."[14]

During his seven years at the *DAB*, Malone had an opportunity to ponder the question, What is greatness? One of the first things he did after completing his editorship was draw up a list of the "forty greatest Americans" based on the criteria Johnson had used for the *DAB*, that is, no living Americans could be included. Then he wrote an article about the list, which was printed in the April issue of *Harper's* magazine. A great number of critics of the article had their own ideas about who were the greatest of their fellow countrymen. Some complained that Malone was sexist because no women were on the list. Others complained that no inventors had made the list. Some historians complained that there ought to be more than one clergyman and one educator among the forty. Others criticized the order of rank within the group of statesmen, soldiers, and jurists. For example, why did Malone rank Ulysses S. Grant ahead of Robert E. Lee, Jefferson Davis ahead of Theodore Roosevelt, Stephen A. Douglas ahead of Daniel Webster and Henry Clay? Critics also questioned his judgment in including William Jennings Bryan on a list that included only a third of the presidents.

Malone was not surprised that his selections caused controversy. He said that his list might easily be revised by making substitutions and changing the order in which he had placed the forty. But there was one part of his list that he said he "would defend with his life." They were the first five names—Washington, Lincoln, Jefferson, Franklin, and Wilson. Among professional historians, there was no disagreement as to Washington and Lincoln, and only slight disagreement as to the relative positions of those two other versatile Americans—Jefferson and Franklin.

Malone explained his choices in a subsequent lengthy article:

> 1) Washington—he still seems more a statue than a human being, but without him the Republic would not have come into being when it did; 2) Lincoln—who has come to symbolize the Union and, in a sense, democracy. A very human figure with plenty of faults; 3) Jefferson—the most versatile of great Americans. All parties claim that he is on their side, but he really preferred science to politics; 4) Wilson—still a controversial figure, but of unquestionable historical eminence because as President during the World War he was for a long time the first citizen of the world.

Malone concluded these five shared a historical quality: "The man who will be remembered tomorrow is the man who looks beyond today."[15]

There was strong objection to Malone's selection of Woodrow Wilson as the only American since Lincoln to stand among the five greatest. Many argued that position belonged to Theodore Roosevelt, who was tenth on Malone's list. "Roosevelt thought of himself as a man of action and Wilson as a man of words," Malone explained in his defense. But the record showed rather that Wilson was the man of action, Malone contended. "T. R.

talked a great deal, but he couldn't put things through. Wilson's first two years are comparable to George Washington's administration. At no time after the beginning of the republic did any administration ever get things done as Wilson did. He assumed a new role in the Presidency, comparable to that of Prime minister," Malone contended.[16] As a war president, Malone wrote, Wilson was a better administrator than Lincoln. The Great War was better conducted than any other war in which the United States had fought. When the Republicans came back to power in 1920, there was practically nothing they could stir up out of the conduct of the war. But moreover, Wilson was the first American in history who was the most important man in the world. "That . . . never happened before," Malone explained.[17]

As Malone expected his selection of Wilson to cause dispute, so did he expect to draw grief with the absence of women from his list. "But it is actually no reflection on them at all," he explained. "Until recently there has been no chance for women to achieve prominence in America. Until the Civil War, their only chance for distinction was as a hostess, like Dolley Madison, or as writers. There weren't many writers. Harriet Beecher Stowe is the best known but she falls short of the nine men on my list of writers."[18]

Under Malone's direction, the *Dictionary of American Biography* was completed with its twentieth volume in 1942. Characterized by competent critics as "the greatest work of historical scholarship yet produced in this country," the dictionary contained the biographies of 13,633 Americans who, in the opinion of Malone and the two thousand biographers who aided him, were important enough in history to entitle them to a place in this permanent record.[19]

This period was memorable in Malone's personal as well as professional life. He often wearied of office routine and sometimes found the immense task he had assumed overwhelming. But as a participant in what he termed "the great historical and patriotic enterprise," Malone enjoyed the experience. He could hardly have picked a more exciting time to be in Washington.

The *DAB* headquarters was located in a building at 17th and I Streets, three blocks from the White House. These quarters fitted the residence staff snugly, Malone recalled. During their coeditorship, Malone and Johnson shared a relatively large room that Johnson had previously had to himself. In addition to a choice selection of his books, this room contained several shelves of reference works that Malone consulted constantly. There were eight or nine editors and staffers altogether. The assistant editors came to the office in the morning to receive their assignments and then proceeded to the Library of Congress to conduct their research.

Malone recalled that Johnson ran "a tight ship." It was not a gossipy office, and social visitors were rare. Johnson had a quick temper, but he was also considerate of those who worked with him and "he was certainly considerate of me," Malone observed. There was no particular need for interviews, and Malone's business was conducted almost entirely by mail. Malone noted that Johnson's handwriting was even "easier to read than that of Thomas Jefferson. It reflected the clarity of his mind."[20]

When Malone arrived on the scene, the enterprise was proceeding steadily on a course that had been carefully surveyed and determined in advance. Twenty volumes, with articles about 675 persons included in each, had been planned. Johnson had compiled a list of names from which the persons to be profiled were selected.

The category entrusted to Malone exclusively was titled "Civil and Military Officers." This included civil officials such as the president and chief justice as well as military and naval officers. These were the people Malone had studied when teaching general American history and, therefore, the sort of people Johnson thought Malone was best qualified to deal with. Malone recalled that since they were working under the self-imposed limit of twenty volumes and 675 articles to a volume, the editors had to be careful in deciding who should and should not be included in this assembly of notables. Some sort of achievement was required. Johnson's only change to the list of notables Malone compiled for his category was to add five hundred words to one biography. The top group that Malone assembled in chronological order included George Washington, Thomas Jefferson, Abraham Lincoln, and Woodrow Wilson. They later added Benjamin Franklin as a figure of monumental accomplishment in the "top five."

Throughout his tenure as editor, Johnson made it abundantly clear to Malone that the highest standards of scholarship must be maintained. Malone would often joke that Johnson had saved him much trouble by putting the fear of God in the minds of the editors at the beginning. "He was known to be an exacting man and had the prestige to make strong demands," Malone wrote.

In his unfinished memoir, Malone recalled in detail his editing protocol. Before an article came to his desk in its properly labeled folder, the number of words in it was calculated by one of the secretaries. The articles were nearly always too long. One of Malone's first editorial tasks was to reduce an article to its prescribed length or, as not infrequently happened, to raise the word count somewhat and pay the author accordingly. Literary editors prepared the articles for press. Malone did the major editing of a good many articles with his own pen and edited all the sketches of the presidents. The group of contributors to the articles, all mature scholars and distinguished writers, numbered 2,243 in the end.[21]

Malone's gratitude to Johnson both personally and professionally was immense, yet the two men could not have been more different. In contrast to Johnson, Malone was a genial man who related to people well. He liked to engage people and talk to them. He was of the deep southern culture, courteous to a fault, and people always responded favorably to him. "I never heard him say a rude or angry word to anyone," his son, Gifford, recalled. "That would have been completely out of character."[22]

Malone regarded it as an honor to work on the *DAB* and recalled that his boss was annoyed when anyone complained about the paltry pay.[23]

It seemed only fair to Malone to leave Allen Johnson's name on volume 7. It should have been left on a good many more volumes, according to Malone. In his memoir, he recalled an incident about Johnson that, as far as he knew, had never been told.

Johnson was determined that every article in the *DAB* be as honest and truthful as humanly possible. If necessary, the editor entered the fray in person. He himself wrote the article about Mary Baker Eddy, the controversial founder of Christian Science, knowing full well that he would displease her followers. Johnson did not assume this task because he was interested in Mrs. Eddy but because he was determined to go wherever the evidence led him and to take whatever consequences might be, Malone recalled. Anticipating trouble in this case, Johnson had his article checked with unusual care and asked every member of the Committee of Management to read it. He sought their approval in advance and told them that he would resign if he did not receive it. Unanimous approval followed, and the article appeared in volume 6. It proved to be one of the most controversial in the entire series, but the criticism was muted to some extent because of Johnson's untimely death.

Under Malone's stewardship, the dictionary's standards remained high. In fact, he improved the procedure for ensuring the accuracy of the articles. The staff of library assistants, whose business it was to check each article, increased considerably under Malone. The method of checking the *DAB* articles under his editorial direction was distinctive. The rival *Dictionary of National Biography* had no comparable policy. Malone had the impression that relatively few scholars checked their titles and references with the care that he did. He later admitted that there were some minor errors in virtually all the articles, and the burden to catch these errors "fell on me."[24]

Malone found that veteran writers generally accepted corrections more readily than anyone else. Practically all authors were sensitive about changes in form. It was Malone's custom to send to each author a carbon copy of the final draft of his article so that he could comment on it as he liked. Because of the limitations of space and the need to obtain a considerable degree of consistency in the articles, Malone had to do a great deal of meticulous editing himself. Nearly all his authors were cooperative, but occasionally somebody thought that Malone had gone too far. "I found it necessary to remind myself and the literary editors," Malone said, "to make no changes on grounds of mere personal preference. 'The style is the man,' as Buffon said, and a wise editor will respect it as long as he can."[25]

At no other time in Malone's life did he have such contact with writers and scholars as he had in this period. He corresponded with people in almost every state and practically every university. "The friends and acquaintances I made in these years," he later wrote, "were invaluable to me in my later professional life."[26]

Malone's years as editor were professionally fulfilling, but he grew weary. The dictionary was supposed to be completed in ten years but was actually finished in more than ten and a half years. Malone found the earlier phases of the work more interesting than the final ones. "It was more fun to select names and to assign articles than it was to crack the whip over delinquent contributors," he recalled. "It was an unforgettable experience. Editing other people's writings certainly taught me to be more careful of my own."[27]

Malone's managerial duties became so absorbing that he had little time to write. In the autumn of 1930 he did emerge from his confinement long enough to read a paper that was later published in the *Virginia Quarterly Review*, titled "Polly Jefferson and Her Father," to a women's club in Richmond. It was in researching and writing this article that Malone learned a great deal about Jefferson's relationship with his daughter. "I have never ceased to look back on this little paper with special affection," he confided in his memoir.[28]

Malone then wrote a few articles for the dictionary about people connected in some way with Jefferson. He had begun his article on Jefferson before Johnson died, and it turned out to be one of the three longest in the *DAB*. His articles for the dictionary formed the basis of his biography of Jefferson and were the genesis of Malone's reputation as a Jeffersonian scholar.

During the seven years that Malone edited the *Dictionary of American Biography*, the Malone family lived in four different places. Malone's reluctance to leave UVA was suggested by the fact that they spent the first year in Alexandria, Virginia. The house they rented on Prince Street was once occupied by Dr. Dick, one of George Washington's doctors; it came furnished with one of Dr. Dick's historical tablets in it. "It may have been the most distinguished house we ever lived in, but it was not in very good condition," Malone remembered.[29]

Gifford was born in the spring of 1930, and in the fall the family moved to an apartment in Washington, D.C., just off S Street, "for greater comfort and convenience." Malone explained that the location "was admirable and our quarters were bright and sufficiently commodious. There was no elevator, however, and we were on the top floor, the fourth. We ran into difficulties getting the baby carriage up and down stairs and decided to move again."[30] They rented a house on McKinley Street in Chevy Chase, the chief advantage of which was the safely enclosed backyard where "Giffy" could play. After two more years, the Malones moved to Bethesda, Maryland, where they remained for the last three years Malone was editor of the *DAB*. Their second child, Pamela, was born while they lived in Bethesda.

Malone's years in Washington were not without tumult. He lived in the nation's capital during the transition from the Hoover administration to the Roosevelt administration, and everything seemed to be in flux. It was the time of the Great Depression, which the Malone family escaped in large measure because Dumas was secure in his position at the *DAB*.

Malone had previously spent a summer in Washington when he was working on his doctoral dissertation, and at that time he had been able to observe the Senate in action. When he grew tired of editing manuscripts for the *DAB* in the late afternoon, he ventured over to the Senate chamber and listened to the debates. Before the end of the summer, he knew each of the senators by sight and name. They impressed Malone as a "group of lawyers contending against one another in the interest of their respective clients or constituencies." He later wrote that he could not help wondering "who was looking after the general interest."[31]

Malone was fortunate enough to meet several senators in person. His good friend Virginius Dabney of the *Richmond Times-Dispatch* was in town and suggested they go to the Senate. Once there, Dabney introduced him to the infamous senator from Louisiana, Huey Long, "the Kingfish." While waiting for Long, they also met Senator Pat Harrison of Mississippi, sometimes described as the gadfly of the Senate and the chief tormentor of the Republican majority. Malone found Harrison to be "an affable gentleman to whom I warmed because he knew my grandfather." When Huey Long appeared, he stayed with Malone and Dabney just long enough to create a distinct impression. "I thought him one of the most conceited men I had ever met. He was absolutely sure of himself," wrote Malone.[32]

In his memoir some years later, Dabney recalled, "Huey was hungry for publicity and he consented to meet me in a room off the Senate floor. I took my wife with me and also her friends, the Dumas Malones. In a few minutes, the Kingfish rushed in, with hair disheveled and waving his arms like a windmill. 'Sit down lady,' he said to my wife, and he almost pushed her into a chair." It appeared to Dabney that Long had chosen to put on a hick act for their benefit. He used bad grammar and spoke in an accent so thick that it sounded as though it oozed up from the Louisiana canebrakes. Dabney wrote,

> We were in the process of asking him a few questions, when somebody came in with a note. He glanced at it and rushed out, still waving his arms, never pausing to say goodbye. He impressed all of us as crude and vulgar to the nth degree. Shortly afterward, he was on the Senate floor shouting

furious criticism of postmaster general James A. Farley, one of Roosevelt's right-hand men, and professing in the most sanctimonious terms to be shocked at something or other. Long's assault on the postmaster general was delivered in faultless prose, and without the bogus down-home accent that he had employed in his conversation with us.

He concluded, "If this ruthless and brilliant man had not been assassinated the following year, he might have become the country's first dictator. He had furnished the blueprint in Louisiana."[33]

Malone never lost his interest in the workings of Congress. In 1965 he and Elisabeth visited the White House as a guest of the esteemed Virginia senator Harry F. Byrd, who wrote, "My dear Doctor . . . it gives me pleasure to enclose your passes to the Senate Gallery. I hope very much you will have the opportunity to drop by to see me when you are here in Washington, as this would give me a great deal of pleasure."[34]

The Malones' social life, however, did not consist of the cocktail or congressional party circuit. But they did have congressmen over for dinner on occasion. One night, expecting to spend an evening trading gossip with old friends, Malone made the mistake of asking a congressman what he thought of the Depression. He responded by giving a lengthy summary of his economic analysis of the matter. "He did not let down his guard all evening," Malone recalled, "but remained the politician on parade in our drawing room."[35]

On occasion, Malone would also visit the Supreme Court to hear oral arguments. During the Hoover administration, the Malones had a connection in the Department of Justice: Charles P. Sisson, an assistant attorney general who had married one of Elisabeth's cousins. Sisson provided Malone with a certain amount of inside gossip about the administration. Malone accompanied him several times to the Supreme Court and attended sessions of the court presided over by Chief Justice William Howard Taft. Malone later witnessed Taft's funeral procession as well as that of Oliver Wendell Holmes Jr.

"My most distinct memory of the Hughes Court was a skit of it in a musical comedy," Malone wrote. "I believe this was called *Of Thee I Sing*. The Justices, all wearing black robes and all bearded like their Chief, went into a huddle on the stage like a football team."[36]

Malone also met future Chief Justice Harlan Fiske Stone at a luncheon at the Library of Congress. When there, Malone often lunched at the table of the librarian, Herbert Putnam, although in his presence Malone felt "diffident and immature."[37]

The Malones also became good friends with Justice Louis Brandeis and his wife and enjoyed dinner with them several times. The invitations were always given over the telephone by a butler who turned out to be a "rather decrepit black man dressed for dinner," Malone recalled in his memoir. He gained the distinct impression that these hosts were indifferent to protocol and did not go in for style. Some of their china was chipped, and the curtains in the living room did not hang just right. "It seemed safe to say that the justice gave no heed to such trifling imperfections," Malone remembered. "The evening was always short. About nine o'clock one got the signal from Mrs. Brandeis that it was time to go. I don't know that the Justice went to bed immediately thereafter, but he certainly guarded his strength. They made it a practice to go out for dinner, and he told me that it was his policy to make no decision of any importance when he was tired."[38]

Malone recalled that in the course of the evening every guest had a personal chat with the justice. Elisabeth, who originally viewed the prospect with consternation, found him to be friendly and unpretentious. Malone talked to Brandeis about the specific duties of the *DAB*.

One afternoon late in the spring of 1932, Elisabeth reminded her husband that they had not visited the Brandeises in quite some time. Because their daughter, Pamela, was due in the summer of that year, the expectant mother remained at home while Malone set forth as the representative of the family. He proceeded to the Brandeis apartment on what he believed was the proper day. At the door Malone was met by a handsome young clerk who informed him politely that the "season" was over and "I was a month too late. He asked if I would like to see the Justice and . . . he ushered me into his study." Brandeis received Malone with the utmost cordiality, but "I may have lingered longer than I should have."[39]

His contacts with Louis Brandeis were too few and his opportunities to observe him too limited, according to Malone. "But from few men whom I have met in the course of my long life have I gained such a strong and distinct impression of greatness. Besides being kind and good he had, as it seemed to me, the nobility and grandeur of a Hebrew prophet."[40]

While in Washington, Malone also socialized with Franklin Delano Roosevelt. He had first met the Roosevelts earlier, on Cape Cod the summer after he and Elisabeth were married. "I think it was in the summer of

1926 and I lunched with the Roosevelts at Marion, Massachusetts, across from Buzzard's Bay in West Falmouth," Malone wrote in his memoir.[41] One morning that summer Malone had been surprised by a visit from Mrs. Roosevelt and Henry Toombs. Malone had known Toombs as a boy in Cuthbert, Georgia. Toombs was one of his most cherished friends as well as godfather to Gifford. He was also intimate with the Roosevelt family, having first become acquainted with them through a relative involved in Democratic politics in New York. Toombs later became a successful architect in Atlanta and was chosen by Eleanor Roosevelt to design homes for her family. He had designed the Roosevelts' dream house at Hyde Park and the buildings at Warm Springs, Georgia, where FDR later died.

That summer morning in 1926, Eleanor Roosevelt invited the Malones to lunch "with the family the next day and this we readily agreed to do." This was before FDR became governor of New York and after his attack of polio. As Malone recalled, "Roosevelt was at Marion in order to be near a particular doctor. He had recently suffered a fall. He remained in it [wheelchair] while we lunched with Eleanor Roosevelt and the children, who seemed to be swarming all over the place." More than half a century later, when Malone saw Franklin Roosevelt Jr., he related the story of their first meeting when Franklin was a little boy. Roosevelt did not remember the occasion, but he remembered the summer in Marion and Henry Toombs.[42]

"We talked with F.D.R. in his wheel chair. He was friendly and approachable, but in his weak physical state he was not particularly impressive. He may have been and certainly had good reason to be deeply depressed at this stage. At any rate, I was depressed for him," Malone thought of the lunch. As the Malones were driving away, Dumas said to his wife, "There is a man who is through. Precisely when I retracted this egregious prophecy I do not know."[43]

Some years later, when Roosevelt was seeking the nomination for the presidency, the Malones attended the Democratic National Convention. "I don't remember why Elisabeth and I were there. The speech itself was in no sense memorable, but the speaker was unforgettable. For an agonizing moment, as he sought to pull himself up by the arms of his chair, it seemed doubtful if this cripple would ever stand erect. When he did so at the podium, strong and handsome, the audience gasped with relief."[44] FDR assumed heroic proportions for Malone at that moment, and this image of courage never grew dim.

About a year later, he attended FDR's first inauguration: "Although I've seen many others on TV, this is the only one I ever attended in person. It was the most memorable of them all. What most impressed me at the time was the new President's courage when he spoke of driving the money-changers from the temple. Thus he appeared as not only a man of indomitable will but also of dauntless courage."[45]

Malone attended the first Gridiron Club dinner of the Roosevelt administration. He owed his invitation to Robert Lincoln O'Brien, a former editor of the *Boston Herald*, then living in Washington. Malone later admitted he remembered little about the occasion beyond the impression that the actor Ed Wynn was a "jokester and that the new President entered heartily into the merriment. As I recall I had to purchase 'tails' for this full dress affair and wore them only once thereafter—at a dinner given Elisabeth and me by President Conant soon after I became Director of the Harvard University Press."[46]

Soon thereafter, the Malones attended a White House dinner:

> We were guests at a musical one evening at the White House. It had been a very cold day and when about to set out we found to our horror that our car was frozen. Finally we procured what seemed to be the only vehicle available in Bethesda—a disreputable looking taxicab. It got us to our destination with two or three minutes to spare and the gate keeper let us in, but I am confident that of all the guests we made the most unimpressive entry.[47]

The last time Malone saw FDR alive was at a tea party Eleanor Roosevelt gave the Literary Society. "That was the last time I saw him in person and all I said to him then was 'Good afternoon, Mr. President.' It seems surprising that he should have been there. As I recall, he seemed rather bored."

In later years Malone often said that the days immediately preceding and following the inauguration of Franklin D. Roosevelt were the most exciting he had ever lived through—the two world wars not excepted. The air of Washington was vibrant during the rest of Roosevelt's tenure, he recalled.[48]

"For us it was as pleasant as was an exceedingly interesting place to live. Our children were young and thriving and these were among the happiest of all our years. We would have been glad to extend them but as has happened in the case of many individuals, my term ran out."[49]

10   Harvard University Press

I am not sure going to the Harvard Press was a wise decision. With the benefit of hindsight and from the purely professional point of view, it may appear that I took the wrong fork of the road.

—Dumas Malone[1]

Harvard is the oldest institution of higher education in the United States, established in 1636. It was named after the college's first benefactor, the young minister John Harvard of Charlestown, who upon his death in 1638 left his library and estate to the institution. The university has grown from nine students with a single master to more than twenty thousand degree candidates, including undergraduate, graduate, and professional students. According to Harvard's website, more than 360,000 alumni live in the United States and in over 190 other countries.[2]

Harvard has had a distinguished publishing history as well. In 1643, Henry Dunster, the first president of Harvard College, inherited his wife's printing press. Yet, it was not until 1913 that Harvard established the distinguished entity known as the Harvard University Press. The press was unusual in that it was not a distinct corporation but a constituent part of the university. Its books were copyrighted in the name of the president and fellows of Harvard College. The press's first director was C. C. Lane, who was succeeded by Harold Murdock, a Boston banker. Murdock oversaw the press's vast expansion of book series it published as well as scholarly books arising from academic lectures at Harvard.[3]

Unfortunately, Harvard University Press was the venue of one of the most turbulent times in Malone's professional career, which ended with his forced resignation by Harvard president James Conant. Malone became the press's third director in December 1935. He hired the press's first manuscript editors and established the high editorial standards for which the press has become known. Under Malone, the press published such prominent works as Arthur O. Lovejoy's *The Great Chain of Being*, Chester I. Barnard's *The Functions of the Executive*, and Susanne K. Langer's *Philosophy in a New Key*. In 1939 it garnered its first Pulitzer Prize for the second and third volumes of Frank Luther Mott's *A History of American Magazines*. A second Pulitzer came in 1941 for Marcus Lee Hansen's *The Atlantic Migration, 1607–1860*.

"I am not sure going to the Harvard Press was a wise decision," Malone wrote in 1985. At the *DAB*, he had been a manager who dealt with authors.

> If I ever thought I had executive ability, that was the time. The academic market was frozen. When President James B. Conant asked me to take the job at Harvard, I viewed it as a challenge. I hope I did something to bridge the gap between scholars and the public. But I felt frustrated after a time. I was more remote from the work than at the DAB. So it wasn't satisfying to me, but I learned a lot. In the end, I had a disagreement with the administration and resigned. That was very fortunate, however, because if I had stayed on, there would probably have been no Jefferson book.[4]

Author Max Hall, in his book *Harvard University Press: A History*, chronicled in detail the hiring and, ultimately, firing of Dumas Malone. Hall reported that in 1935 President Conant was planning his final attempt to find a press director from outside Harvard's ranks, before he promoted someone from within. In August he received a letter from Mark Antony De Wolfe Howe of the class of 1887. Howe was a prolific author and former editor from Beacon Hill, as well as a member of the influential Harvard Board of Overseers. He was also a major contributor to the *DAB*. Knowing that the final volume of the dictionary was nearing completion, he suggested Malone as director. In his glowing letter of recommendation, Howe gave Conant some background on Malone: he was forty-three years old, a southerner, and a Yale-trained historian. With his letter, he enclosed a copy of Malone's entry in *Who's Who in America* and said he thought that few American scholars knew more about publishing. Conant queried several editors and scholars about Malone. The responses were persuasive. Maxwell Perkins of Scribner's, the publisher of the *Dictionary of American Biography*, observed "that Malone would be an excellent appointment."[5] At the time, the Harvard history department was unsurpassed, with notables such as Samuel Eliot Morison, John Fairbank, Charles H. Taylor, Arthur Schlesinger Sr., and John Kenneth Gailbraith in economics.

In late 1935 Conant offered Malone the position—and extended a challenge to make Harvard University Press into an independent publisher of fine scholarly books. In fact, during his seven turbulent years at the helm, Malone substantially increased the number of press-owned books and doubled its income from sales.

Before accepting the job, Malone told Conant that he could not yet leave the *Dictionary of American Biography*. Seventeen volumes had been published, but the remaining three were in the final stages of production. Conant agreed to allow Malone to serve part-time at first, and the Harvard Corporation formally voted to appoint Malone as director of the press, effective December 1, 1937 (even though Malone was offered and accepted the position in December of 1935). The university announced Malone's appointment on December 4 and at the same time named David Pottinger as associate director. Pottinger wrote Malone a warm letter of welcome, pledging his support and enclosing a list of employees in the Publishing Department with their salaries and duties. In what would turn out to be a colossal understatement, he said the job "may seem, in the beginning at least, to have difficulties," but, he added, "I can assure you that it also has its durable satisfactions."[6]

The press's headquarters was located on Quincy Street, just off the Harvard Yard in a building that is no longer standing. Malone thought he "had a better set up than I had had in Washington. My office was in a large and pleasant room on the first floor in a large room at the front of the house. My own secretary received visitors, pitted her typewriter and answered the telephone." The associate director and his secretary were across the hall while the sales manager and the editors were upstairs. "I regarded myself as the Editor and looked on them as my assistants, but actually I did far less editing in this position than I had done on the DAB."[7] Most employees at the press thought Malone "gracious, learned, articulate, strong-minded, and willing to make unpopular decisions."[8]

Malone had no doubts about the nature of his mission. He was a "middleman of learning." The press existed not only to transfer the results of investigation from one scholar to another but also to serve as "a bridge between the whole group of scholars and the outside world."[9]

In January 1938, at a banquet dinner in the Fogg Museum celebrating the press's twenty-fifth birthday, Malone called for books going beyond "barren displays of erudition."[10] The lavish dinner attracted a large number of carefully chosen representatives of the various schools and departments. Malone sat between former president Lowell and President Conant, who introduced Malone as "the right man in the right place."[11]

In his speech that night Malone used the now famous expression "scholarship plus" several times, according to Hall's account. By this he meant that Harvard's publications should meet both the literary and the human interest test; in other words, he wanted to publish books for everyone, not just for scholars. During his tenure as editor, the critical spirit became highly developed at Harvard University Press, "but occasionally, on a Departmental recommendation, we published a book which hardly anybody wanted to read . . . approval of Departmental books was virtually automatic, however, and there was really little that we could do with these except prepare them for the printer."[12]

Later that month, in an address titled "The Scholar and the Public," Malone reiterated his sentiments. At the American Philosophical Society in Philadelphia, he argued that academic publishers should be more rigorous in selection, not only for financial reasons but also for the sake of scholarship. No publishing house could perform its more important functions if it were swamped with dissertations and other "minor monographs." University presses ought to publish major works of scholarship, Malone concluded, "even if the sales prospects were relatively discouraging—a sentiment that would soon run afoul of Conant and the Board of Syndics."[13]

Malone saw the Harvard University Press as an intellectual and literary endeavor, rather than as a business or for-profit publishing house. Over time, however, the Printing Office, which was a service agency, became a continuing headache for him. It incurred upon the press "the ill will of some of the departments and consumed his time and energy with administrative problems that he had not foreseen in accepting the Directorship."[14]

One of Malone's first acts was to execute decisions regarding the Printing Office that had already been made. "I was a sort of lord high executioner," Malone explained. Herbert Jacques, the accountant who headed the printing operation, was terminated. So was J. Tuckerman Day, the editor who headed the proof room. About this time the press bought its first linotype machines. All this reorganizing and equipping was supposed to expedite the work and reduce the prices charged to university departments.[15]

One of the biggest changes at the press was the replacement of the syndics. Never in the press's history had there been another such turnover in the board. According to Hall, President Conant instructed Malone to "start from scratch. All of the old members submitted their resignations, and the Harvard Corporation accepted them as of July 1, 1936. . . . George Lyman Kittredge turned seventy-six that year. Conant thought he had been too long a power at the Press and indeed should retire from the faculty. He privately asked Kittredge to do this. Kittredge reluctantly complied."[16]

The corporation had already appointed Malone as board chairman. In addition to Paul Sachs, a professor at Harvard who eventually became chairman of the Syndics of the Press, it appointed the following faculty members chosen by Malone: Edward S. Mason, on his way to becoming one of Harvard's most distinguished economists and administrators; Thomas Barbour, a naturalist who directed the Museum of Comparative Zoology; Zechariah Chafee Jr., professor of law; A. Baird Hastings, professor of biological chemistry in the Medical School; James B. Munn, professor of English; and Ralph Barton Perry, professor of philosophy and winner of a Pulitzer Prize for his biography of William James. In 1938 one more faculty member joined the corporation: Malcolm P. McNair, a professor of marketing at the Business School. Malone later regretted this move because McNair became one of his sharpest critics.[17]

At first, the syndics, Conant, and Malone worked smoothly together. Conant did not question Malone's ability to perform the functions of his chairman position while he was working at the press, but he believed that as a house master (internal matter), Malone should have an academic title. Accordingly, "he offered to appoint me a professor of history. After discussing with incumbents the costs of being a House Master, I concluded that I simply could not afford it."[18]

The syndics backed Malone in several policy changes, including implementing a firmer attitude toward the other entities of the university.

Invoking the press's authority over its own imprint, "he insisted that the Press control the printing, the typographical formats, and the editorial standards of all the books it published, even series books owned and financed by Harvard schools and departments. Malone also began the practice of bringing series books before the Syndics along with other manuscripts."[19]

He also installed his own editorial staff at 38 Quincy Street. The action was perfectly in line with his idea of "scholarship plus." "Surely," he wrote, "the Press has no more important function to perform than that of helping to make good books better."[20] To that end, he imported two manuscript editors from his completed *Dictionary of American Biography*: Eleanor Dobson and Dorothy Greenwald. Both were earnest and meticulous and had high standards. Malone instructed that all manuscripts would pass through the hands of the new editorial staff members and be edited by them. "Later we found," Dorothy Greenwald remembered, "that the really admirable proofreaders had for years done a wonderful job of catching inconsistencies and preventing errors, and I sometimes wondered whether we were achieving more." But, in time, the editorial department became widely recognized for helping to make "good books better."[21]

With the arrival of one more secretary, the old yellow house on Quincy Street, with its fireplace in every room and its peeling wallpaper, had nine occupants, a small group compared to the typesetters, pressmen, proofreaders, bookkeepers, and shippers crowding Randall Hall. The nine were Malone, Pottinger, and their secretaries on the first floor and Warren Smith, Horace Arnold, Eleanor Dobson, Dorothy Greenwald, and Grace Alva Briggs on the second. This staff published an average of seventy-seven books a year during Malone's editorship.[22]

During four of the seven years Malone was at the press, the Malone family lived in Lincoln, Massachusetts, a serene and relatively unspoiled village near Boston. They rented a white house that was just being vacated by Bernard DeVoto, who was going to New York to assume the editorship of the *Saturday Review of Literature*. Built in 1815, the house was the stateliest and most commodious house in which the Malones ever lived. "Elisabeth developed a lovely garden and we had an apple tree that was glorious in the spring. Having grown up in the deep South, I myself never became fully reconciled to the snow and the excessively long winters," he later wrote.[23]

Lincoln seemed unusually pleasant, and Dumas recalled it was an especially good place for children. Gifford was six and Pamela was four when they arrived. Lincoln was small enough to have town meetings of the old-fashioned type, and Malone attended several of these to the benefit of "my historical education."

The hurricane of 1939 occurred while they were living there. Dozens of elm trees were uprooted during the storm, and they lost their beloved apple tree. Elisabeth's father and mother were by then retired and living in Cape Cod year-round. After the hurricane, when the roads were sufficiently cleared, Elisabeth drove down to see how her parents had fared. On her way back, she suffered an extraordinary accident. Her car skidded after hitting a slew of rocks in the road and jumped a low stone wall. Fortunately she suffered no injury. The accident was not the reason the family left Lincoln, although the "loss of our apple tree was a consideration," Malone later wrote.

In 1940, when gasoline was becoming scarce because of the war in Europe, the Malones bought a house on Belmont Hill, where they lived for the next three years. According to Malone, there was "a small but admirable day school almost behind our house and this proved just the place for our children. The years prior to the American entrance into the War were good years."[24]

After the United States entered World War II in 1941, a fundamental change occurred in the life of the Harvard community. President Conant traveled a great deal to perform a scientific service for the federal government. He had greater things on his mind than the press's financial problems. "I saw him rarely and our private relations became more impersonal," Malone wrote.[25]

Yet among the influential works published during this period, two books won Pulitzer Prizes and several exceeded $100,000 in sales over the course of many years. Not until many years after Malone's departure was it fully realized how "big" these books were. As author Max Hall concluded, "When a university press publishes the scholarly equivalent of a best seller, the accomplishment may take shape in small increments over decades, during which the book demonstrates its enduring value."[26]

Under Malone's stewardship, the books that drew the most publicity and attained the largest sales were in the fields of business, law, philosophy, and architecture. The press's rise in the field of business became especially impressive. The Harvard Business School, "the scene of intense intellectual ferment, took a central part in this rise, but the book that led the rest in circulation and influence was written by the president of the New Jersey Bell Telephone Company."[27]

Under Malone, national recognition came to the press in the form of distinguished prizes. In 1938 *We Americans*, by Elin L. Anderson, won the John Anisfield Prize for the best book on "racial relationships." Morison's unfinished history of Harvard brought him the Loubat Prize, offered by Columbia University every five years for the best work on "the history, geography, archaeology, ethnology, philology, or numismatics of North America."[28]

The press's first Pulitzer Prize under Malone's direction came in 1939 for a work by Frank Luther Mott. He won the award in U.S. history for the second and third volumes of *A History of American Magazines* (1938). Mott headed the journalism school at Iowa State and later at Missouri. The press's second Pulitzer came in 1941 for *The Atlantic Migration, 1607–1860.* The author, Marcus Lee Hansen, died in 1938 before his prize could be awarded. Arthur M. Schlesinger Sr., who worked in Harvard's history department at the time, turned Hansen's rough draft into a polished manuscript and delivered it to Malone. Schlesinger gave the following account in his autobiography: "Marcus Lee Hansen of the University of Illinois, dying when but forty-five, had spent two decades gathering material, mostly in Old World archives, on the social and economic background of emigrant groups to America from colonial days to the Civil War; and in his last hours he expressed the wish that I put the manuscript into final shape or that it be destroyed, an alternative which would have entailed a grave loss to knowledge."[29]

By 1948 the press's sales had passed $45,000 for the year. In the "emotional atmosphere of the war effort," Hall wrote, "the Press published two eloquent little books by Harvard leaders. One was *Our Fighting Faith*, by President Conant, consisting mainly of talks he had given to undergraduates. The other was *Our Side Is Right*, by Ralph Barton Perry." The sale of both books came as a disappointment. Conant's sold about thirty-five hundred copies, and Perry's, about two thousand copies. *Our Fighting Faith* was Conant's first book since he had become president nine years previously.

Hoping for a wide audience, he first offered the manuscript to Roger L. Scaife of Little, Brown, who turned it over to Malone. The press published it quickly. But Malone's critics "felt he mishandled the project. An assistant to the president complained that he could not find *Our Fighting Faith* on display in Harvard Square, whereupon Warren Smith persuaded all the bookstores in the vicinity to put it in their windows. According to Smith's recollection many years later, nearly all those books were returned unsold."[30]

After Malone had left the press and *Our Fighting Faith* had sold three thousand copies, Conant learned that another publisher had published a book with the same title. Hall wrote of Conant's reaction: "[He] took this to mean that the other publisher had never heard of his book. He complained in a letter to Malone's successor, 'I am afraid this is only one more bit of evidence to indicate that as the Press has been run one might just as well drop the book into the Atlantic Ocean as to have it published through that medium.'"[31]

The atmosphere had not always been hostile between Malone and Conant. In fact, at the twenty-fifth anniversary of the press in January 1938, Conant, presiding over seventy banqueters, proposed a toast to "the future of the Harvard University Press—solvent, significant, successful."[32] The next day he congratulated Malone on his "scholarship plus" speech at the banquet and said the university was fortunate to have him.

Malone, however, had already been cautioning the Harvard administration about the press's bleak financial outlook. In its March 1937 study of overhead expenses, the press not only found that publishing overhead amounted to 45 cents on each dollar of sales income but went on to explore the implications of this. More important, the worrisome questions about the press's finances and its function in the university hung unresolved for another year or so while the war raged in Europe. Meanwhile its reputation for good books continued upward, and as late as May 1941 Conant told Malone, "The general history of the Press for the past year is certainly one of which you may well be proud. My congratulations and best wishes. Keep it up!"[33]

But relations between the Malone press and the administration began to disintegrate. The single crucial factor in this deterioration was the appointment of William H. Claflin Jr. to preside over the press's business affairs. Claflin, the university treasurer, had been president of a sugar company and a partner in a Boston brokerage firm. Arthur Schlesinger Jr. wrote that just before World War II began, Claflin told President Conant, "Hitler's going to win. Let's be friends with him."[34] In wartime, the treasurer ran the university's financial and business affairs with a frugal iron fist. This circumstance, Hall noted, "together with Conant's preoccupations elsewhere, gave Claflin a high degree of authority. He had no close knowledge of publishing problems and probably had little opportunity to appreciate the importance of the books Malone was publishing. Not being the most patient of men, he was not likely to go about the matter in the gentlest of ways."[35]

Claflin's prescription for the press's ills and difficulties was the practice of "strict economy." He erupted when he learned that his predecessor had authorized a $50,000 loan account for working capital and that the press had drawn $35,060 of it by June 1941. "Claflin ordered that no more money be paid out of this fund," author Max Hall wrote. "Malone believed that Conant did not have an adverse view of him as a publisher until after the president returned from one of his wartime absences and received a report from Claflin."[36]

"Dealing with Bill Claflin was a very different matter . . . he was a tough-minded businessman, rather intimidating in manner and he knew nothing whatever about publishing. As a guardian of the finances of the University in a troubled time, he was unquestionably effective, but he seemed to me rather like a bull in a china shop, and I am quite sure that I fell a good deal below his standard as a businessman," Malone later wrote with some bitterness.[37]

Malone requested the syndics' support. In July 1942 he held a special meeting, during which he told the syndics something had to be done and asked them to draw up a memorandum to Conant. Conant had indicated to Malone seven years before that he wanted the press run on an academic, and not sales, basis, and therefore "it should now be judged not from a commercial standpoint but for its contribution to intellectual and academic life."

The syndics' memorandum to Conant was everything Malone hoped for. "Whether Conant ever saw it is unclear," Hall wrote. The committee members invited Claflin to dinner and expressed confidence that they could work things out with Malone. The committee made the following points about Malone and the press, according to Hall's account:

- The press had lived up to its expectations for issuing quality books.
- The syndics were prepared to examine finances and any other problems.

- The press was as deserving of support in wartime as in any other time.
- The press should not be expected to end each year in the black and should be one of the small group of "deficit departments," along with the library.
- The corporation needed to make a definite statement on its policy. The tentative status of the press was "demoralizing, discouraging, and unfair from any point of view."[38]

Years later, in his unpublished memoir, Malone reflected on his troubles at Harvard:

> With the benefit of hindsight, I can see that I was much too trustful. I did not realize how insistent the financial authorities of the University were on the principle that every tub must stand on its own bottom. But the main task of a University Press, as I perceived it, was to publish meritorious works which commercial houses could not afford to handle. Therefore, I naively assumed that the richest University in the country would provide [some sort of subsidy]. Claflin regarded the Press as a business and judged it almost exclusively in business terms. I don't believe he gave much thought to its services as a disseminator of learning.[39]

All this time Malone himself was "basically a lame-duck leader. I did not regard myself as wholly lacking in managerial ability, but it seemed that I was now expected to be more of a businessman than I wanted or was qualified to be. I was uncomfortable in this situation but was in no position to resign."[40] The academic market had again become stagnant, and student enrollments were declining sharply. Faculty appointments were few and far between. Malone had a family to support and nothing but his salary to depend on. "It was a time of deep gloom in the Western World," Malone admitted, "and there was plenty of fear in the atmosphere of Cambridge, but with characteristic optimism I believed the Press could muddle through."[41]

In January 1943 he proposed to the syndics that both his salary and his routine tasks be reduced. In April the syndics agreed. Conant responded via the syndics on whether they had confidence in Malone as director. Conant groaned that Malone had proposed, in effect, "that he abdicate as Director and become literary editor" with considerable time for his own scholarly and literary activities. This was not Conant's concept of the position to which the corporation had appointed Malone.

Even syndics who liked Malone and admired his accomplishments doubted his future effectiveness. Conant told the syndics that if the result were a vote of no confidence, Malone would be paid his full, one-year salary. After the poll, Sachs told the president that a large majority had voted "no confidence."

Conant met with Malone in June. Hall writes, "Conant may have had this meeting in mind when he said to an interviewer thirty years later: 'I remember having a session with him and he suggested that we'd better call it quits. He was thinking around that time of a better basis for his work on Jefferson. I think it was a sort of mutual decision. For all I know, Dumas might say that his departure was accelerated.'"[42]

Malone submitted his letter of resignation on July 17. In it, he wrote that he could not be satisfied in a position "where the major criteria by which my work is judged differ materially from those applied to the academic departments of the University." He had no desire to head an organization that approximated a commercial publishing house. In his defense, he argued that during the last seven years the literary standards of the press had greatly improved and that it had reflected well on Harvard.[43]

The corporation promptly accepted Malone's resignation. At their next meeting they voted for a year's severance. The university issued a news release saying that Malone had resigned to devote himself to his Jefferson biography and that Roger Scaife would be acting director until a new director was appointed.

In his memoir, Malone lamented on his Harvard tenure:

[When] I was editing at the DAB, I had no financial responsibility. I had a salary and that was it. But at the Harvard Press, I was responsible for all the finances. When I was on the dictionary, at least I edited a lot, but on the Harvard Press, I didn't even edit. I had other people to edit, and I couldn't even read all the books. Other people did that, and I had to judge their judgments. I was getting more and more remote, and I finally decided that was too much and quit. Business responsibility is a great burden to me, and I don't like it. I like to write. But it took me half my life almost to find out what I most like to do. That's not so surprising, I guess. That's just the way things are.[44]

For many years Malone had almost no communication with the press and had tried to block the Harvard experience out of his mind. In 1970 he was invited to a dinner for an editor that he had hired, Eleanor Dobson Kewer. Around that time, he also wrote a letter to Mark Carroll, then director of the press. In the letter, Malone became almost nostalgic for his years at Harvard, and he praised colleagues he had worked with there: "Few can remember as well as I how admirably [Eleanor Dobson] met the needs and bore the responsibilities of her important post in that day of small things. . . . I am sure that the high quality of her work has been unvarying. Fortunately there come times when credit can be given where credit is due. . . . This is one of them and I am happy on this occasion to pay tribute to an ideal editor."[45] This was a trait that ran throughout Malone's life—amiability and an almost herculean effort to name and give credit to others for work that he had undertaken himself.

In July 1981, when Malone turned eighty-nine—and much in the public eye because volume 6 of *Jefferson and His Time* had just appeared—one of the messages he valued most was a telegram that read, "Undoubtedly one of the great moments in human events is the publication of the last volume of your Thomas Jefferson biography. Warmest congratulations from the Harvard University Press to its distinguished former director."[46]

Malone ultimately moved back to Charlottesville and worked on his Jefferson biography during the twelve months covered by his Harvard salary. He had "had to make difficult and painful readjustments in my private affairs" on leaving the press, "but it proved to be an exceedingly fortunate occurrence. It enabled me to resume my interrupted journey with Mr. Jefferson."[47] Five years later, in 1948, *Jefferson the Virginian*, volume 1 of his epic, was published. This event must have pleased Roger Scaife, his interim successor at Harvard, because it was he who had signed Dumas Malone to the Little, Brown contract for his Jefferson biography.

11   Columbia

*Somebody said he couldn't imagine anyone foolish
enough to write a biography of Jefferson. The poor devil
would enter a labyrinth of architecture, science, politics
and never come out.*

—DUMAS MALONE, 1981[1]

*The first generation of American public men was the
greatest [generation]. I particularly addressed myself to
the Virginians. They had the largest numbers of these
leaders and the most distinguished group.*

—DUMAS MALONE[2]

When Little, Brown's managing editor, Roger Scaife, signed Malone to the most important book contract in either man's career, the title of the project was *A Life of Thomas Jefferson*. The contract, signed on June 1, 1938, called for two to four volumes; it was amended to six volumes years later. In his letter to Scaife, Malone outlined five reasons why he was writing the book: "I want to write an extensive biography of Jefferson and to make this if I can the most important literary and historical work of my life. In view of what I've done on the subject already my deep interest in it would be little short of tragic not to carry out the plan I made 15 years ago."[3]

Malone explained that he could not "give an appreciable amount of time to the project for another year and perhaps for two years and even after a good start. . . . [It] will be necessary to complete the work distinctly as a long-range proposition. The offer of Little Brown in your letter of March 22, 1938 is a generous one, and as good as I can ever hope to receive." But Malone did not feel comfortable accepting the cash advance "before, I have cleaned up pending tasks and begun to work in earnest on the project. After a year or so, perhaps, I might avail myself of this part of your very generous offer. But at the moment, I don't think I would be right to do so."[4]

Scaife responded to "my Dear Malone" and wrote that his letter "pleased us all greatly. We are delighted at the prospect and the honor of publishing your biography of Jefferson, although we realize some years may lapse before completion. We are quite ready to wait. I quite understand your reluctance to accept any money until the work is progressed to a certain point. We are, however, quite ready to carry out our original offer if you should change your mind."[5]

"He offered me a generous contract," Malone confessed. "This turned out to be a fortunate action, but it may seem surprising that I took it at this particular time." What Malone considered generous was the original offer of $1,000 for an option to publish the work, on the basis of an advance of $2,500 per volume against a royalty of 15 percent. The book was originally to be printed at the Harvard University Press, but that plan was abandoned when Malone resigned.[6]

Scaife outlined his thoughts on the book in regard to potential publicity and sales: "I have discussed the matter of bringing out the first volume of Jefferson in 1943, and I find the general agreement that this would be a good thing to do, but it is important that not too long an interval elapse between the publications of the first volume and the others." Scaife reasoned that if the first volume could be published in 1943, it would have the threefold value (1) "of securing the additional publicity value, which will come from the bicentennial celebration of Jefferson's birth in 1743; (2) of the time and timeliness of bringing Jefferson into the picture during the period, which is destined to be one of great political and world significance; and (3) of paving the way for a really substantial sale of the work as a whole." Scaife, always the businessman, further pressed Malone to finish the book as soon as possible: "I don't suppose there's any chance of your having say the first volume of Jefferson ready for publication during the year 1943 at which time the Bicentennial celebration will be held. If so, you and we together would gain an added publicity value, which might mean larger sales."[7]

Book sales were not an altogether foreign subject to Malone. While he worked at the Harvard University Press, he had become cognizant of how important they were to an author's reputation. In a letter to Larned Bradford of Little, Brown years later, he wrote, "I am more and more persuaded of the desirability of getting *Jefferson the Virginian* out in paper as soon as possible. My present feeling indeed, is that you might also get out *Jefferson and the Rights of Man.* I'm not so sure about volume three. I believe we're missing out on a good deal by not having these volumes available in a cheaper and more saleable form."[8]

Early in 1944 Douglas Southall Freeman, the renowned Civil War historian, suggested that Malone's Jefferson project might receive a grant from the Rockefeller Foundation, of which Freeman was a trustee. Malone's lack of an institutional connection would be an obstacle, for the foundation did not make grants to individuals. President John Newcomb of the University of Virginia and Harry Clemons, the UVA librarian, worked out a scheme with Malone that satisfied the foundation. Malone was appointed honorary consultant in biography in the Alderman Library, and a grant to the University of Virginia in support of his Jefferson biography was requested. Freeman paved the way for Malone by discussing the project with David H. Stevens, who handled such matters for the foundation. Freeman arranged for Malone to interview and advised him sagaciously at every turn.

The Rockefeller grant was important because Malone's income had to be supplemented. His account book for this period has been preserved, and

> it tells a story, much of which I have tried to forget. In the spring of 1945, about a year after I went on the grant, I drew up a list of loans on life insurance and advances by the publishers by means of which I had supplemented my income during the two years that I had been working on the Jefferson project. . . . Looking at this list after nearly forty years, I found it appalling and wondered how I could possibly have got myself into such a situation.

By this time, Malone was intimately familiar with Jefferson's own finances and knew that he bore a heavy burden of debt during most of his life. "This was one respect in which I did not want to emulate him."[9]

In the midsummer of 1943, leaving his family on Cape Cod, Malone returned to Jefferson's home country and the university he had fathered. Malone had written no part of the comprehensive biography for which he had signed a contract five years earlier and which he had envisaged a dozen years before. He had a considerable collection of notes, however, made at one time or another, and in due course he was to make use of these. "I was resuming an interrupted journey and my distinguished companion was no stranger," he remarked.[10] Malone embarked on his new beginning after his personal and professional disappointment at Harvard. He now meant to go through life and history with Thomas Jefferson step by step, guided by the archives.

Although there was no specific timetable for the delivery of the manuscript, at Malone's request, Little, Brown delayed the announcement of the book. "I did not want anybody else to undertake a comprehensive biography of Thomas Jefferson, and I dared hope that the formal announcement of my project would serve as a deterrent. But I certainly did not think that I could stake out an exclusive claim."[11]

While Malone had been at Harvard, his situation had not been favorable to extended research on the Jefferson book or its writing, but he found time to compose an imaginary letter from Mr. Jefferson to President Roosevelt. Jefferson's imagined response to the Depression and World War II was first presented at a meeting of the Examiner Club in Boston. Among those in attendance were Justice Felix Frankfurter; Mark A. De Wolfe Howe, dean of the local literati; Judge Charles Zanski of the U.S. District Court; and Frank Buxton, editor of the *Boston Herald*.

Shortly before Jefferson's two hundredth birthday, Malone's letter appeared as the leading article in the bicentennial issue of the *Virginia Quarterly Review*. Presumably Malone felt compelled to write it because of anti-British sentiment in Boston during the war and his fear that Jefferson would be quoted in support of this. As Malone noted, Jefferson strongly favored cooperation with the British by the time of the Monroe Doctrine. Malone wanted to make it abundantly clear that Jefferson would have supported the British against Hitler at the time of World War II:

> I had tried to sum up and interpret his domestic as well as his foreign policy. Thus I had him say: If I were living now, you may be sure that I should oppose with all the force at my command whatever should seem to be the

greatest tyrannies of the age, the chief obstacles to the free life of the human spirit and I should favor what seem to be the most effective means of bringing appropriate opportunity within the reach of all, regardless of race or economic status. But I must protest against the use of my name in defense of purposes that are alien to my spirit. If there is anything eternal about me it is the purposes that I voiced and the spirit that I showed. So far as methods are concerned, the supreme law of life is the law of change.[12]

The editor of the *Virginia Quarterly Review* sent a copy of Malone's article to Stephen Early, an aide to President Roosevelt, expressing the hope that Roosevelt would read it. Malone did not receive any indication that Roosevelt ever did, but when going through his papers many years later, Malone's startled secretary discovered a handwritten letter signed by FDR. "This I had entirely forgotten," Malone told his secretary.[13] Malone suspected, however, that the letter may have been authored by Charles P. Sisson, who was then at the Judge Advocate General School at the University of Virginia. He had been an assistant attorney general in the administration of Herbert Hoover and had often bantered with Malone about the Democratic and Republican parties.

On April 13, 1943, a crowd of five thousand gathered on the blustery shores of the Tidal Basin in Washington, D.C., to witness the dedication of the new Thomas Jefferson Memorial. A towering likeness of Jefferson gazed out from the rotunda as President Franklin D. Roosevelt delivered a speech from the steps below. "Today, in the midst of a great war for freedom," Roosevelt began somberly, "we dedicate this shrine of freedom to Thomas Jefferson, apostle of freedom." Jefferson was now officially admitted into the "trinity of immortals," that is, Washington, Lincoln, and Jefferson.

The U.S. Marine Band ("the President's Band") played music, and then Bishop Peter Ireton gave the benediction. Those in attendance included the legendary Speaker of the House Sam Rayburn; Cordell Hull, the secretary of state; Colgate Darden, then governor of Virginia; and the Honorable John Newcomb, president of the University of Virginia.

As Roosevelt spoke, Dumas Malone listened intently to his eloquent words. The next day Malone participated in a symposium on the founding father at the Library of Congress. Among those present besides Archibald MacLeish, librarian of Congress, were famous journalist Walter Lippmann, Professor Allan Nevins, and Julian P. Boyd, curator of Princeton's Jefferson papers. Justice Frankfurter gave an address titled "The Permanence of Jefferson" in the Coolidge Auditorium at the library. His remarks were followed by a concert by the Budapest String Quartet.

Malone observed,

> Almost the only other thing beyond my own blundering that I remember about this symposium was a remark of Walter Lippmann's to the effect that the Jeffersonian principle of self-government was too strong a dose for many of the peoples of the world. Actually Jefferson himself said that about the French in 1789. . . . The symposium had reminded me as a historian that I had accumulated a good deal of administrative rust. I was soon to have ample opportunity to brush this off.[14]

In the fall Malone brought his wife and two children from Massachusetts to a furnished house he had rented from a UVA professor who was away on war leave. "For all of us a new chapter had begun," he wrote.[15]

While Charlottesville was a haven for his family during the last two years of the war and the Alderman Library was the center of his professional activities, Malone spent much of his time in Washington. This was chiefly in the Manuscripts Division of the Library of Congress, but for a time, in the winter of 1943–44, he was occupied at the Pentagon. Malone served on a secret committee of historians set up by Gen. Henry "Hap" Arnold to advise the Air Force about its bombing policy. The committee included Carl Becker, Bernadotte E. Schmitt, Louis Gottschalk, and other scholars of distinction with whom Malone considered it a pleasure to associate. "None of us thought our counsel would be of much value but we dutifully repaired to the Pentagon, where we were regaled with inside information about air raids. The horrors of war we seem to have taken as a matter of course," Malone confided.[16]

In fact, Malone had been chosen to head the committee as "chief historian" by Col. Frank Monaghan. In a letter to Malone, Monaghan revealed, "Several months ago, I thought that I had found a most exciting position for you: chief historian of Allied Military Government. I gave your name first, and they were delighted. Then . . . they informed me that the chosen person would have to be in uniform." Monaghan apologized but ended by saying he hoped that "[you] find it possible to stop off in Washington, so that we can talk of things, including Jefferson and Hamilton."[17]

After six weeks, Malone's secret committee managed to produce a report. Malone recalled "that we fully recognized the necessity of an invasion of the Continent. In fact, we were confident that one had already been decided on and were somewhat fearful of finding out when it would occur. Daylight savings time was continued through the year in this period of austerity and . . . the winter of 1943 and '44 in Washington was grim."[18]

On completion of his duty, the War Department sent Malone an honorary certificate and expressed "its appreciation for patriotic service in a position of trust and responsibility to Professor Dumas Malone. As a member of the Army Air Forces Secret Committee of Historians to study Germany's war potential, dated March 1, 1946."[19]

As the war drew to an end, the academic market, which had been frozen, began to thaw. At some time during the spring of 1945, Malone received a visit from Professor John A. Krout, chairman of the History Department at Columbia University. Krout had been a contributor to the *Dictionary of American Biography*, and Malone had corresponded with him frequently.

Krout boldly offered Malone a position as professor of history at Columbia. Malone initially declined on the grounds that he was obligated to the Rockefeller Foundation to give full time to the Jefferson book for two more years. In fact, the foundation had reason to believe that Malone would continue to give full time to it until he had finished. A few months later Malone received a visit from a determined Allan Nevins, an esteemed professor at Columbia. Nevins added his arguments to those of his colleague and was largely responsible for the outcome. The Rockefeller Foundation agreed to an arrangement—Malone could give part-time teaching service to Columbia during the lifetime of the grant, but the grant would be administered by the University of Virginia. When it expired, it was renewed for a year at a reduced rate and administered by Columbia.

At the time of Krout's offer, Columbia's History Department was one of the strongest in the country. Malone thought it a privilege to even be considered for the position. Nevins was Columbia's most prolific member and its most colorful. Like Douglas Freeman, Nevins was determined never to waste a minute, Malone recalled. But unlike Freeman, Nevins gave the impression of always being in a hurry; he was a man who never walked but always ran. He was notoriously reluctant to tear himself away from his research and writing. Nevins and his wife, Mary,

> were very hospitable, but he had a way of remaining in his study just as long as he could, hoping to write a few more sentences. On one occasion that I remember he did this until all the guests had assembled. We were standing in a sort of circle. Allan gravely shook hands with each one of the group, including his own son-in-law. Our host was probably still thinking of the last sentence he had had written. . . . His absorption in his work and his concentration on it bordered on the obsessive.[20]

Malone never doubted that any other American historian of his generation directed more doctoral dissertations than did Nevins. "I never regarded myself as very good at supplying topics for others, but Allan seemed never to be at a loss," Malone said. His enthusiasm for research and writing was contagious. Nevins stimulated many a novice and probably "did more than any other professor of his day to popularize history. Some of his more cautious colleagues viewed him with disfavor, and at times he seemed to be moving too fast for safety, but he was a remarkable man by any reckoning and unquestionably a great historical reporter."[21]

Nevins also had a vast library. His study, which adjoined Malone's, had ten thousand volumes. Henry Steele Commager, a professor down the hall, also had "a goodly number," Malone remembered. "We did a lot of borrowing from each other and there wasn't much need to go to Butler Library. I was assigned a carrel there, but I practically never used it and therefore gave it up. My study was a good place to work on the second volume of the biography, if only I could find time to do so."[22]

Next to Nevins, Malone became best acquainted with Krout. As a contributor to the *DAB*, Krout had a rare distinction, Malone recalled. His articles seemed virtually errorless and required little or no editing. This was more than could be said of the numerous articles Nevins wrote, "excellent as those were in most respects." When Malone eventually became Krout's colleague at Columbia, he learned that Krout was regarded as the best lecturer in the department. "He was a wise and good man whose friendship I greatly prized."[23]

Initially, however, Krout had a difficult time persuading Malone to come to Columbia. In fact, Malone rebuffed him several times. He reasoned, "I should regard it as a privilege to be associated with such a stimulating and friendly group, and I have no doubt that you will do great things in history. It would be a great pleasure for me to share . . . [but] until I finish the book, this will continue to be the best place for me to be, on both professional and sentimental grounds."[24]

Krout would not take no for an answer:

I can't tell you how sorry I am—we are all—that you won't come here and be with us. We had all looked forward with enthusiasm to having you as a colleague and companion and we had hoped that you might re-create here that interest in the study of the South, which has long been neglected. Yet I can understand your reluctance to leave any place [like] Charlottesville and to move away from the living spirit of Jefferson to the stronghold of Hamilton, or perhaps even to Babylon.[25]

Krout remained persistent in his May 1945 letter: "I am glad that I postponed an answer to yours, for I have now had a chance to talk with Professor Nevins and other members of the department. I need not tell you that all of us want you to become a member of the department of history at Columbia. . . . We hope you will be able to accept an appointment as professor of history at a salary of $7500 per annum."[26]

Ultimately, Malone relented and formally accepted the offer. Krout was ebullient: "I'm delighted that you've finally decided to throw in your academic lot with us at Columbia. I think you and yours will like it and I know we are all very happy that you will be able to be with us. . . . Everyone here at the University with whom I have talked is delighted to know that you are really coming to Columbia. It will be good to see you whenever you come."[27]

A number of colleagues also expressed delight with Malone's appointment, most notably Julian Boyd, who lived in Princeton. He hoped to see more of Malone and Elisabeth, he said. Ralph Gabriel, Malone's old professor, wrote, "My heartiest congratulations. I think Columbia also is to be congratulated. . . . Chrisse and I are happy to have you and Elizabeth near by. When the war is over and it is possible to travel once more, I am sure that we shall be able to get together with reasonable frequency."[28]

Malone's beginning part-time salary was $3,000 for the academic year 1945–46. His annual pay climbed several years later to $10,500, and this would remain in effect until July 1, 1952. It would rise only to $15,000 when he returned permanently to UVA in 1959.

"I'll never forget one incident when I was teaching up at Columbia," Malone related.

> We had a lot of graduate students who taught in the local New York schools. And one day I said, let's just forget all this historical stuff for a while and tell me, "is this doing you any good?" And one fellow said, well no, he needed the MA to get a raise, but the PhD was no help. He couldn't raise any fine points in class, there was no time. Well I asked him "why the dickens are you doing it?" First he said, I do it because I like it. Second, there's an awful lot of politicking in the New York schools, people snooping around to see what you're doing, what you say. I come into this room, though, I'm a free man.

Malone said he wanted to cry when he heard that response.[29] Yet, under these circumstances, Malone finished *Jefferson the Virginian* in 1947 and "published it on the great man's birthday in 1948."[30]

12 On Writing and Politics

*But writing has never ceased to be hard work. You can't
have the unalloyed pleasure of just doing research. When
you sit down to write, you just have to do it.*
—**Dumas Malone (1985)**[1]

Malone wrote all, or nearly all, of the first volume of *Jefferson and His
Time* at home. "Mr. Jefferson may have been surprised to find himself translated from the red hills of Albemarle to a Westchester suburb,"
Malone quipped. "And it must have been something of a strain on my wife
to have me home for lunch much more often than before."[2]

Although Malone could compose on the typewriter, he regularly wrote
the first draft of a chapter in longhand. He then proceeded to the typewriter, editing the draft as he went along. He triple-spaced lines to facilitate
further editing and generally did a good deal of editing before making a
fresh copy. His notes remained in the text in parentheses, and he let this
draft lie fallow as long as he could before having a typist make a final copy.
There was virtually no limit to the amount of editing Malone did. He
would try to stop when the law of diminishing returns began to operate.
More important, he was under contractual obligation to submit something
to Little, Brown within a reasonable period.

Malone's writing pattern varied at each stage of his work. For example,
he did not have a research assistant when he wrote his first volume, and

I did absolutely everything myself. That was a very different pattern from the one in the last volume when I had highly competent assistance. Also, there was a good deal of difference in my procedure when I was teaching and when I was not teaching. In the early days, I actually worked when I could, and I would often work at night, at any hour. But in [those] latter years, I stopped writing at night because I found that it affected my sleep.[3]

Malone's philosophy of writing became simple as it evolved over nearly forty years: "never press, but keep eternally at it." Researching his subject thoroughly, he consulted all available sources and let them speak through his writing. He restrained himself from further interpreting the information. Perhaps most important, Malone wrote in a readable style that could appeal to all readers. One did not need to be a historian to understand Malone's prose. The detail flowed endlessly, and the style of writing encouraged the reader to continue.

Years later, when Malone had a secretary, she would date a chapter after she copied it in what Malone believed to be its final form. At this early stage in the volumes, however, "I kept little record of my writing and can speak of progress only in general terms. I did 'keep books' on my research." Thus, by 1943 Malone had already gone through the Jefferson papers in the Massachusetts Historical Society to the year 1801. Whenever he finished "one of the interminable folio volumes of Jefferson's papers in the Library of Congress, I made careful note of it."[4]

The research Malone did on Jefferson's early life "was particularly enjoyable. Suffice it to say that during the bright springtime of Jefferson's life I found him an even more exhilarating intellectual companion than I had expected," Malone confirmed. Although Malone did not read all the books Jefferson read, he dipped into a good many of them and found ample evidence of Jefferson's enthusiasm for knowledge and the confidence in the human mind that characterized his entire life.[5]

Malone could not remember a time during his long association with Little, Brown when his editors objected to the substance of his writing or to his interpretation of events. "They were notably trustful as well as patient, and very rarely did they make critical editorial comment on my writing," he commented.[6]

Through most of the volumes Malone did not have a deadline, but he regularly delivered the copy to his publishers "a good many months before the book was published," and before his deadline.

The person Malone dealt with the most at his publisher was Roger Scaife, who had negotiated his original contract "and but for whom I might never have been associated with this fine old publishing house." Scaife had also handled author Albert J. Beveridge's *Life of John Marshall* and took immense pride in that book. Malone "gained the impression quite early in the game that he didn't think my book was going to come up to it." After Scaife had read a few of Malone's early chapters, he asked Elisabeth on Cape Cod "if she thought my book was interesting!" To match Beveridge's work in interest would have been difficult, Malone thought. "I had approached this task as a scholar, and my first concern was that the book be good history, but I was not writing solely for scholars. . . . I wanted it to be good reading."[7]

Malone was somewhat distraught that Scaife did not think the book was "interesting." Scaife even went so far as to say that Malone's writing was archaic. He knew Scaife might have a point. "I recognized immediately . . . that an author who is dealing with an earlier age and drawing on its documents must be on guard not to write in the style and manner of that age."[8] Much as Malone admired Jefferson as a writer, he did not want to use as many long words and complicated sentences as Jefferson did. He wanted to bridge the gap between the scholar and the public with his Jefferson biography. "On the other hand, I had no intention of embracing the literary fads and fancies of the moment in the effort to be popular."[9]

Much to his chagrin, Malone's first manuscript ended up in the hands of a junior editor, a young man that he had never met. "He was not one of the regular editors, and if he remained with the firm I never heard of him afterward," Malone confided in his memoir with some bitterness. As he recalled, the editor had recently emerged from graduate school. His comments and suggestions were all relayed to Malone through Scaife. "Many of these were excellent," Malone conceded, and he gladly accepted them. "The young fellow was particularly helpful in suggesting cuts. He was a good editor, but he went too far," Malone insisted, alluding to changes that reflected the editor's own taste and personal literary preference.[10]

In Malone's view, some of the changes the editor made actually altered or modified the meaning of a specific passage. "After a time, I became annoyed with the liberties that were being taken with my writing, and I asked that the manuscript for the entire volume be returned to me." Malone had retained carbon copies of his manuscript and had already marked many changes, "which I myself wanted to make. I considered the suggestions of the young editor, accepting those I liked and rejecting the others, and took a fresh look at the book as a whole."[11]

In midwinter, Malone went through the full manuscript from beginning to end. In correspondence with Scaife, he elaborated on his own editorial changes but also instructed Scaife on his idea of "the editorial function and particularly upon its limitations." Malone wrote confidently that he had arrived at these views "on the basis of long experience." Giving solace to one of their prized authors, the president of the publishing house, Alfred McIntyre, told Malone "privately that he agreed that the young editor had overreached himself."[12]

The editorial issues, coupled with the dismal state of Malone's finances, took their toll on the author. "I took a lot of punishment that winter at a time when my fortunes were low," he confessed. "And this did not serve to elevate my spirits." Malone had been warned by others that the Jefferson project may be too big for one author, and also for one editor. His fears seemed to be coming true. "At times I wondered if I had not let myself get lost in the Jeffersonian labyrinth. My full manuscript went to the copy editor in May, 1947. It was not until I saw the book in proof weeks later that I could judge whether the pain and effort had been justified."[13]

In his memoir Malone confided that he was in a quandary about the title of his first volume. It dealt with the American Revolution, but he did not like the original title, *Jefferson the Revolutionary*, because the latter term had gained a connotation "in our age that it did not have in his, and thus might give a false impression. *Jefferson the Democrat*, a title of which I once thought, would have been somewhat premature, and he [Jefferson] hardly ever used the word democrat anyway. He called himself a republican, but in view of the use of that term to designate a later party, I was not satisfied with it. What I finally came to was *Jefferson the Virginian*."[14]

While Malone completed the first volume of the book and during the next three years of his connection with Columbia, the family lived in the attractive suburb of Bronxville, New York. They had moved there at the suggestion of Allan Nevins, and one of the fruits of their stay was a deepening friendship with Nevins and his wife, Mary. Since their two children were away at school—Gifford at Princeton and Pamela at the Putney School in Vermont (en route to Smith College)—and the Malones spent their summers on Cape Cod, "there was no reason for Elisabeth and me to continue to reside in the suburbs. We found quarters in an apartment house belonging to Columbia, on Claremont Avenue just across from the campus of Barnard College and only a stone's throw from the campus."

Malone recalled the arduous move:

> Any move is time-consuming, upsetting, and expensive, and this one was no exception. We had to move in before we had sold our house, and we had to carry the house for several months. We had to pay for the bookcases we installed and other minor improvements. By New York standards, however, the rent was moderate and we were to find this a pleasant place to live. We saw no reason to move again until I retired from Columbia ten years later.[15]

Since Malone was teaching only one course his first year at Columbia, he rarely needed to go to the city more than two days in the week. He taught one of two sections of a colloquium in American civilization. This was a reading and discussion course in intellectual and social history. The other section was taught by Dwight C. Minor, whom Malone knew and liked. These subjects had received a great deal of attention from historians during the years that Malone had been absent from the classroom, and "I had a good deal of catching up to do."[16]

Malone's course required a disproportionate amount of preparation on his part at first. However, in the end, he felt it had enriched his classroom experience, and his contacts "with students and professors were distinctly rewarding."[17] During the two wartime years Malone had worked in the Alderman Library, before his move to Columbia, the University of Virginia had been virtually deserted. He had considered life as a freelance scholar a rather lonely one, and after the austerity of the war years, the intellectual climate of a big university like Columbia stimulated Malone. But his move to Columbia and the metropolitan district had not solved any personal financial problems. Indeed, it created a number of new ones. Salaries at Columbia were relatively low at this stage, and Malone received only part of a salary because of his commitment to the Rockefeller grant. Still, the move to Columbia was unquestionably to his professional advantage.

"I became a better historian as a result of it, and, presumably, a more fitting companion for Mr. Jefferson," Malone explained. "Of necessity, in this period [my] participation in the life of Columbia was sharply limited. I was living on the periphery of the university as well as that of the city. My professional life centered on an unfinished book."[18] In a manner of speaking, Malone had actually finished the first major stage of his long journey with Mr. Jefferson during his first year at Columbia. Although he had only partially written the draft of volume 1 in longhand, he had finished all the research.

It was not until the autumn of 1948, however, that Malone regarded himself as a member of Columbia in the full sense. He was now a member of a graduate faculty who shepherded candidates through to advanced degrees. At the time, Columbia consisted of three graduate faculties: political science, including history and the social sciences; philosophy, including the languages; and natural science and mathematics. The undergraduates, who were fewer in number than the graduate students, attended Columbia College. In Malone's group the emphasis was on research rather than instruction. "I doubt that I ever became truly reconciled to this. Teaching was more to my taste than directing research, and I missed the undergraduates. I gave up the colloquium. Instead, I gave a lecture course and conducted a seminar on the 'Age of Jefferson' the first semester, and the 'Old South' the second. I always liked lecturing, and the topics were thoroughly congenial."[19]

When Malone assumed his full-time academic duties at Columbia, the chief matter of general interest was the presidential election. Malone thought that the American political system had "produced two admirable candidates in Eisenhower and Stevenson. I could not support both of them, however, and I was actually an active member of a large group that had been organized at Columbia in support of Stevenson."[20]

Gifford classified his father as a "moderate Democrat" most of his life. "My father [was not] flamboyant, ostentatious, radical or highly opinionated. He was a moderate in thought and behavior and indeed rejected extremism in any form. His behavior was totally consistent with his philosophy and was even reflected in his personal tastes."[21] A letter in Malone's papers illustrates this point. In corresponding with John Oakes of the *New York Times* in 1964, Malone was asked his opinion of presidential candidate Barry Goldwater and the Republican convention. "There is hardly anything to say about this political coup that somebody hasn't said in print already but . . . I'm taking this very seriously, being terribly afraid of the impact of this man, especially in the South. I've been thinking for a considerable time that the crackpots were gaining, but had not expected such a triumph of irrationality. This is nihilism, not conservatism."[22]

When Dwight Eisenhower had retired from the presidency of Columbia to become a candidate for president, Malone wrote that he had always liked "Ike, as almost everybody else did," and that he was better qualified to be president of the United States than to be president of Columbia. "There was good reason to expect him to take a broad-minded view of international affairs. He was the sort of man one trusted," Malone wrote.[23]

When Eisenhower assumed the presidency of Columbia, Malone wished to present him with a copy of *Jefferson the Virginian*. Malone sought an appointment with him, which took place first thing in the morning and lasted half an hour. Malone recalled that Eisenhower talked a good deal about George Washington, whom he greatly admired. Eisenhower had read many of Washington's war letters and found them pithy, with little frivolity or small talk. Washington wanted his letters so immaculate that he had them rewritten many times by his aides. Malone responded that even Jefferson, a fluent wordsmith, praised Washington's correspondence saying, "He wrote readily, rather diffusely, in an easy and correct style."[24]

In fact, Malone told Eisenhower that he "did not gain the impression that Washington was intimate with Jefferson or any other official, but the two Virginia planters had much in common and appeared to be on admirable personal terms."[25] Eisenhower had even contended in a speech that "Washington was the greatest man ever produced by the English-speaking race." Malone agreed but retorted that "he would have stuck to this side of the Atlantic."[26]

Eisenhower had a proper sense of the subordination of the military to the civil authority, in sharp contrast to his rival, Gen. Douglas MacArthur, Malone observed. Whether Eisenhower got this from Washington, Malone could not know, but "it was in that great man's spirit."[27] The general was less familiar with Jefferson, Malone recalled. He told Malone that he would love to read his book but added that except for westerns, he had not read a book in five years. "He must have said the same thing to somebody else," Malone wrote, "for he was quoted in much those same words afterwards. It was not I who gave him away to the press, though I did tell the story on several occasions. I liked him for his candor and lack of pretense but wondered how he came to be the head of a university."[28]

Malone recalled that Eisenhower conducted himself with dignity but actually participated little in academic affairs. He set up an organization under which he was spared the ordeal of presiding over faculty meetings, and he was summoned to the North Atlantic Treaty Organization (NATO) in the midst of his administration. Malone thought he seemed overwhelmed at times by the burdens that befell him as a public man. Eisenhower deserved much sympathy, Malone thought, because he was clearly not at home in an academic community and stood in some awe of the professors.

The faculty members actually liked Ike personally and were willing to accept him at face value, Malone declared, from his academic vantage. "But he gained little money for Columbia and added nothing to its prestige as a seat of learning. Judging from the enthusiastic reception he received when attending football practice, he would have been popular as Dean of Students, and he probably would have been effective in that role."[29]

Malone, however, was greatly impressed by Adlai Stevenson. He had met Governor Stevenson in Springfield, Illinois, on Lincoln's birthday in 1949, while Malone read a paper to the Abraham Lincoln Association. He owed his invitation to the event to Professor James O. Randall of the University of Illinois, who wrote the article on Abraham Lincoln for the *DAB* and with whom Malone had established a cordial friendship. Malone was introduced to Stevenson and his sister when he passed through the hall that afternoon.

The great event of the birthday celebration was a speech by Vice President Alben Barkley in the evening. Malone had dinner with six Lincoln experts and heard "the veep" over the radio. Barkley made a nonpolitical speech of about an hour's length in which facts and legends about Lincoln were indiscriminately commingled, Malone remembered. "The experts squirmed in their seats when he told stories which they had been unable to verify and some of which they had actually discredited. The next day the Vice President himself said that he had made a terrible speech, but the crowd presumably liked it all right as everybody liked him."[30]

When Malone returned to his hotel that night, he found a note from Stevenson inviting him to breakfast at the governor's mansion the next day. When Malone arrived he was met by a maid who asked him to "rest my things just as they used to do in Virginia." Malone recalled that Stevenson himself had ancestral connections with Albemarle County and that he presided at the breakfast table with grace and charm. Senator Lucas[—whose first name was not referenced in the memoir] and the vice president were also present, and "I found that I had many ties with Barkley. My mother had been born in his part of Kentucky, and he had gone to school with one of her cousins. I had taught his son at the University of Virginia, and we had common acquaintances all over the South."[31]

Barkley, living up to his reputation as a storyteller, did most of the talking. Malone did not recall what, if anything, Stevenson said, but he carried away from this breakfast an impression of a delightful personality. "I am sure that when I got back to New York I told some of my colleagues that I had met a man of distinct presidential potentiality."[32]

Malone was sure that the Democrats had made the best possible nomination. Of all the presidential candidates of the postwar era, Malone regarded Stevenson as the most literate and articulate and as the one whose values most closely resembled those of Jefferson. Whether Stevenson was tough enough to meet the problems of that harsh period Malone did not know, but he continued to support him in 1956 and never ceased to admire him. Malone did not actually meet him again until 1960, when he was back at the University of Virginia. Stevenson made a speech in the exercises on Jefferson's birthday, "and of course it was a good one." This was the year when the directors of the Thomas Jefferson Memorial Foundation, of whom Malone was one, inaugurated the custom of celebrating this occasion with a dinner at Monticello. Adlai Stevenson was their first honored guest, and "no one could have fitted the occasion better," Malone wrote.[33]

In retrospect, it appeared that Stevenson faced virtually insurmountable odds in his contest with Eisenhower. He battled a legendary hero. Military fame has often been exploited for political ends in the course of our national history, Malone recorded, and "the results have sometimes been unfortunate."[34]

While he taught at Columbia, Malone yearned to get back to his Jefferson biography, and he missed the South, especially Charlottesville, terribly. Throughout his long years of absence, he kept in touch with the University of Virginia.[35]

While on sabbatical from Columbia in the summer of 1952, Malone and his wife went to Europe, something they had not done for nearly a quarter of a century. Both their grown children were in Europe most of that summer. Gifford was working in the south of France under the auspices of the American Friends Service Committee, and Pamela was living with a family in England under the Experiment in International Living. Malone and Elisabeth spent six weeks in Salzburg, Austria, where Malone was a member of the faculty of the Salzburg Seminar in American Studies. This was housed in the Schloss Leopoldskron, a large, baroque building on the outskirts of the little city.

The Malones stayed in a lesser building, called the Meierhof, with a couple of other American professors and their wives. The idea was to relieve the Malones from climbing the vast stairs in the main building. But the Malones' building had only one bathroom, and as Malone recalled, there was no way to lock the door. As a protective measure, Elisabeth placed a postcard picture of Mozart on the outside of the door when she was inside, a sign well understood by the other residents.

They visited the birthplace of Mozart in Salzburg and attended the music festival. Malone later wrote that this was probably the first time he had heard *The Marriage of Figaro*, "but it was certainly the first and in fact the last time I ever heard *The Magic Flute*. I have never ceased to prefer the music of Mozart to all others, and I have retained a special affection for Austria."[36]

Malone did a great deal of work on volume 3 of his biography during his sabbatical from Columbia. But he concluded that he could not afford to work on the book exclusively until "I had done something to restore my shattered finances." In the long run, the Jefferson series was a distinct financial success, but such was certainly not the case at the beginning. "I was deeply in debt while doing the first two volumes. In a time of great inflation, when my expenses were at their height because of the education of my children, assured income was insufficient. The research and writing took much longer than I had anticipated." Malone reflected that his experiences during these years were good preparation "for a study of Mr. Jefferson's finances, although his did not turn out as well as mine did in the long run."[37] Malone had to borrow extensively on his life insurance and accepted sizable advances from his publishers, always hoping that the royalties would restore the balance.

The timing of his second volume, *Jefferson and the Rights of Man*, turned out to be unfortunate. Malone always described each volume as a unit in itself, but each covered only a segment of Jefferson's life. Volume 2 had to compete with a single book that covered Jefferson's whole life, Merrill Peterson's acclaimed *The Jefferson Image in the American Mind*. When Malone checked with the publishers, he learned that fewer than six thousand copies of his volume had been sold, and it was clear to him that the returns would be insufficient to cover the advances he had received from the publishers. "I could not expect any further advances from them under these circumstances. I gave them my note for the amount I owed them and on this I paid interest. I doubt if Alfred McIntire would have required that, but I do not blame the responsible official for being businesslike."[38]

Volumes 1 and 2 remained in print during the long period of waiting for volume 3, and the royalties somewhat paid Malone's gradually increasing debt.

In 1959, eight years after volume 2 was published, Malone accepted a full professorship position with salary at his academic home, the University of Virginia. Like Thomas Jefferson, he thereafter never left Virginia to live anywhere else until shortly before his death in 1986.

Malone had previously been asked to return to the UVA faculty by Presidents John Newcomb and Colgate Darden, but for professional and financial reasons, he had been unable to do so. Now, the opportunity seemed little short of providential. Although he had great respect for Columbia, his personal and professional situation had improved as time went on, and both of his children had grown up.

Malone could not have remained at Columbia much longer, even if he had wanted to. He would have had to retire when he reached the age of sixty-eight in 1960. "I would have had to give up my big study at that time and would have had no place to do my writing and keep my books," he noted. At the University of Virginia, Malone could remain a member of the faculty until he reached the age of seventy, and then it "would remain to be seen what would happen after that. I had reason to believe that the Thomas Jefferson Memorial Foundation would continue to sponsor my biography, and I did not believe that I would be ejected from the Alderman Library."[39]

As things turned out, Malone left New York at the age of sixty-six and technically remained a member of the Columbia faculty during the next academic year. He was entitled to sabbatical leave, and with the aid of a Guggenheim Fellowship, he was able to spend 1959 in Virginia. He then became the Thomas Jefferson Memorial Foundation Professor of History at the University of Virginia, and "I was still occupying a commodious study in the Alderman Library a quarter of a century later."[40] It was the easiest decision Dumas Malone ever made.

13   Jefferson, the Virginian

By keeping this account of Jefferson, true to his own chronology, I mean that I have not viewed him as a static personality like a portrait on the wall, but as a living, growing, changing man always the same person but never quite the same.

—DUMAS MALONE[1]

Mr. Jefferson was six feet two and half inches high, well proportioned and straight as a gun barrel. He was like a fine horse—he had no surplus flesh. His skin was very clear and pure—just like he was in principle. Mr. Jefferson was always an early riser. The sun never found him in bed.

—CAPT. EDMUND BACON[2]

By the time Malone returned to UVA full time in 1959, the Thomas Jefferson Memorial Foundation had already been established. It had purchased Jefferson's home, Monticello, at a cost of a half million dollars. Fund-raising became its major occupation during its early years. Chartered in New York in the early 1920s, the foundation had as its early members largely businessmen. It had no connection with the University of Virginia then, and even by midcentury the foundation had no academic representatives.

Malone wrote in his memoir that the foundation had an expert in Jefferson -ian architecture in member Fiske Kimball, director of the Philadelphia Art

Museum. Kimball became the most influential member of the committee on the Jefferson bicentennial in 1943. In fact Kimball and his wife, Marie, a historian, had nominated Julian Boyd as the historian of that committee. Fiske became the dominant member of the Jefferson Memorial Foundation in the 1940s "and did more than anybody else for the restoration of Monticello," Malone wrote. Marie, the curator of Monticello, wrote several pamphlets on the furnishings of the home, in addition to her own three-volume Jefferson biography. "The Kimballs were an aggressive pair and their attitude toward Monticello and its master was considered by some as possessive," Malone observed. "They undoubtedly resented my entrance into the field as a biographer."[3]

Although there was no formal connection between the foundation and the University of Virginia, greater rapport between the two grew when Malone accepted a seat on the foundation's Board of Directors in 1956. Several of the directors were alumni of the university, including William S. Hildreth, president of the UVA Alumni Association, who was an avid sports fan; Thomas J. Michie, a liberal lawyer who afterward became a federal judge; and Henry J. Taylor, a right-wing columnist whose headquarters was in New York but who had a country home in Albemarle County. Malone remembered Taylor as the most talkative member of the board. According to Malone, "I think he was the person who first suggested that it honor Jefferson by promoting historical scholarship, and especially Jeffersonian scholarship, at the University."[4]

Malone felt there were strong personal as well as professional reasons for him to make his headquarters at the University of Virginia. The close relationship he had established with Harry Clemons, the university librarian, as a young professor remained through the years. Malone considered the university library to be "his laboratory, workshop and almost second home." He had the honor of speaking at the dedication of the Alderman Library in 1938 and had often visited it when preparing the biography of Edwin Alderman, for whom it was named. In his remarks at the dedication, Malone observed, "No structure that has been erected by an institution with which I have ever been connected has brought me such joy as this one."[5]

Clemons had invited Malone to lodge in his house in the room normally occupied by John Wyllie, the curator of rare books who was away on war service in 1943. But Malone ended up staying at the Colonnade Club on the Lawn, as he had when he was a bachelor a score of years before. Then, the university promptly provided him with a study in the library. This office was not comparable in size to the one in which his ambitious project was completed nearly forty years and more than a million words later, but it proved an adequate workshop during the next two years.

Malone was often asked why he picked Thomas Jefferson as the subject of a comprehensive biography. In 1974 he wrote, "I was attracted to Mr. Jefferson as a subject of inquiry because he was not only a controversial figure, but also one of extraordinary diversity. To live with him intimately is a liberal education."[6]

The proof of Jefferson's diverse interests was self-evident. Malone related a story about the Italian ambassador's private tour of Monticello in the 1970s. Surveying every room, book, and painting, the ambassador had kept muttering to himself, "Leonardo, Leonardo." The ambassador then commented that there would not be another man like Thomas Jefferson in five hundred years. Then he revised his statement: "Make that 1000 years."[7]

H. S. Randall had published a three-volume life of Jefferson in 1858. But to Malone, these three volumes were not enough. He thought an exhaustive work on Jefferson, a man he ranked with Washington and Lincoln as one of the three greatest Americans, was long overdue and explained that Jefferson deserved extended and careful treatment.

The Jefferson memorial in Washington was tangible evidence of Jefferson's recognized membership in the trinity of American immortals, Malone reported. Others may deserve to stand beside them, but the supreme eminence of these three was practically unchallenged at the time when Malone published his first volume in 1948. While Washington and Lincoln were the major symbols of the independent republic and the preserved union, respectively, in Malone's view, Jefferson surpassed both of them in the rich diversity of his achievements. No historic American, except possibly Benjamin Franklin, played so notable a part in so many important fields of activity and thought: government, law, religion, education, agriculture, architecture, science, and philosophy.

It was doubtful, Malone wrote in his memoir, that any other public man in all America's annals was equally interesting to so many sorts of minds. Jefferson was never regarded as the first citizen of the world, as Woodrow

Wilson was for a brief time, but after the passing of Franklin and Washington, no American of his period matched him in international reputation. And as "a major apostle of individual freedom and human dignity Jefferson has long belonged, not merely to his own compatriots, but to the human race," Malone wrote. "His fame was probably greater in our generation than it had been at any other time since his death."[8]

It was historical justice that Malone should finish his work at the school that Jefferson, the scholar, created and Jefferson, the architect, designed. "I was not very conscious of Jefferson's personality until I came here," Malone admitted.

> William Howard Taft once said, "They talk about Mr. Jefferson here [at UVA] as though he were in the next room." There is that. His mind still lives because architecture is living. To gaze at his campus at the university and his home, Monticello, on a hilltop outside of town is to have an unspoken dialogue with their creator. His reasoning is there, before your very eyes. Part of his appeal is that Jefferson was a universal man. That lasts. His politics don't. But his architecture, his writings are timeless.[9]

Malone conceded that Benjamin Franklin was the more entertaining American and might have been better company. But he liked Jefferson from the start and still liked him at the end of their "long journey." "If you're going to spend years with someone, you've got to like him."[10]

To summarize or even begin to synthesize the six volumes of *Jefferson and His Time* is beyond the scope of this book. But there can be no doubt that Malone was most proud of the first and last volumes of his biography and for the same reasons. He saw them actually printed after much professional delay, blood, sweat, tears, and finally, old age.

The first volume, *Jefferson the Virginian* sold for $2.95 when it came out and met with immediate acclaim. Arthur Thornhill, an editor in Little, Brown's New York office, brought Malone advance copies of the reviews in the *Herald Tribune* and the *Saturday Review of Literature*. Malone later wrote that he found these reviews "to be very good reading. I was exceedingly fortunate in my reviewers. These . . . were all friends of mine and highly competent scholars."[11]

"Prodigiously researched and felicitously written," said the *New Republic*, "Dumas Malone's multi-volume *Jefferson and His Time* is one of the great biographies of the 20th century." Historian Adrienne Koch, who had recently published a book on Jefferson's philosophy, wrote, "There is no question in this reviewer's mind that Mr. Malone's JEFFERSON supersedes all previous biographies." Gerald Johnson predicted, "If the succeeding volumes sustain this high level, it will endure as one of the imperishable monuments of biography—and take note that I don't say American biography, I say biography period." Yet, one critic warned, "Unfortunately this biography, while always interesting and sometimes instructive, is seldom exciting. The fault may be Jefferson's rather than Malone's."[12]

Malone also received congratulations from various Jeffersonian scholars, including Professor Douglass Adair of the College of William and Mary and Professor Thomas Jefferson Wertenbaker of Princeton, who was an authority on the colonial history of Virginia and a descendant of one of the first librarians at the University of Virginia.

This first volume was dedicated to the University of Virginia. A few days after the reviews appeared, Malone went to Charlottesville for a little ceremony in the Alderman Library. There he presented an autographed copy of the book to President Colgate Darden. In his speech, Malone told the audience that as a scholar he had been privileged to work in some of the world's greatest libraries: those of Yale, Harvard, and Columbia; the Library of Congress; the British Museum; and the Bibliotèque Nationale. He was grateful to have had access to all of them, "but the one I liked the best was this one. If Mr. Jefferson was listening, I'd think he must have been pleased. He started the University of Virginia Library. In effect, [Jefferson] had also started the other one in which I had worked longest alongside of him, the Library of Congress."[13]

Malone had no idea how the book would be received outside of academia, and he was extremely apprehensive: "Our judgment was that of scholars. However, it remained to be seen whether the book over which I had labored so long would appeal to anybody else."[14] The popularity of the book became evident when sales figures revealed that more than 13,583 copies had been sold by 1952. The Mississippi Valley Historical Review placed it fifth on the preferred list of American biography.

Jefferson the Virginian follows Jefferson through his first forty-one years, from 1743 to 1784. For more than half of that time, Jefferson was growing up, going to school, reading law, and fitting himself for his inherited station as a leading planter of Virginia, Malone wrote. Then he practiced his profession while acquiring further legal learning, performed the public duties that went with his position in society, began to build a famous house, made a happy and advantageous marriage, and started a family. Jefferson was at the height of his private fortune and personal happiness in his early thirties, when the storm of the American Revolution gathered and broke. Being a Patriot by conviction, Jefferson devoted himself largely, but not wholly, to public tasks for the next ten years.[15]

Jefferson's youth presented the biggest challenge of the entire biography because scant records existed for the young Thomas Jefferson. The man who, at the age of thirty-three, wrote the Declaration of Independence on a folding writing box in his bedroom-and-parlor apartment in Philadelphia was born in 1743 at Shadwell, Albemarle County, Virginia. He had a reflective, rather than active, character and was a thinker more than a leader. Although he enjoyed the elegant social life of Williamsburg under Governor Francis Fauquier, he did not marry until he was twenty-nine. Jefferson preferred law to love. While his chief contemporaries during the Revolution were making military reputations, he was occupied principally with parliamentary affairs.[16]

Young Jefferson was influenced by many, Malone told readers, but none more so than his early teachers, James Maury and William Small. They gave Jefferson his classical training. George Wythe provided his legal education and Patrick Henry his politics. Jefferson studied the writings of Isaac Newton, John Locke, and Francis Bacon on humanitarianism, and Andrea Palladio on architecture. Malone traced all of these influences in careful detail in the 484 pages of *Jefferson the Virginian*.

In the foreword, Malone wrote, "About twenty years ago I promised myself that I would write a big book about Thomas Jefferson someday. I was teaching history at the University of Virginia, which he founded, and any time that I wanted to I could look up and see Monticello in the dim distance."[17]

Malone did not flatter himself that he had mastered Jefferson. He wrote that "I do not claim that I have yet done so, and I do not believe that I or any other single person ever can. Nobody can live Jefferson's long and eventful life all over again, and nobody in our age is likely to match his universality."[18]

Malone found that the materials bearing on Jefferson's early life were relatively scanty because of the fire at Shadwell when Jefferson was twenty-seven years old. Consequently, when dealing with the early part of his life, Malone did not want to miss anything that was available:

> The place where the sources were most lacking was in the first volume, the early part of Jefferson's life. You see his papers at the house at Shadwell burned when he was 27 years old, and we have hardly any papers before that. We don't have much record of what he actually did when he was in college of William and Mary, but I could try to find out about the college, what sort of place it was. I knew that he went to the Palace in the time of Governor Fauquier. I don't have very much information about what he did, but I could find out about the governor and about the sort of life Jefferson probably led. There aren't many periods in Jefferson's life for which abundant material is not available. I often wish I knew what was going on in his mind. He is not subjective. He doesn't unbossom himself. He did not keep a diary where he recorded his feelings. You can't read his mind. Perhaps that is generally the case with men of affairs. I don't want to read things into Jefferson which are not there. I don't know anything to do except to use your common sense.[19]

Before he completed the first volume, Malone had gone through the entire Princeton collection of Jefferson papers for this period. Afterward Julian Boyd, the editor of Jefferson's papers at Princeton, and his able assistants, Lyman Butterfield and Mina R. Bryan, did Malone another great service. They read through the entire proof of volume 1 "and undoubtedly saved me from many errors."[20]

Malone cobbled together a fascinating personal and physical portrait of a young Thomas Jefferson. He recorded Jefferson's physical description from several sources. For example, Joseph Story, a contemporary of Jefferson's, described him as "tall and thin, of a sallow complexion, with fine, intelligent eyes."[21] Another described Jefferson as "tall and of slender make, possessing a fresh complexion and a clear and penetrating eye. . . . His manner is modest and affable."[22]

Malone described Jefferson as tense and intense in his basic character. Of a quiet temperament, he was shy and often ill at ease with strangers. A poor orator, but a superb writer, Jefferson had a brilliant intellect even at a young age. He also had an abiding capacity for hard work, deplored indolence and "idle chatter," and welcomed periods of solitude. He guarded his private life as much as possible, and violent outbursts of temper were rare if nonexistent.[23]

According to Malone's research, Jefferson's recorded papers began to be abundant only when he became governor of Virginia at the age of thirty-six, and they become progressively richer as the years went by. Although the sources were meager for the years before he was thirty, Malone managed to uncover some fresh details about this period in Jefferson's life. "I rest content with the hope that the early story will seem somewhat fuller and truer as the result of these relatively unrewarding labors."[24]

Malone first needed to put the young Jefferson properly in his setting of place and time. He detailed Jefferson's relationship with Virginia and Virginians at considerable length. One of the most interesting chapters deals with Jefferson's college days at William and Mary, where he formed his intellectual and political genius.

Malone noted that before arriving at William and Mary in March 1760, young Jefferson had been fortunate to study for two years under James Maury at a little school near Fredericksburg, Virginia. Apparently it was a stimulating educational adventure for the boy of fifteen to seventeen. In two short years, Jefferson gained the ability to read the Greeks and Romans (learning ancient Greek and Latin) and developed his love for the classics, which continued throughout his long life. Maury himself had attended William and Mary as a student and had served there as an usher and at the Grammar School. Jefferson's education also involved associations in Williamsburg with two more superb teachers: William Small and George Wythe.

In his autobiography, Jefferson reflected on his relationship with Professor Small in the spring of 1760:

> I went to William & Mary college where I continued for two years. It was my great good fortune and will probably fix the destinies of my life, that William Small of Scotland was then professor of mathematics, a man of profound and most of the useful branches of science, with a happy talent

of communication, correct and gentlemanly manners, and an enlarged and liberal mind. He most happily for me became attached to me and made me his daily companion when not engaged in the school, and from his conversation I got my first use of the expansion of science and of the system of things in which we are placed.[25]

According to Malone, these two college years had a tremendous influence on Jefferson. They reinforced his civilized upbringing and decorous manner. Jefferson was never profane, neither as a youth nor as an old man. A few years after college, he described his study of mathematics and natural philosophy under Small as "peculiarly engaging and delightful." Fifty years later, when he was trying to help his grandson in a mathematics course, Jefferson wrote, "Thanks to the good foundation laid in college by my old master and friend Small, I am doing it with delight and success beyond my expectations."[26]

In 1767, when Jefferson was twenty-four years old, he began to keep a pocket account book, the first in a series, year by year, that he kept as long as he lived. From these it was possible for Malone to determine where Jefferson was practically any day in his life. They were not diaries, but they contained a vast amount of nonfinancial material. Malone discovered that these little account books became widely scattered in repositories from Boston to California. It was a great inconvenience to anyone desiring to use them, until Malone hit upon the idea of having photostatic copies made. Eventually, the Alderman Library acquired a set, as did the Library of Congress. Of course, Malone had an annotated set of his own.

Some people, Malone wrote, in seeking to explain how a man of Jefferson's democratic spirit could have come out of what was commonly regarded as an aristocratic society, took the position that while Jefferson was an aristocrat on his mother's side, he was a yeoman on his father's. Malone never accepted this simplistic explanation. His studies showed that Peter Jefferson, Thomas's father, had achieved a position of recognized distinction and was a fully accredited member of the Virginia gentry. Malone traced the line further back and found a place in the English gentry for Peter's father as well. Peter gave his son an assured place in society and the means to maintain it. The son, through his mother, Jane Randolph, was related to almost everybody of importance in the province. In almost every sense of the term, Malone concluded, Jefferson was well born, and his biographer had the impression that he had surprisingly few enemies in his young adulthood.

During Jefferson's college days, William and Mary had six professorships distributed among four educational entities: the Grammar School, the School of Philosophy, the Divinity School, and the Brafferton, a school for educating Native American youth.[27] One faculty position was accorded the Grammar School, where young boys learned the catechism, perfected writing skills, and attained proficiency in the "Latin and Greek tongues." Throughout the colonial era, this basic course of instruction remained the largest component of the college.

Students who had completed a classical education entered the School of Philosophy, which had two faculty positions. The professor of natural philosophy taught physics, metaphysics, and mathematics, while the professor of moral philosophy offered instruction in rhetoric, logic, and ethics. This was the school Jefferson entered, because he had already studied for five years under the Reverend William Douglas and for two more years under Maury.[28]

After completing studies in moral and natural philosophy, students who had been "put up on the Foundation" (that is, placed on scholarship) moved on to the Divinity School, where they learned Hebrew and received instruction in "the literal sense of the Holy Scripture" before being put in "Orders." The Divinity School was chartered with two professors, one skilled in Oriental languages and one in divinity. As a faculty member, the president was expected to "explain the common Places of Divinity" and to read one theological lecture per week.[29]

Essential to Jefferson's experience was the physical setting that organized the daily activities of this college "family." By 1760 the main building of William and Mary had achieved its present form—a three-story range fronting the Duke of Gloucester Street, with two rear wings housing a hall and chapel. From Duke of Gloucester Street, one approached the compound by way of an impressive forecourt framed by nearly identical brick piles housing President William Dawson to the north and the Brafferton to the south. Two rooms deep and two stories in height, these flanking structures were similar to recently built houses of Virginia's richest gentlemen. Equally splendid was the space these buildings enclosed, "a formal garden adorned with graveled walks and symmetrically arrayed topiary. Together, these elements presented an impressive face to the town of Williamsburg."[30]

By 1773 a library and an infirmary were established on the third floor, probably near the center of the building. Faculty and students lodged on this level. Each professor had a private apartment of two finished rooms, corresponding with the hall and chamber of a private dwelling. Leftover spaces were distributed among the "better Sort of the big Boys," who lived three or four to a room, while Grammar School students slept in the undivided dormitories over the hall and chapel. Thirteen windows lit each of these barracklike rooms, and a fireplace was the only source of heat. Curtains afforded some visual separation between individuals or groups. Those who occupied these common sleeping rooms enjoyed little privacy.[31]

Important as institutional and physical arrangements were to Jefferson's experience of the college, it was the ebb and flow of life that most influenced his views about higher learning. At the time, William and Mary's daily routine included a number of ritual observances. The student's day began with prayers in the chapel, scheduled at 6:00 a.m. in the summer and at 7:00 during the winter. Led by one of the masters, scholars read from the Book of Common Prayer, as mandated by Virginia law.[32]

Jefferson later called William and Mary "the greatest school of morals and manners that ever was in America." He saluted the edifying example of such men as Peyton Randolph, William Small, George Wythe, and Francis Fauquier. This enduring thought figured prominently in Jefferson's later attempts to create an ideal setting for higher learning at the University of Virginia.[33]

Young Jefferson described himself as a "hard student" with a "canine appetite for knowledge." Years later John Page recalled how his boon companion "could tear himself away from his dearest friends, to fly to his studies."[34]

The death of two professors reduced the faculty at William and Mary to only two masters. One of these was natural philosophy professor William Small, a graduate of Marischal College at the University of Edinburgh and the only layman who had ever served on the faculty. Small had become Jefferson's de facto tutor. In later years, Jefferson paid heartfelt tribute to his teacher and to the circle of learned friends he made available to his students:

> Dr. Small was . . . to me as a father. To his enlightened and affectionate guidance of my studies while at college, I am indebted for everything. He procured for me the patronage of Mr. Wythe, and both of them, the attentions

of Governor Fauquier, the ablest man who ever filled the chair of government here. They were inseparable friends, and at their frequent dinners with the Governor . . . he admitted me always, to make it a *partie quarrae*. At these dinners I have heard more good sense, more rational and philosophical conversations, than in all my life besides.[35]

In researching his subject, Malone made some interesting observations about Jefferson's personal characteristics. He noted, for example, Jefferson's sense of humor. Malone concluded,

He wasn't devoid of it. Yet more than Washington, certainly the sort of grim humor and he liked tall tales. One of the things that Tucker says . . . is that Jefferson was almost reckless in expressing his opinions. Everybody noticed this about him, you'd ask him and he come right out with it. That was not true of his public papers. They're carefully guarded, but he says some extravagant things in his private letters. . . . You have to distinguish between what's private and what was in public. I'm sure I've said things in private letters, which I never would have said public. You've got to know to whom the letter was written and should know all the circumstances."[36]

Malone agreed that almost all of Jefferson's biographers spoke of him as being "amiable"—they use the word again and again. Strangers, people who met him for the first time, said he was a little stiff at first, however. "He was not effusive, he was not demonstrative, and there was a certain restraint about him always."[37]

Thomas Jefferson was much more conspicuous after the American Revolution than he was during it. When Jefferson said "my country," he meant Virginia. Jefferson was a Virginian before he became anything else, and as Malone reiterated in subsequent volumes, he never ceased to be one. Jefferson was deeply rooted in that soil. His ancestors had lived in the colony for at least three generations before him. Jefferson received the whole of his formal education there, and until he was forty, he had spent scarcely a year outside the borders of the province and state. His own "country" was almost the only scene of his activity until he had entered into middle life.

Jefferson knew more about it than anybody else, and he described it in his *Notes on Virginia* far more fully than anyone else had ever done.

Against this background, Malone delved into painstaking detail on how and why Jefferson was chosen to draft the Declaration of Independence. The day of America's birth, July 4, 1776, dawned bright and pleasant in Philadelphia, Malone wrote. Thomas Jefferson, at thirty-three the youngest member of the Virginia delegation to the Continental Congress in Philadelphia, noted that the temperature was 68 degrees at 6 a.m., the wind was from the southeast, and the mercury rose to 76 in the heat of the day. In Pennsylvania's brick State House, now revered as Independence Hall, forty or fifty representatives of America's original colonies and common-wealths had been discussing the adoption of an independence declaration for several days. On this day, their debates did not end until evening.[38]

Above them in the State House hung a one-ton, twelve-by-fifteen-foot bronze bell, now known as the Liberty Bell. Made in England, it had cracked once while being tested in Philadelphia and had to be remolded twice before its installation in 1753. Around its crown, the bell bore an inscription from Leviticus: *Proclaim liberty throughout all the land unto all the inhabitants thereof.* An old bellman is said to have been stationed in the steeple, patiently awaiting a signal from a boy posted at the door below. When, finally, in the hush of evening, the boy clapped his hands and shouted, "Ring! Ring!" the aged patriot yanked the rope that was to signal the birth of a new nation. (Contrary to popular legend, Malone confirmed, the bell cracked again, not during this historic tolling, but fifty-nine years later, while it was being rung for the funeral of Chief Justice John Marshall.)[39]

A resolution of political independence had been adopted by the Congress on July 2, and John Adams of Massachusetts had written his wife, Abigail, that he felt sure this day would be commemorated by later generations. But the birth certificate of the infant republic bears the date July 4, when a full charter of freedom was formally approved. Broadsides of the authenticated Declaration were ordered and hastily run off by a local printer, John Dunlap, on the night of July 4. His punctuation and capitalization were so erratic that the first printed version was described as following "neither pre-vious copies, nor reason, nor the custom of any age known to man."[40]

Malone wrote that the official parchment of the Declaration of Independence in the National Archives was not ordered engrossed until

July 19. It was headed, "In Congress, July 4, 1776. The unanimous Declaration of the thirteen united States of America." (The word United was inscribed in small letters to make a line fit.) But only twelve states actually voted for it on July 4 because New York's delegates were not empowered to do so until July 9. And the fifty-five signers who subsequently inscribed their names (on August 2 and thereafter) were not identical with those who had voted for the resolution on July 4. Some of the latter had since left the Congress, and new members had appeared on the scene.[41]

Jefferson was chosen to write the Declaration because of his "felicity of expression." He composed the historic document, without recourse to reference books or pamphlets, on a portable writing desk of his own design, in the second-floor parlor of a Philadelphia bricklayer's home, where he had lodging. By June 28 he submitted a rough draft to John Adams and Benjamin Franklin to enable them to write in their suggestions. The Congress later deleted references to the slave trade and Scottish mercenaries, along with some of Jefferson's more high-brow passages.

But the rough draft, "scored and scratched like a schoolboy's exercise," was treasured by its author all his life. The signers of the Declaration included twenty lawyers, fifteen planters and large land holders, seven merchants, four doctors, three businessmen, two farmers, a judge, a surveyor, a clergyman, and a scientist-philosopher-diplomat (Ben Franklin). Their ages ranged from twenty-six to seventy. The average age was under forty-five. They ran the gamut from the continent's wealthiest men to plain "men of the people." Some signers were doubtful. John Adams observed that some "signed with regret, and many others with many doubts." As he affixed his signature, Franklin is supposed to have remarked, "Yes, we must all indeed hang together—or most assuredly we shall hang separately." Portly Benjamin Harrison was reputed to have boasted to the slender Elbridge Gerry of Massachusetts that his own great weight would ensure his neck's snapping instantly, "whereas Gerry would probably be left kicking in the air for over half an hour."[42] John Hancock, who inscribed his famed signature about a third larger than usual, is said to have commented that he did so to enable John Bull to read it without his spectacles and to double the British price on his head.

John Dunlap worked through the night and into the next morning printing the text of the Declaration onto broadsides—single-sided, printed sheets. Early on July 5, John Hancock dispatched these broadsides to be read and posted in order to announce the colonies' independence. Only twenty-five Dunlap broadsides are extant today.[43]

After signing, some of the men withdrew into relative obscurity, leaving scarcely a trace behind. A considerable number lost most of their fortunes in the subsequent Revolutionary War, but the majority continued in public service.[44]

The first to die was John Morton of Pennsylvania, in April 1777. The last was Charles Carroll of Carrollton, Maryland, often described as the country's richest man and the sole Catholic among the signers. He died in 1832 at the age of ninety-five and was the only signer who survived long enough to see anything faster than a horse—a railroad train.[45]

14   Douglas Southall Freeman

Stephen Vincent Benet said that [Douglas Southall Freeman] should be given at least ten Pulitzer Prizes and then should be chained to his desk to write a biography of [George] Washington.
　　　　　—MARY TYLER FREEMAN CHEEK McCLENAHAN[1]

I recognized him as one of the masters of our craft.
　　　　　—DUMAS MALONE[2]

During the last week of January 1962, John Glenn delayed for the third time his attempt to rocket into space to become the nation's first earth-orbiting human. Bill "Moose" Skowren, the Yankees first baseman, was given a $3,000 raise that elevated his annual salary to $35,000. *Franny and Zooey* was at the top of the fiction bestseller list, followed a few spots down by *To Kill a Mockingbird*, and Barbara Tuchman's *The Guns of August* was said to have been a favorite of John F. Kennedy's.

In those long ten years between Columbia and Malone's official return as professor to the University of Virginia, he received assistance and mentoring from several scholars, but from none more so than Douglas Southall Freeman, the great Civil War biographer, best known for his four-volume biography of Robert E. Lee.

"At this stage of my own work I received much help and encouragement from Douglas Southall Freeman," Malone wrote. Malone had not met Freeman during his first tour of duty at the University of Virginia in the

1920s but knew that he was the esteemed editor of the *Richmond News Leader* and had heard him speak.[3] In the early summer of 1953, when Malone was at Cape Cod, he learned of the untimely death of Freeman. Five volumes of Freeman's magisterial work on George Washington had been published by that time, and Malone had reviewed all of them in Sunday's book section of the *New York Herald Tribune*.

Despite his incessant labors, Freeman had been unable to finish his biography of Washington before his death. In due course, Malone learned that Freeman had nearly completed the sixth volume that had carried Washington into the beginning of the year 1797. Malone was researching Jefferson's life in that very year and was actually more familiar with the events covered in Freeman's sixth volume than any of the others he had reviewed. Malone did not review it but was asked by Freeman's widow and publisher to write a lengthy afterword. He gladly agreed because he so appreciated what Freeman had done for him and sincerely admired his work. His 1964 afterword, titled "The Pen of Douglas Southall Freeman," described Freeman's methods in considerable detail.

Dumas Malone was to Thomas Jefferson as Douglas Southall Freeman was to Robert E. Lee. Both historians were biographers of two of the greatest southerners, Virginians, and patriots who ever lived. Growing up, Malone recalled that the period of American history he was most aware of was the Civil War. His favorite historical character became Robert E. Lee. "Father Ryan's poem about his sword was a favorite throughout the former confederacy. Whenever I read it . . . the thrills ran up and down my boyish backbone," wrote Malone in his memoir.[4]

Malone had known Douglas Southall Freeman well throughout the years. "I got acquainted with him also through the DAB," Malone said in a 1985 interview. "His book on Lee had not then been published, but we knew he was writing it, so we had him write articles for the DAB on Lee, Jackson, Longstreet, and a few other Confederate generals."[5]

When Freeman's *R. E. Lee* came out, Malone was one of the editors of the *American Historical Review*. He asked his managing editor if he could review it. "I still think it is my favorite American biography. It's a little long, but it is a remarkable book," he commented. "I have never been disposed to modify the praise I gave the work at that time. I still rank it first among American historical biographies."[6]

When Malone returned to UVA to start working on Jefferson in 1943, Freeman "was wonderful. He got me a grant from the Rockefeller Foundation. He was parsimonious with his time, he didn't lose a minute or a second, but he gave me a lot of it."[7]

Malone recognized Freeman as one of the masters of their shared craft, and his influence on Malone's research and methodology became profound. Malone had lost none of his admiration for *R. E. Lee*, and he had avidly read the three volumes of *Lee's Lieutenants*. Freeman himself regarded *Lee's Lieutenants* as his best work, and Malone believed it was his most popular. Although the volumes on George Washington had been received with scholarly acclaim and approval, they were less popular than the books on Lee and his generals. In spirit, Malone later wrote, Freeman had lived all his life in the Confederacy and not as comfortable in the eighteenth century as he was in the nineteenth. Perhaps that would have required another lifetime.

As a reader of Freeman's books, Malone had been enormously impressed and influenced by his mastery of detail. Malone would emulate Freeman's precision in his biography of Jefferson as well. In his tomes on Lee and Washington, Freeman traced with unerring skill the development of the characters and his subjects. In each case he examined and verified a heroic legend. By the slow and painstaking processes of scholarship, he showed that Lee and Washington were as noble in fact as in tradition. He had placed on fresh pedestals the greatest hero of the ill-fated Confederacy and the first and greatest hero of the Republic. Both as a patriot and as a scholar, Malone rejoiced in Freeman's notable work of historical conservation.

Freeman had asked Malone whether he still planned to write a biography of Jefferson. Freeman's editor had suggested both Jefferson and Washington to him as subjects, and he did not want to encroach on Malone's territory. As it turned out, Freeman turned his attention to Washington and was deep in his biography when Malone returned to Virginia in 1948.

"Freeman was the greatest historical craftsman with whose methods I was familiar," Malone explained, "and I picked up more helpful suggestions from him than from anybody else. I could not be as systematic as he was and did not try to be."[8] For example, Freeman often suggested he was not writing a history of the Civil War but instead described historical events only as they became known to Lee. Thus, he writes Gettysburg as a Confederate defeat, not as a Union victory. Malone was well aware of the necessity of keeping his own story centered on Jefferson, and although he kept Freeman's process in mind and used it occasionally, he did not follow it strictly. Readers can see Freeman's influence in Malone's retelling of the Lewis and Clark expedition, which is reported only as Jefferson learned of it. Malone followed much the same course in his account of the Burr conspiracy.

No contrast could have been sharper than that between Freeman's tempo and Malone's. Being a full-time editor at the *Richmond Times-Dispatch* during the years in which he did most of his historical writing, Freeman became an exceedingly jealous guardian of his time and did not want to waste a moment. One historian noted that Freeman rose every day at 2:30 a.m. and was customarily at work by 3 a.m. He planned to work on the biography of George Washington eight hours each day, seven days per week. At the end of each week, he tallied the number of hours actually logged and calculated the grand total to date. On June 7, 1953, six days prior to his death of a massive heart attack in the late afternoon, Freeman recorded a total of 15,693 hours invested in the project. He had nearly finished volume 6 of the biography of Washington at 1:00 p.m. on the day he died in June 1953. No doubt George Washington, who also rose early and kept a diary, would have applauded Freeman's compulsiveness.[9]

Malone, however, was not compulsive. "I was never that careful," he admitted. "Of course I had no way of knowing whether I would last long enough to complete such an ambitious project, but I realized that I was entered in an endurance race and was disposed to assume a pace I could maintain."[10] Malone's policy, therefore, was never to press but to keep steadily at it. Freeman kept a daily record of his research and writing. He knew the exact number of hours he spent on *Lee's Lieutenants*. Freeman urged Malone to keep a similar type of book, but Malone never measured his labors with such exactitude. Instead Malone devised a more elaborate system of records than he had previously employed. In this connection he profited from Freeman's example and suggestions.

Malone described Freeman's system in detail in the afterword he wrote to volume 6 of Freeman's biography of Washington. Freeman constructed a detailed outline of a chapter before he wrote it. Either because Malone's materials did not lend themselves to this treatment or because of his personal limitations, Malone never did this. As Malone's biography of Jefferson progressed, his preliminary outline grew simpler and the chronologies more detailed. Continuity and chronological sequence assumed major importance for Malone.

Douglas Southall Freeman had a provincial life, nearly all of which was spent in Richmond, Virginia. His newspaper editorials and his twice daily radio broadcasts made him the most influential man in his native state. In addition, his daily analysis of the campaigns of both world wars made him famous throughout America, particularly in military circles. Presidents and leading commanders, such as Adm. Chester Nimitz, Gen. George Marshall, Gen. Douglas MacArthur, and Gen. Dwight Eisenhower, sought his friendship and advice. Indeed, Eisenhower later said that Freeman first persuaded him to think seriously about running for the presidency. Freeman was a leader of opinion in the South's move from the Democratic Party into the ranks of its hereditary foe, the Republican Party.

Freeman was born in Lynchburg, but his family moved to Richmond when he was a little boy. He grew up in the former seat of the Confederacy. In stories, he often referred to the "Jeems" River (James River), which flowed by both these small cities. Even Richmond was small in his boyhood, and his own tone always retained the flavor and humor of the Virginia countryside. His father, Walker B. Freeman, was a Confederate veteran who had served in the ranks throughout the war and was at Appomattox at the surrender. In later years, he was known as "General" Freeman, but he gained this title as an officer of the United Confederate Veterans, not as an officer in Lee's army.

Douglas Freeman was a deeply religious man, and in his youth, he gave serious thought to becoming a minister. As a boy, he listened to stories of the Army of Northern Virginia at his father's knee. He himself attended Confederate reunions, where he saw gnarled and wounded men, and from an early age Freeman cherished the ambition to tell their full story.[11]

Freeman received all his formal education through the college stage. He attended the University of Richmond, a Baptist institution, and was always loyal to it. He served for many years as head of the Board of Trustees.

Freeman was a good student, and his interest in history may be described as innate, quickened by Professor Samuel Chiles Mitchell, a teacher who encouraged him to pursue the subject further.

While an undergraduate, Freeman became a newspaper correspondent and contributed to the college literary magazine. Once he had "printers ink" in his veins he could never get it out. For the moment, however, history had the priority. He gained a fellowship at the Johns Hopkins University, where he studied history and economics, and at the unusually early age of twenty-two, he received his PhD. For the rest of his life, the title "doctor" was fastened to him. Freeman picked up a good deal of medical knowledge in Baltimore from medical students and from his older brother, Allen, who became a doctor. The only copy of the young graduate student's dissertation—on the Virginia Secession Convention—was destroyed by fire before it was ever published, but his "Calendar of Confederate State Papers" appeared in 1908, the same year he earned his degree.[12]

Leaving Baltimore, Freeman returned to Richmond. For a time, he was on the staff of the *Times-Dispatch*, but his enduring connection was with the afternoon paper, the *News Leader*, where he began working when he was twenty-five. In 1915, at the age of twenty-nine, he became the editor of the *Times-Dispatch*, and he held this post until he was sixty-three. His edition of Lee's dispatches also appeared in print in 1915. Shortly thereafter, he signed a contract for a biography of the great captain, but nearly a score of years was to pass before he could publish it.[13]

In 1986 the *Virginia Magazine of History and Biography* published reflections by Freeman's daughter, Mary Tyler Freeman Cheek. She noted that Freeman wrote every word of his books in longhand. He typed his editorials, but he never wrote any of his books on a typewriter. He felt that the typewriter encouraged prolixity. Freeman wrote in his tiniest handwriting on special lined paper with one inch between lines, which allowed for many revisions. He revised every book, usually as many as seven times. He also made notes on cards, arranged them in chronological order, and numbered them with a machine.

One time Freeman received a letter from a doctor in Harrisonburg. The doctor wrote that when he was a student at the University of Richmond,

Freeman had come to speak. He hadn't known who Freeman was at the time, but he had never forgotten something that he said. In the speech Freeman had likened education to entering a dark tunnel. You travel and work, and you begin to see a little light at the end of the tunnel. You keep on working, and you see more light, and finally, you are out in the sunlight, and you are a success. The doctor explained that he had been an indifferent student, but Freeman's statement carried him through the university, medical school, and his years as an intern. He contended, "I have never forgotten it."

Perseverance was something Freeman felt strongly about, his daughter explained, and Malone felt the same way. Cheek wrote, "I am sure he [Freeman] would disapprove wholeheartedly of the instant gratification that we all expect today. The 'me' generation would have appalled him. He felt that selfishness was man's greatest limitation and hindrance. To him patience and perseverance were virtues on which one could depend. He lived that creed."[14]

In Malone's afterword to Freeman's Washington biography, he paid a semi-formal tribute to his mentor's achievements. Malone observed that one of Freeman's associates on the *News Leader* estimated by the time of his death he had written at least 600,000 words every year—equivalent to three books and perhaps a hundred altogether. Yet his associates remembered him as one who always emphasized the virtue of brevity in a journalist. "With this went an emphasis on restraint," wrote Malone. "'Don't gush, and don't twitter,' he told his juniors. Play it straight."[15]

Most stories about Freeman as a newspaperman come from his later years, after his working habits became widely known and he became a legendary character on the national as well as the local scene. He worked behind an uncluttered desk and under a sign that read, "Time alone is irreplaceable . . . Waste it not." Freeman was characteristically genial, Malone wrote. He told a good story, and there was plenty of laughter at his staff conferences.[16]

Freeman became a national literary figure and gained a sure place in American historiography with the publication of *R. E. Lee* in 1934–35, when he was forty-eight. The one-volume work he had contracted for in 1915 had grown to four large volumes. It had been many years in preparation. To those who were unfamiliar with the slow processes of research and writing, this seemed like a long time, Malone confessed, but to the initiated, who were also aware of Freeman's other tasks, it was a notable performance by any reckoning.[17]

"I shall never forget the impression his *R. E. Lee* made on me at the very first reading," Malone wrote.

> By that time, although I had no such acquaintance with the man as I gained later, I had firsthand knowledge of his scholarship, for I had seen the articles on Lee, Stonewall Jackson, and others that he had prepared for the Dictionary of American Biography. He afterwards told me that he found the writing of these sketches, under sharp restrictions of space, a cruel task. These were miniatures, but they left no doubt of his historical craftsmanship and his skill in portraiture, whatever the scale might be, and I awaited with confidence the appearance of his long-heralded life of Lee. Great as my personal expectations were, the realization far surpassed them, and never did I devour a major historical work with such insatiable appetite and more unalloyed satisfaction.[18]

Malone observed that Freeman's work was a blend of biography and military history. It had the exhaustiveness and judiciousness that became Freeman's hallmark.[19]

While performing his daily task as an editor, Douglas Freeman had produced a major work, immediately hailed as a classic. He received more invitations to make speeches than he could possibly accept. He could have been forgiven if he had rested on his laurels after his financial success, and he did not begin another major historical undertaking for three years. He had not yet completed the task he set himself in his youth. "This was to preserve the record of the Army of Northern Virginia," Malone reported.

In a real sense, Malone thought Freeman's *R. E. Lee* told the story of that army, but in that military biography he had wisely adopted the device of viewing the field from headquarters. Thus, Freeman had been unable to give a full account of the actions of Lee's officers. Fearing that unwittingly he had done them an injustice, Freeman wanted to redress the balance and fill out the story. The result was a second major work, *Lee's Lieutenants*, which many regarded as a supplement to its predecessor but which turned out to be even more popular.

On June 14, 1936, Freeman began work on *Lee's Lieutenants*. In his diary that day, Malone noted, Freeman made this entry: "Outlined scope on train between N. Y. City and Meriden, Conn., and finished broad outline at Middletown, Conn., this A.M." Almost eight years later, Freeman completed the work, having spent 7,121 hours on it. It was published in three volumes, from 1942 to 1945. "This is the most colorful of all Freeman's works. It has been accepted as a classic in the field of tactics; and it will long live as a penetrating study of military personalities," Malone declared.[20]

Two weeks after his fifty-eighth birthday, Freeman finished *Lee's Lieutenants*, and six months later, he began outlining the first chapter of another major work, his biography of George Washington. He worked on this biography for the rest of his life. In the midst of this period of eight and a half years, he retired from the editorship of the *News Leader* on June 30, 1949. He continued his radio broadcasts and many other public activities, but now became a full-time historian. As a rule, he worked at history fifty-six hours a week. Remarkably, his labors on *R. E. Lee* and *Lee's Lieutenants* spread over a period of twenty-nine years. It is impossible to make exact mathematical comparisons between the time spent on these two works and on George Washington, but Freeman's third major undertaking may be compared to the two others in bulk and in hours.

Stephen Vincent Benet once commented that Douglas Freeman ought to be chained to his desk and forced to write a life of George Washington. "There was logic in this, beyond a doubt," Malone wrote. Materials on Washington that were available by the 1940s had not been fully exploited. An authoritative military estimate of him was needed, and Washington was the fountainhead of the tradition that had been inherited by Lee as a man and soldier. Freeman's acceptance of this challenge may be attributed, perhaps, to the "quenchless ambition of an ordered mind, which Freeman was soon to perceive in [George] Washington."[21]

Freeman's methods can be commented on most appropriately in connection with his last work, Malone observed. They developed through the years, and it was not until after he had begun to work on Washington that Malone ever talked with him about the mechanics of research and writing. Like many other people, Malone knew a good deal about Freeman's schedule, but he did not know just how Freeman spent his time in his third-floor study. In the late 1940s Freeman explained to Malone—and showed him— his research and writing methodology, emphasizing his detailed outlining of each chapter. Malone emerged from these conversations with enhanced humility, but a number of excellent ideas that he would employ with his Jefferson book. It was a great pity that Freeman did not write an article on the subject of historical method, Malone observed, for it could have been a classic of its kind. Freeman's procedure was systematized to a degree that "I have never seen equalled, but no one should say that he was engaged in mass production. He had more help in his last years than when doing his Confederate books but, considering the scale of his operations, his staff was always small," Malone wrote.[22]

In his work on Washington, Freeman had a regular research assistant who looked up things for him and traveled to places where he could not conveniently go. But he never saw people or events through anyone else's eyes. An abstract written by an assistant never relieved him of the responsibility of looking at an important document, and no scholar whom Malone had known was more conscientious about a personal examination of source material. In fact, Malone adopted this painstaking method himself. Freeman took nothing on secondary authority and carried his independence to the exclusion of others. He mastered the facts for himself, expressed his own opinions, and wrote his books with his own pen. Freeman always remained a master craftsman, "and the significance of his methods lies chiefly in his skill in making himself effective without loss of motion."[23]

In his library, Freeman's books were always in order, so he wasted no time in finding one of them. He had weights to keep books open at the proper place, and he had a place to write standing if he tired of sitting. He could tell almost at a glance how many words were on his specially ruled paper. He could tell what time it was from the clock in the back of his head. Freeman could also tell within a page how long a chapter would be before he had finished it. His elaborate outlines of each chapter helped with this last feat. Malone found these detailed outlines one of the most interesting items in Freeman's procedure: "He [Freeman] was convinced that it was a great time-saver."[24]

Freeman visited Malone frequently and gave him more ideas about historical craftsmanship than any other writer or historian. Malone did not think he was as good as Freeman as a "craftsman himself. [Freeman] was organized to a point beyond my ability to be organized. I couldn't function that way, but he gave me a lot of good ideas that benefited me enormously."[25]

Malone had his own methods with the Jefferson book and obtained some of them from Freeman. Yet, some habits Freeman practiced, Malone did not think himself capable of. For example, Freeman would spend days creating an outline of a chapter and write the chapter almost verbatim from the outline. "I couldn't do that," Malone recalled. "But I had very great respect for Freeman as a scholar and historian."[26]

When death came to Douglas Southall Freeman in Richmond on June 30, 1953, he was sixty-seven years old. "He delivered his regular radio broadcast on the morning of the day he died," Malone eulogized, "speaking like a father to his fellow Virginians in his familiar drawl, and, almost at the end, he finished the last chapter in this volume. Lying on his desk in his third-floor study was a framed quotation from Tennyson's 'Ulysses' which included these words:

> *Something ere the end, Some work of noble note may yet be done,*
> *Not unbecoming men that strove with gods."*

This quiet man, Malone wrote, whose tireless pen had traced the marches and described the battles of so many great captains, did not quite have time enough to finish his own last work of noble note. He did not live quite as long as George Washington did, and his own labors ended before he could carry that hero through his second term as president and bring him home to Mount Vernon.

Yet, by the simple measure of labor and achievement, Freeman had lived several lives already. He himself gave no sign of a split personality, but for purposes of description, "we will say that he lived at least two lives—as an editor and as a historian. Either one of these would have been far too full for most mortals, but this incredibly effective man serenely proceeded from task to task with unhurried step," Malone noted.[27]

No one can fully explain how Freeman did all that he did for inner springs of power are invisible to the observer. "By mastering himself [Freeman] made himself the master of his destiny," Malone concluded. "He revealed a quality that he assigned to young George Washington: the quenchless ambition of an ordered mind." Also, he was a living illustration of certain truths that Thomas Jefferson proclaimed to his young daughter:

"No person will have occasion to complain of the want of time who never loses any. It is wonderful how much may be done if we are always doing."[28]

In Malone's view, "[Freeman] did not romanticize the past and the first families. Once in private conversation, I remarked to him that he was the most efficient Virginian since Jefferson—a charge that he smilingly denied. I still regard this particular parallel as close, but I doubt if this Richmonder got his major inspiration from Jefferson, even in matters of industry and order. If he consciously modeled himself on anyone—it was on Robert E. Lee."[29]

Freeman had his Lee, and Malone had his Jefferson. Both men shared a passion for historical, linear biography that left no fact unchecked, no detail unconfirmed. Both historians produced books that shared an honest and full attempt to restore legendary figures to engrossing human dimensions; they told with rich insight based on a storehouse of information. Freeman's encouragement of Malone inspired him to search for the "living, breathing person" underneath the icon. In the end, Malone plumbed the life of Jefferson under Freeman's considerable influence.

15 Sally Hemings

A myth's power does not depend on its plausibility.
—GEORGE WILL[1]

Refutation can never be made.
—JAMES CALLENDER, 1802[2]

In 1974 the national speed limit of fifty-five miles per hour became law, Richard Nixon resigned as president, the "streaking" fad hit the United States, and the Symbionese Liberation Army kidnapped heiress Patty Hearst. Three American singles topped the pop charts: "The Way We Were" by Barbra Streisand, "Seasons in the Sun" by Terry Jacks, and "Love's Theme" by the Love Unlimited Orchestra. A new home cost $38,900, and a new car, $4,440.

By this time, Dumas Malone had released three more volumes of his Jefferson biography (five in all). But his tranquil world of academia in the Blue Ridge Mountains was about to be toppled by the publication of Fawn Brodie's salacious biography, *Thomas Jefferson: An Intimate History*, which reignited the controversy over whether Jefferson had an ongoing sexual affair with his fourteen-year-old slave, Sally Hemings.[3]

The Sally Hemings controversy hit the "Jefferson establishment" like a thunderclap. The allegation would test the very fabric of Malone's character, patience, and reputation. His southern gentleness cringed at what he considered a vulgar rumor, and he would be severely tested over the next decade, defending Jefferson's reputation from evisceration. In short, Malone considered Brodie's book and her charge that Jefferson had had an affair

147

with Hemings, or any slave for that matter, as "psychiatric paraphernalia." Malone spent the final years of his life debunking the accusation and buffering Jefferson's image from what he considered unwarranted, intense derision. "Suffice it to say," he wrote with determined composure, "that much of it is bad history, in my opinion, and much of it is not history at all. In using documents [Brodie] disregards some fundamental rules of evidence, and her psycho-history is largely a work of imagination."[4]

Malone's handwritten notes, research, and letters shed new light on the hyperbolic Jefferson-Hemings controversy. But more important, they reflect Malone's role as a historian. He did not believe that historians had free license to roam through the past handing down moral verdicts on individuals. He agreed with Arthur Schlesinger Jr.'s assessment that "all persons, including historians, were trapped in a web of circumstance that should curtail moral pontification. History is not a redeemer, promising to solve all human problems in time."[5]

Malone believed the allegation that Jefferson fathered several of Hemings's children and had a continuing relationship with her "is without foundation and is wholly out of character." The more likely suspects, according to Malone's research, were Jefferson's nephews, Peter and Samuel Carr, or Jefferson's own ne'er-do-well brother, Randolph Jefferson, whom one historian described as a "half wit."[6]

Malone himself had made an oblique reference to the Hemings story as early as 1956 in a *New York Times Magazine* article: "In later years, political enemies spread wild stories, but there is no evidence that Jefferson was ever corrupted by the exercise of arbitrary power under a system he always deplored. His relations with his slaves were marked by no cruelty or sensuality. He was a responsible master in the best patriarchal tradition."[7]

One reason Malone did not believe Jefferson had an affair with Sally Hemings was the state of his health at the time. Multiple folders in Malone's official papers detail Jefferson's declining health. Jefferson died from a wasting, internal infection, Malone wrote. By May 1808, when Eston Hemings was born, Jefferson had lived to an age that was double the life expectancy for men born in 1743. His age, illnesses, prescribed treatments, stress level, habits, and lifestyle certainly had an adverse impact on his fertility and potency.[8] For the last two decades of his life, his health declined at an accelerated pace and affected two of his physical passions: hunting and horseback riding. In fact, he was frail at sixty-five years old and suffered from excruciating migraine headaches, debilitating rheumatoid arthritis, prostate problems, diarrhea, and numerous intestinal infections—all of which would have prevented him from having sex with twenty-two-year-old Sally.[9]

In 1795, at age fifty-two, Jefferson wrote to James Madison, "My health is entirely broken down and my age requires that I should place my affairs in a clear state." He wrote this a few months after Sally's first confirmed child, Harriet I, was conceived, in January 1795. In 1796 he told a friend, "I begin to feel the effects of age. My health has suddenly broken down, with symptoms which give me to believe I shall not have much to encounter of the *tedium vitae*."[10]

Although Jefferson lived thirty-three more years, at the time he felt that he had only a few years remaining. Malone concluded that his decrepit health, among other documented reasons, would not have permitted a sexual relationship with anyone.

The rotting corpse bobbed up and down in a muddy, shallow stretch of the James River. Through peeling flesh and hair matted like seaweed, the man's gray face was still recognizable. He was the eighteenth-century version of a tabloid reporter, devoid of honor or decency. Hours earlier, the combustible man had staggered in and out of Richmond's finest taverns, slurring words of rage against President Thomas Jefferson. The next day a coroner heaved the alcohol-saturated body onto the autopsy table. The cause of death was registered as drowning. Amid rumors of foul play, the formal inquest noted that the deceased had been drunk and his waterlogged body drowned in three feet of water on a Sunday in June 1803. The coroner then scrawled a name on the death certificate: James Thomson Callender.[11]

Ten days later the *Examiner* announced that Callender's death was a drunken suicide and continued, "This unfortunate man had descended to the lowest depths of misery after having been fleeced by his partner."[12] His onetime collaborator recalled years later that Callender had resorted to "unwarrantable indiscretions" begun amid "paroxysms of inebriety."[13] And so the foul life of the most ignoble James Callender came to an end; he had self-destructed like an overloaded circuit without a breaker.

This is where the Sally Hemings controversy began, according to Malone. The most direct statement that can be made about the alleged sexual relationship between Jefferson and Hemings, Malone observed, is this: it was invented by the fractured psyche of an alcoholic, incendiary journalist, James Callender.

Malone explained that the alleged affair between Jefferson and Hemings began as a vindictive political attack during Jefferson's first term as president. Callender, a disappointed office seeker, the "most deadly of all political animals,"[14] first published the story in 1802. As was the common practice of those times, the allegations were spread for political purposes, even though they had no foundation in fact. The pestering rumors were initially promoted by Jefferson's Federalist enemies and were then accepted by some historians and offered to the public as fact.

Who exactly was Sally Hemings? And what did Malone know about her? The simple answer is that Sally is a historical enigma. As biographer John C. Miller commented, "We know virtually nothing of Sally Hemings, or her motives [and] she is hardly more than a name."[15]

Born in 1773 at a Charles City plantation, Sally was allegedly the illegitimate daughter of John Wayles, Jefferson's father-in-law and a well-known businessman, lawyer, and occasional slave trader for a British supplier. Her mother was Betty Hemings, one of Wayles's slaves. It was rumored that Wayles took Betty as his concubine, and if the rumor is true, Jefferson's wife, Martha, was Sally's half-sister.[16]

A Monticello slave described Betty as "as bright as a mulatto woman."[17] Jefferson recorded that she had had several children, some fathered by someone other than Wayles. The oldest child was Mary, born in 1753; Nance was born in 1761, and the youngest of this group, Bob, was born in 1762. Betty's other children, including Sally Hemings, were born in 1773, the year John Wayles died.

In that same year Jefferson inherited, on his wife's behalf, all of Betty Hemings's family (including Sally as an infant), several large parcels of land, and 135 slaves from Wayles. Most of the Hemingses, including Betty, became house servants at Monticello; this may indicate that the family had special status because of Wayles's relationship with Betty. It seems clear that the Hemings family was considered "special" throughout the plantation, Malone wrote. The Hemingses were trusted and indispensable servants to Jefferson's family. They were nannies, cooks, carpenters, dressmakers, and seamstresses and filled almost every support role at Monticello.[18] Malone agreed with historian Donald Jackson's take on the origin of the Hemings controversy:

That the Hemings matriarchy was well thought of by the Jefferson family made the children and grandchildren more conspicuous than the other slaves in the Monticello neighborhood. Add the facts that miscegenation did exist in the South; that men of such probity as George Washington were falsely but commonly believed to engage in it; and that Sally and her children were all but white in appearance, and it is little wonder that Jefferson's opponent would eventually produce a story conferring on him the paternity for those children.[19]

After her return from Paris as a maid to Jefferson's daughter, Sally lived with her older sister Critta on Mulberry Row, the slave quarters closest to the big house. Four years later, they moved, in all probability, into one of the three new log cabins built in 1793. Finally between 1803 and 1807 Sally moved into a masonry room near the "south dependency," then the kitchens and stables. There is not a shred of credible evidence, Malone concluded, that Sally lived inside Monticello or occupied some secret rendezvous room there.[20]

Sally died in 1835 or 1836, at age sixty-two. She had no burial marker or obituary in the newspaper. Malone reported no evidence or letters suggesting that she ever spoke about her relationship, if any, with Jefferson. Nor is there any evidence of her activities in the post-Monticello period. There is no indication that Sally was approached by anyone about whether she had been Jefferson's sexual partner, Malone wrote.[21]

In *Thomas Jefferson: An Intimate History*, Fawn Brodie approached Thomas Jefferson's personal life from a perspective completely different from that of most historians before her. Brodie, then a biographer and UCLA history professor, had experimented with psychological models long before they became popular. Her 1943 biography of Joseph Smith, written in this mode, led to her excommunication from the Mormon Church. In the late 1960s Brodie turned her attention to Thomas Jefferson. She suggested that the Sally Hemings story need not be considered a charge against Jefferson or a threat to his heroic stature: "It could be that Jefferson's slave family, if the evidence should point to its authenticity, will turn out under scrutiny to represent not a tragic flaw in Jefferson but evidence of psychic health.

And the flaw could turn out to be what some of the compassionate abolitionists thought long ago, not a flaw in the hero but a flaw in society." By
making these points in a lecture at the University of Virginia and an article in the *Virginia Quarterly Review*, Brodie was venturing into the lion's
den, hoping to declaw her opponents before they attacked her.[22]

While Brodie praised the work of Jefferson scholars such as Malone and
Merrill Peterson, she made it clear that she wanted to cut a new groove in
Jeffersonian academe, to search for something other scholars had overlooked
in their exhaustive but idealized biographies. In a review of what she considered Peterson's heroic-icon biography, *Thomas Jefferson and the New Nation*,
Brodie complained about the absence of "any kind of probing into Jefferson's
inner life for sources of his ambivalences toward blacks, which might explain
his increasing apathy toward slavery."[23] Here was a clue to her own evolving
thesis: perhaps Sally Hemings held the key to Jefferson's thinking on slavery.

Brodie chafed under what she called "the Jefferson establishment." In a
1971 article, "Jefferson Biographers and the Psychology of Canonization,"
she suggested that Malone and Peterson had succumbed to the impulse to
sanctify without knowing it. "Both biographers teach at the University of
Virginia, live virtually in the shadow of Monticello, and walk each day in the
beguiling quadrangle Jefferson designed 150 years ago. Jefferson is so much
a 'presence' in Charlottesville, and so omnipresent a local deity, that one cannot help wondering if this in itself does not exercise a subtle direction upon
anyone who chooses to write about him." Brodie charged that the Jefferson
biographers had focused almost exclusively on his public life and left his private life untouched: "There is important material in the documents which the
biographers belittle; there is controversial material which they flatly disregard
as libelous, though it cries out for careful analysis. And there is what one may
call psychological evidence which they often ignore or simply do not see."[24]

Brodie concluded "that something is at work here that has little to do
with scholarship," something that called for "speculation and exploration"
and perhaps even Freudian analysis. Jefferson's male biographers could not
seem to accept the possibility that Jefferson engaged in affairs of the heart
outside of marriage. Perhaps a female biographer could restore Jefferson's
masculinity and accept the possibility that he had a sexual relationship with
one of his slaves.[25]

Brodie castigated Malone and Peterson for being too close to their subjects
and for "canonizing" Jefferson.[26] She seemed more intent on demystifying

"the Jefferson establishment" than on debunking the Jefferson myth. She suggested, once again, that an intimate relationship between Jefferson and Sally Hemings could be seen in a positive light. Perhaps Jefferson, a lonely widower, "had turned to the 'dashing Sally' for solace," and she, in turn, found him attractive. "None of this has to be described as 'ruthless exploitation of the master-slave relationship.' He had then been for years a widower." Jefferson need not have been condemning his children to slavery, Brodie added, since they were, by his own definition, white.[27]

In her 1974 biography, Brodie supplemented documentary sources with Freudian psychoanalysis and concluded that Jefferson both enjoyed a long-term, loving relationship with Sally Hemings and fathered several of her children. The book received favorable reviews in many publications, which infuriated Malone, who considered its evidence inconclusive, its methodology questionable, and its thesis implausible. Malone's supporters depicted Brodie as a woman obsessed with sex and as a marginal historian who had made a "scholarly specialty of oddballs." Brodie's supporters, in contrast, depicted Malone as a hagiographer and a conservative defender of the national self-image.

Malone was "surprised and pained" by charges of his racial insensitivity. "To me the story would be no more credible (and no more creditable) if the supposed object of Mr. Jefferson's amours had been white," he added in response to Brodie's book. "So far as I am concerned," he wrote later, "the question of race is entirely irrelevant." On this matter, Malone agreed with Brodie: the issue was gender, not race. "From my understanding of his character, temperament, and judgment I do not believe that he would have done that with a woman of any sort. If I find the story unbelievable it is not because of Sally's color."[28]

Brodie continued to correspond with Jefferson scholars in Charlottesville even after the publication of her controversial book. On December 18, 1975, she wrote James A. Bear, curator of the Thomas Jefferson Memorial Foundation:

Dear Mr. Bear,

I promised to keep you up to date about new material on the children of Jefferson and Sally Hemings. But at the moment I did want to tell you that the descendents of Eston Hemings have given me permission to tell the story of their family, and it is indeed fascinating. They have furnished me scrap books by the two sons of Eston Hemings. . . . I have some new data from a family which claims to be descended from Thomas M. Woodson. . . . Several branches of this family have a strong oral tradition that they are descended from a Thomas Woodson, who was a son of Jefferson "and the slave girl who went to Paris" who was half-sister of Jefferson's wife. There is still not enough material to authenticate the claim absolutely, but the historical sources which could throw further light on the family have not yet been exhausted.

All good wishes for the holidays, Fawn Brodie.[29]

It is interesting to note that Brodie and Malone met several times prior to the publication of her controversial book. Initially Brodie seemed in awe of Malone and echoed the sentiment to him on March 10, 1969:

It was good of you to give me so much of your time in Charlottesville, and I wanted to thank you also for the kind invitation to cocktails. I wish very much that I could have stayed over an extra day, but I had to return to teach a class. I had to combine so many good things in a short visit—seeing old friends at a conference, seeing our son, Bruce . . . and getting acquainted with the fabulous collection of documents at the Alderman Library. I felt it was one of the richest five days of my life. I do hope to return for an extended stay if my Jefferson research gets as complicated as it promises to be.[30]

Malone was cordial, if not effusive, when he told her,

It was a very great pleasure to talk with you the other day, and I only wish that we could have talked longer. My wife and I were disappointed that you and your husband left town before you had a chance to have a drink with us. I hope, however, that you will be coming this way again. . . . If I can help you out in any way, I shall be most happy to do it. Meanwhile, you have been a great deal of help to me.[31]

Brodie candidly admitted her fascination with the Hemings affair in a 1968 letter to Malone, some six years before her infamous book: "I have for some time been collecting material for a paper on Thomas Jefferson and slavery, and in the course of my research have become fascinated by the

Dumas Malone as a professor at the University of Virginia, 1959. *Courtesy of the Albert and Shirley Small Special Collections Library, University of Virginia*

University of Virginia, faculty photograph, 1959. *Courtesy of the Albert and Shirley Small Special Collections Library, University of Virginia*

Thomas Jefferson, by Jamie Wyeth, 1975. *Courtesy of the Albert and Shirley Small Special Collections Library, University of Virginia*

Dumas Malone, The College of William & Mary Dinner, Williamsburg, Virginia, 1976. *Courtesy of the Albert and Shirley Small Special Collections Library, University of Virginia*

Elisabeth Malone, wife of Dumas Malone. *Courtesy of Gifford Malone*

University of Virginia Dinner, in honor of Queen Elizabeth's bicentennial visit, 1976. *Courtesy of the Albert and Shirley Small Special Collections Library, University of Virginia*

RIGHT: Dumas Malone, in his office at the University of Virginia, 1981. *Courtesy of the Albert and Shirley Small Special Collections Library, University of Virginia*

BELOW: Dumas Malone, UVA office, finishing the sixth and final volume, *The Sage of Monticello*, 1981. *Courtesy of the Albert and Shirley Small Special Collections Library, University of Virginia*

Dumas Malone in his UVA office with his Visualtech magnifying machine for reading, 1981. *Courtesy of the Albert and Shirley Small Special Collections Library, University of Virginia*

Dumas Malone with his assistants, Steve Hochman and Kay Sargent, 1981. *Courtesy of the Albert and Shirley Small Special Collections Library, University of Virginia*

Gifford Malone, son of Dumas Malone, Westwood Country Club, Vienna, Virginia, 2012. *From the author's collection*

Grave Marker—Dumas Malone, University of Virginia Cemetery. *From the author's collection*

folklore surrounding the alleged 'slave family' of Thomas Jefferson and Sally Hemings, and other less well known legends. I should like very much to talk to you about this problem."[32]

After her book was published in 1974, Malone rarely mentioned Brodie or her book by name. As a respected scholar, he preferred to stay above the fray. Occasionally, however, he spoke out publicly against her. In May 1974 he wrote an op-ed column for the *New York Times* titled "Jefferson's Private Life," in which he made public a letter written in 1858 by Jefferson's grand-daughter, Ellen Randolph Coolidge. In the letter, Coolidge stated that Jefferson could not possibly have carried on a relationship with Hemings at Monticello without raising the suspicions of his family, so closely quartered. She suggested that the Hemings children were fathered by Jefferson's Irish workmen and his nephews, Peter and Samuel Carr. Here was a theory that could not be "dismissed lightly," Malone argued.[33]

A few months later Virginius Dabney asked Malone for a public state-ment on Brodie's book. Dabney needed to quote Malone and the other leading Jefferson scholars in his Charter Day speech at the College of William and Mary. He wanted to take the gloves off and launch a public barrage against Brodie, but he lacked the stature to do it alone. "For me to say Brodie is nuts would mean little or nothing," he told Malone in October 1974, "unless I could quote you, Julian Boyd, Peterson and Adair. That would be a blockbuster!" Dabney cited the nation's upcoming bicentennial celebration in 1976 as a reason to respond quickly. "Since nobody has made any effective answer to Brodie and Vidal, and this is the beginning of the Bicentennial, it seems appropriate . . . for someone to point out the dis-service that these writers are performing in attacking the very people to whom we are indebted for the Bicentennial."[34]

The "Vidal" Dabney referred to was the flamboyant author Gore Vidal, who had authored the bestselling, historical novel *Burr* in 1973. Dabney tethered Vidal with Brodie because he felt both had taken liberties with historical facts. He confided in his memoir years later that "what we were interested in were facts, and facts establishing Jefferson's paternity of the children were nowhere to be found in Brodie's vulnerable thesis."[35]

In an interview after his speech at William and Mary, he said,

Finally, it popped into my mind that nobody, as far as I knew, had really confronted Gore Vidal and Fawn Brodie about their two books, which I thought were pretty awful in many ways. . . . I consulted various people, Dumas Malone, Julian Boyd, and Merrill Peterson, and got them to comment on Brodie's book. All their comments were unfavorable. I convinced them that it was their duty to come out and say what they thought about anything as distorted as this which was giving people such perverted ideas of Jefferson's career. Malone was the most hesitant because he felt that he would be attacking another author in his field, but I agreed to put in the speech that he was reluctant, and so he came through with an awfully good statement including the one about graffiti, which I thought was about the best thing that anybody said; to the effect that "anybody could write graffiti on walls, anybody could write dirty words, but it was shocking that they were so richly rewarded," which got him a brickbat from Brodie in *Time*. I'm sorry about that because I didn't want to get him in that sort of a controversy.[36]

Malone supplied Dabney with a three-page statement in which he called the Brodie thesis "highly objectionable." Jefferson was no "plaster saint," according to Malone, "but this author, in her obsession with sex, has drawn a distorted picture. In her zeal to demonstrate that Jefferson's sexual activity continued after his wife's death—until almost the end of his long life—this determined woman runs far beyond the evidence and carries psychological speculation to the point of absurdity." Malone closed with a metaphor. "Fawn Brodie and Gore Vidal cannot rob Washington and Jefferson of their laurels, but they can scribble graffiti on their statues. It is unfortunate that dirty words are so hard to erase, and it is shocking that the scribblers should be so richly rewarded."[37]

Dabney thanked Malone for his help with the speech, which "was received astonishingly well. I've never been so congratulated in my life." Malone asked Dabney if he had heard anything from Brodie or Vidal. "I haven't had time to hear from Brodie or Vidal," Dabney replied, "assuming that they pay any attention at all." Brodie apparently read about Dabney's speech in *Time* magazine. She responded with an angry letter to the editor, calling the "graffiti" quote "a slap against black people." Dabney called the Brodie letter "extremely silly" and privately assured Malone that her charges could easily be answered if he chose to do so. "I have kept up with the references in *Time*," Malone replied, "and gain the impression that we are doing all right. I shall not give Mrs. Brodie the satisfaction of having a reply from me."[38]

Some years later, Dabney in fact would write his own rebuttal to Brodie's book: *The Jefferson Scandals: A Rebuttal*. Malone offered an endorsement for the book and said, "Dabney's book is a convincing response to allegations against Jefferson's character that have been recently revived but never substantiated. It should appeal to any fair-minded reader."[39]

Both Malone and Brodie were honored for their Jefferson biographies in 1975. While Malone won the Pulitzer Prize for the first five volumes of his biography, Brodie was named "Woman of the Year" by the *Los Angeles Times*. Both were elevated to the status of celebrity historians. But Malone and his allies insisted they were not worried about Jefferson; his reputation was secure from attacks well informed or otherwise, they reasoned. "A bit of chipping around the edges of the alabaster isn't likely to be noticed," Edwin M. Yoder Jr. bristled in the conservative *National Review*. Rather, Malone and the others feared a lowering of scholarly standards. As they saw it, revisionists like Brodie valued ideology above accuracy.

Brodie's *Intimate History* was on the *New York Times* bestseller list for thirteen weeks and sold 80,000 copies in hardback and 270,000 in paperback. In essence, she accepted Madison Hemings's narrative as historically true. Madison, Sally's son, gave an interview twenty years after her death to a partisan abolitionist newspaper claiming that he was the son of Jefferson and Sally. Brodie described the interview as "the most important single document" relating to the story of Jefferson and Hemings. Her psychosexual study concluded that the third president's affair with Sally was "a serious passion that brought both parties much private happiness over a period lasting thirty-eight years."[40]

From the beginning, Malone thought Brodie's controversial book was "curious" on several accounts, the first and most fundamental of which was that it frustrated classification. On the dust jacket, the volume was described as a "biography, a rich three-dimensional intimate portrait that illuminates the relationship between Jefferson's inner life and his public life." But this was not a biography as Malone understood the genre—that is, the book was not a full and balanced account with detailed analysis of all aspects of Jefferson's life. Some significant aspects of the subject's public life received only scant attention, in Malone's view. These, and other departures from the characteristics of the genre, reflected Brodie's purpose—she did not wish to write a conventional biography, Malone observed. Noting that virtually all previous scholars who have written about Jefferson have "centered" upon his mind and its impact on society, she warned that she had a quite different emphasis. "This is a book about Jefferson and the heart," she announced, a history of Jefferson that attempts to portray not only "his intimate but also his inner life." To "illuminate" this relationship required certain biographical techniques, she continued, that make "some historians," meaning, presumably, the conventional Jefferson scholars such as Malone, "uncomfortable."[41]

This technique did not bother Brodie, however, and she explained how a writer can use psychological analysis to determine the inner life of a figure of the past: "One must look for feeling as well as fact, for nuance and metaphor as well as idea and action."[42] In essence, Brodie put the tools of psychology and psychoanalysis to use for historical service. For some reason she did not give these tools their "psycho" label, Malone commented, nor did she admit that she was writing what has come to be called "psychobiography," but this is the genre into which her book most fit, he thought.

One of the problems with psychological techniques, Malone observed, was that often they have to work from indirect, secondary sources and thin evidence. Brodie afforded an immediate example of this danger in discussing Jefferson's relationship with his parents and their influence in forming his personality. Admitting that so little is known about Jefferson's parents as to make any supposition hazardous, she nevertheless proceeded to speculate at length. Brodie noted that in all his copious recordkeeping Jefferson included only two brief references to his mother. She reasoned that he was attempting to "erase" all traces of his feeling for her, and therefore he must have felt hostility toward her. On still less evidence, she concluded that Jefferson admired but also resented his domineering father. Thus, he had a hostile relationship with his parents.[43]

In a 1981 interview, Malone commented on Brodie's use of psychoanalysis:

> I haven't indulged in it at all because I'm not qualified to do so. Psychiatry and psychoanalysis were something I've never gone in for. I've been very careful to avoid using their terms, because I make no claims in those fields. I don't object to anybody using any tool that will help us arrive at a better understanding of people. The trouble about psychoanalysis as applied to

figures of the distant past is that there were practically no materials to work with. Where are your materials when you're dealing with people like Jefferson or George Washington or John Adams? You haven't gotten them on the couch, you can't question them. So I'm a little skeptical of [psychoanalysis'] value in dealing with characters from the distant past.[44]

Malone also discounted Brodie's emphasis on the importance and intensity of Jefferson's extramarital attachments. He firmly believed that Jefferson's marriage to Martha Wayles was a reasonably happy one and that after her death, when he was only thirty-nine, he turned to politics as his principal passion. His premarital foray at Mrs. Walker (the so-called Walker affair, which Jefferson admitted to) was a clumsy and atypical effort. His flirtatious relationship with Maria Cosway and Angelica Church in Paris reflected no more than a playful affection that may have grown into something more but that ultimately did not.

Malone's official papers and extensive research, especially newfound information on Angelica Church, were instructive in this regard. Brodie (and more recent historians) have alleged that Jefferson began his affair with Sally while he was minister to France and living in Paris for five years. Nothing could be further from the truth, Malone concluded, because Maria Cosway and Angelica Church held his romantic interest at that time. And while much has been written about Jefferson and the beautiful Maria Cosway, Malone found that Jefferson's relationship with Angelica Church was perhaps deeper and longer lasting.

Jefferson was introduced to Mrs. Angelica Schuyler Church by the famous artist John Trumball. Church was the eldest daughter of Gen. and Mrs. Phillip Schuyler and a sister-in-law to Alexander Hamilton. She and her husband, a member of British Parliament, traveled to Paris in 1787 with their daughter, Kitty, a girl of five, to place her in private school there. Thomas Jefferson had been alerted to her arrival by their mutual friend Maria Cosway. Cosway inquired of Jefferson, "Have you seen yet the lovely Mrs. Church? If I did not love her so much I would fear her rivalship. But no, I give you free permission to love her with all of your heart and I shall be happy if you keep me a little corner of it when you admit her even to reign queen."[45]

Malone concluded that an entire chapter could have been written on Jefferson's relationship with both Church and Cosway while he lived in

Paris. Both letters and witnesses documented the evidence, which Malone believed initially refuted any rank speculation that Jefferson began a sexual relationship with Hemings. Malone wrote extensively of Jefferson's famous "Head and Heart" love letter to Cosway and also of his affectionate letters to Church. For example, Malone noted that when it was time for Church to venture back to London, Jefferson accompanied her to Saint-Denis. On his return to Paris, he wrote to her that he spent the evening with their mutual friends Madame de Corny and that "they talked over our woes" occasioned by her departure. Church had previously written Jefferson a "note of adieu," and to that Jefferson replied, "You speak, Madame, in your note of adieu of civilities which I never rendered you. What you kindly call such were but the gratifications of my own heart. The morning you left us all was wrong, even the sunshine was provoking, with which I never quarreled before."[46]

In the end, Malone concluded that limited interpretation tools could be useful to writers of biography and should be employed by those who cherish the art. Psychological interpretation, however, must be used with severe restraint and with recognition of its inherent limitations. Malone believed that Brodie had misused psychology in attempting to "illuminate" the inner life of Jefferson.[47] Garry Wills, professor of history at Northwestern University and the author of several books on Jefferson, was even tougher on Brodie. "Two vast things, each wondrous in itself, combine to make this book a prodigy," Wills bristled. "The author's industry—and her ignorance."[48]

Malone found the Sally Hemings legend so abhorrent that he devoted an entire appendix, titled "The Miscegenation Legend," to the controversy in volume 4. He argued that the father of Sally Hemings's children may have been Peter Carr, but more likely it was his dissolute brother, Samuel. "It is virtually inconceivable," he wrote, "that this fastidious gentleman whose devotion to his dead wife's memory and to the happiness of his daughters and grandchildren bordered on the excessive could have carried on through a period of years a vulgar liaison which his own family could not have failed to detect."[49] To charge Jefferson with "that degree of imprudence and insensitivity requires extraordinary credulity," Malone concluded.[50]

Malone, as well as Peterson, attributed the rise of the Sally Hemings legend to three factors: (1) Federalist hatred and the efforts of British critics to discredit democracy; (2) the institution of slavery and, especially, the efforts of abolitionists to discredit it by showing that Jefferson, though himself a conspicuous champion of freedom, was contaminated and victimized by the slave system; and (3) certain factors in Jefferson's own life, including the discreditable Walker affair and his special concern, over many years, for the members of the Hemings family among his slaves. "Quite obviously, the truth must be sought in the life he actually lived," Malone contended, "not in what political enemies or social reformers have said about that life for their own purposes, good or bad."[51]

Malone researched and learned a good deal about the Hemings family. Unfortunately, however, he could not answer with finality the perplexing question of the paternity of Betty Hemings's numerous children. But it is probable that Jefferson regarded himself as especially responsible for the welfare of the Hemings family, Malone explained. "If we can accept the oral tradition, handed down by certain of the slaves themselves, that Betty Hemings was the concubine of John Wayles (Jefferson's father-in-law) after the latter's third wife died, and that he was the father of the six youngest children she brought to Monticello, Jefferson's actions take on fresh significance and poignancy," Malone argued.[52]

If this information is correct, Malone concluded, then Jefferson shouldered and bore quietly for a half century a grievous burden of responsibility for the illegitimate half brothers and sisters of his own adored wife. He wrote,

> There is material here for the tragedian, but the historian must recognize that oral tradition is not established fact. Jefferson himself would have been the last person to mention such a relationship and I should be extremely reluctant to do so here had not others previously mentioned it in print. Since it is already in the public domain, I should be remiss if I ignored it, even though, in my opinion, Jefferson's conduct toward these slaves of his can be explained, though less poignantly, on other grounds. It was quite in his character as a private man.[53]

The question of the paternity of Sally's children remains, Malone observed. "So far as I know, nothing is said about this in any of Jefferson's records. Paternity is exceedingly difficult to prove, and in this case at this distance it may be quite impossible."[54] But Malone was quick to note that Jefferson's grandson, Thomas Jefferson Randolph, made a categorical statement many years ago. Requesting the discretion of biographer Henry S. Randall, Randolph said that while no one at Monticello suspected that his grandfather had affairs with female slaves at any time, "the connection of two of his very near relatives with two women of the Hemings family was notorious on the mountain and scarcely disguised by them." Specifically, Randolph said that Sally was the mistress of Peter Carr, one of Jefferson's favorite nephews whom he treated as a son and that Sally's sister Betsy was the mistress of Samuel Carr, Peter's brother. One of Jefferson's granddaughters shifted the characters. Writing to her husband while on a visit to her brother, Ellen Randolph Coolidge reported a "general impression that all four of Sally's children were the children of Sam Carr . . . the most notorious good-natured Turk that ever was master of a black seraglio kept at other men's expence."[55]

Malone concluded his position on the Sally Hemings controversy when he wrote, "Every true scholar must abhor any manipulations of facts and exploitations of sex or sensation in order to gain popularity and make money. If he enters the marketplace he should be as scrupulous as a judge."[56]

Perhaps, Julian Boyd of Princeton summed up Malone and the Jefferson defenders' point of view best: "You [Malone] have given us the true, authentic Jefferson and you have done so in a way that inspires respect and confidence. Your great biography of this great and good man will be remembered and read, and appreciated long after the shallow and self-serving products of the sensationalists have been forgotten."[57]

16   Malone vs. CBS

*The sad probability is that as long as the majestic bronze
figure stands in its marble temple near the Potomac,
some version of the old Sally story will be periodically
hung round its neck.*

—Historian C. Vann Woodward[1]

*It is difficult to prove a negative. The latter part of the
charge however is disproved by its atrocity and its utter
disagreement with the general character and conduct of
Mr. Jefferson.*

—Dumas Malone[2]

The debate over Jefferson, race, and sex took on renewed vitality in
January 1979, when Malone learned of plans by CBS to develop a television miniseries based on Brodie's 1974 work and a forthcoming book,
Sally Hemings: A Novel.[3] The author of the novel, Barbara Chase-Riboud,
had imagined the alleged affair between Jefferson and Hemings from the
viewpoint of the female protagonist. Chase-Riboud, born in Philadelphia
and also a poet and sculptor, had accepted Fawn Brodie's premise of a deeply
serious, loving relationship and had crafted a story that opened in 1830 in
Albemarle County, not far from Monticello. In the novel, Sally Hemings is
free and living with her two sons, Eston and Madison. The story is told
from several viewpoints and jumps back and forth in time. Chase-Riboud
devotes many pages to Paris, where Jefferson supposedly fell in love with the

fourteen-year-old Sally. And in the fictional account, Martha and Maria (Jefferson's young daughters) are fully aware of the affair. Like Sally, they are in awe of their father, and they never object to the liaison. The novel closes with Jefferson dead and Sally freed by Martha after a bitter exchange.[4]

Chase-Riboud used long interior monologues to explore the slave's doubts and fears rather than the master's inconsistencies. The author had turned to fiction to supply what history could not. Word of the novel distressed Malone and the many Jefferson scholars who did not want to see the Sally Hemings story revived in any form, fictional or otherwise. The miniseries proposal jolted Malone into action.

The struggle between CBS and the Jefferson establishment is explained in detail in Malone's papers at UVA. Two authors, Scot French and Edward Ayers, also summarized the CBS debate in their article "The Strange Career of Thomas Jefferson: Race and Slavery in American Memory, 1943–1993." According to their account, an article in the *Hollywood Reporter* found its way to Malone. The miniseries would tell "the real-life story of the 35-year affair between Thomas Jefferson and his mulatto mistress," as depicted in the novel by Chase-Riboud. Distressed by the advance publicity, Malone decided not to wait until production of the CBS show to act. He mounted a vigorous letter-writing campaign aimed at stopping the miniseries and emphasizing the fictional nature of the book.[5]

"I believe that CBS would render the American public a great service by abandoning the idea for a series based on a tawdry and unverifiable story," Malone told Robert A. Daly, president of CBS Television. "If you go ahead with the project, I would urge you to make it absolutely clear that you are presenting fiction." Malone claimed to speak for countless others who shared his concerns. "I do this not only on my own account, but on behalf of all persons who are concerned with the preservation and presentation of our country."[6]

Malone wrote that the book

on which the series will be based is a work of fiction, but apparently it is being represented as possessing the central historic validity. Actually, the story of Jefferson's alleged liaison with one of his servants is . . . hearsay. It has never been proved, it cannot be proved. Because of human affinity for sex scandal, however, the general public will be predisposed to accept it. No honest historian wants to make a plaster saint out of any national hero but he can and should resent the taking of liberties with the reputation of any of them. The gross liberties . . . taken with Mr. Jefferson in the forthcoming book can be confidently assumed. The publishers say that the author gives free rein to her imagination. If you do go ahead with the project, I would urge you to make it absolutely clear that you are presenting fiction. I hope you will understand my motives in making these comments.[7]

In a similar letter to CBS chairman William S. Paley, UVA historian Merrill Peterson urged the network to "reconsider lending its name and network to media exposure of what can only be vulgar sensationalism masquerading as history." Peterson went on to write that "as an American historian who has devoted thirty years to research and scholarship on and about Thomas Jefferson, no serious student of Jefferson has ever accepted the truth of that notorious black Sal scandal [brought] by violent political enemies after 1800. Presumably Chase Riboud has pirated [Fawn] Brodie, and the Scherick production will occupy the shadowy realm of 'docudrama,' where it is impossible to distinguish between fiction and fact. Even if the truth of this hoary legend about Jefferson could be established, it would still be among the least significant events of his life."[8]

Malone also objected to the way that Viking Press characterized the Chase-Riboud novel in its catalog, treating the "love story" as undisputed fact. "Over three decades their passionate, complex love affair endured and flowered," the promotional blurb declared. "While most documents related to that passion were carefully destroyed by Jefferson's white family after his death, enough remained to substantiate the basic facts of the case. Using this historical premise and data, Barbara Chase-Riboud has fashioned a dramatic—and unashamedly romantic—novel."[9]

Malone wrote to the president of Viking Press, Irving Goodman, saying he was "appalled" by the promotional blurb. He called the assertion that family members had destroyed records "unsupported" and "utterly irresponsible. To be sure, you are publishing a work of fiction," he urged, "but it seems to me that you should make no claim that it has historical foundation."[10] Malone reiterated that the allegation "is made that the descendents of Thomas Jefferson destroyed most of the records of a liaison with that slave. This unsupported assertion is utterly irresponsible. Furthermore, it is entirely incorrect to say that documents exist which substantiate the story. Most serious students of Jefferson can agree with this statement."[11]

Alan D. Williams, the editorial director of Viking Press, apologized to Malone for "what might have been called catalog hype for the sales conference." He promised that "the statement about the non-destroyed or destroyed documents re Thomas Jefferson and Sally Hemings" would not appear on the jacket of the book. Yet, he replied that his publishing house would not stop stressing the historical foundations of the novel. Viking Press claimed *Sally Hemings*, Chase-Riboud's first novel, was a "drama created by an American black woman. It is not an historical treatise." What Chase-Riboud tried to do, according to Viking publicity agent Victoria Meyer, "is convey something symbolic about the relationship between the races in America."[12]

On February 11, 1979, the *Richmond Times-Dispatch* published a front-page story about the book, the miniseries, and the "tremors" emanating from Monticello and Charlottesville. The article targeted the "leading critics of the miniseries as Malone, Peterson, Virginius Dabney, and Frederick E. Nolting, Jr., president of the Thomas Jefferson Memorial Foundation— Jefferson's first line of defense."[13]

Two days later the *Washington Post* reported on efforts by "several of Virginia's more prominent historians" to "protect the good name" of Jefferson. The story quoted Malone, Dabney, and Robert Rutland, the editor of the James Madison papers at the University of Virginia. "What bothers the Virginia historians," the *Post* reported, "is their fear that one woman's symbolism, as transmogrified by Hollywood writers, will become the definitive biography of Jefferson for the millions of Americans who learn their history from television." Malone was quoted as saying that a "gullible public" would believe the televised version of the novel, no matter how romantically it was presented. "What's the use of us trying to get history straight?" he asked rhetorically.[14]

The historian firmly believed that television would exploit history's biggest names for corporate profits. He most lamented the degradation of truth and historical facts to blacken Jefferson's name. Malone argued that an allegation that receives the full television treatment may gain more currency than the magnum opus of a factual biography. "Distortions can't get fixed in the public imagination. It will be a mockery of history," he concluded.[15] "I am very upset," fumed Virginius Dabney. Robert Rutland seethed, "Those television people don't give a damn what they do to the national character."[16]

Yet, the defensive response of Malone, Peterson, and other Virginia historians to what they considered "the Hemings myth" generated a backlash on the editorial page of the *Cavalier Daily*, the student newspaper at UVA. "The Virginia historians seem less interested in scholarship than in the frenzied defense of their hero from imagined slurs," wrote Howard Brody, a doctor who had recently moved to Charlottesville. He accused Malone of ignoring the oral tradition passed down by Madison Hemings and of focusing instead on "denials arising within the Jefferson family."

An editorial in the student newspaper questioned the "local Jeffersonian scholars, who seem to view the book's publication and potential television adaptation as a personal affront." There was something hostile, the writer observed, about the way in which these supposedly detached scholars were defending their subject. He continued, "Chase-Riboud's work certainly is unscholarly. The author admits she gives 'free rein to her imagination' in recreating the love affair. But historians who say they hate to witness criticism of an old, familiar friend like Jefferson run the risk of appearing equally unscholarly." The editorial called for a more balanced response, one based on erudition rather than emotion.[17]

As the controversy escalated, Malone grew uncomfortable with his role as a public protector of Jefferson's flame. He refused to grant television interviews and reluctantly agreed to speak with newspapers. "I am a little sorry that this matter has received so much publicity," he told Harold J. Coolidge, a Jefferson descendant who did not believe the Sally rumor, in March 1979. "While every effort should be made to dissuade CBS from producing a mini-series, we don't want to give any more publicity to Sally Hemings and the forthcoming book than we have to." Dabney voiced similar concern: "The question is whether CBS will think this publicity makes it all the more desirable that they produce the mini-series. We'll just have to keep our fingers crossed." By April CBS officials had distanced themselves from the project, saying they had "a commitment from an independent producer for a 'treatment' of the Jefferson story" but that they were "under no obligation to accept the treatment when and if delivered."[18]

In a letter to Harold Coolidge, CBS vice president E. K. Meade Jr. acknowledged the concerns of the Jefferson descendants and scholars who opposed the miniseries: "As to the apprehensions you express and the objections of such eminent historians as Dumas Malone and Virginius Dabney, let me say that we are well aware of the controversy surrounding this particular work on Jefferson. More to the point, we assure you that those views will receive the most conscientious consideration in determining what, if any, decision we make in the matter." CBS seemed ready to defer to the Jefferson scholars who opposed the miniseries.[19]

Some critics who opposed the miniseries, however, had no problem with Chase-Riboud or her book. "She is a poet, she calls her work fiction, and her agent says it is 'symbolic' of race relations in America," wrote Barbara Stanton, an editorial writer for the *Detroit Free Press*. "Race has been an open sore with us for more than three-and-a-half centuries; and it is the ordained function of a writer to poke our sores where they hurt, until we do something about them."

However, in an article coauthored by Jon Kukla, then assistant director for publications at the Virginia State Library, Virginius Dabney accused Chase-Riboud of manipulating historical fact to serve her own present-day agenda.[20] "Her novel tells of an enslaved, black female being oppressed and intimately exploited by white, male America disguised as Thomas Jefferson."[21] He went even further in his personal and professional attack of author Gore Vidal in his fictionalized book, *Burr*. "I haven't had time to hear from Brodie or Vidal, assuming that they pay any attention at all. I think Vidal spends most of his time engaging in *la dolce vita* in Rome. He is a notorious homosexual, of course."[22] Chase-Riboud denied that her book was a veiled attack on Jefferson or white America. "There isn't a bitter or angry word in the book," she told Flora Lewis of the *New York Times*. "Lots of people found rage in it, but it isn't mine. It's their rage which they're projecting." Chase-Riboud said the book was about "the metaphysics of race" in a "mulatto country," not about the plight of blacks in a white country. "Sally is by no means a black experience book," she explained. "There's no such thing as 'black experience' except in relation to 'white experience.' I don't think we'll even be using those terms much longer."[23]

She acknowledged that a streak of feminism ran through the book, "but I didn't introduce it purposely, it just came in the story of one woman and all her labels." She did not seem disturbed that she had been labeled a black activist by critics of her novel. Chase-Riboud explained that "she had gained a sense of herself 'without labels' while living in Paris, just like Sally Hemings some two hundred years before."[24]

When Chase-Riboud returned to Charlottesville in June 1979 to promote her book, she challenged Malone to prove that the affair between

Jefferson and Hemings did not happen. "They just say that it couldn't have happened but they have to have the data to back it up," she told the local newspaper. "They just don't have it." She explained that she thought the public was ready for her point of view, "especially as it in no way diminishes Jefferson's genius but increases the sense of his humanity."[25]

The CBS executives disagreed. In December 1979 Dabney eagerly informed Malone that CBS had "dropped all plans" for the miniseries. His source was Frank McCarthy, "the Richmond-born Hollywood producer who turned down the idea himself years ago, and now sends glad tidings that CBS has lost all enthusiasm. If you haven't gotten the word already, I know you will be happy to hear that CBS has definitely dropped all plans for a TV program on Sally Hemings. . . . Let's keep our fingers crossed and hope that the whole business is dead."[26]

Dabney did not know why CBS decided to abandon the television movie, but he was pleased nonetheless. "Enough damage has been done by Brodie and Chase-Riboud without TV also," he chided. Malone congratulated Dabney on his efforts: "It seems to me that you deserve more credit for this fortunate result than anybody else." Still, Malone worried that the Hemings story might be revived by someone else. "As you say, we must keep our fingers crossed. Eternal vigilance will be necessary."[27]

In March 1980 Dabney wrote to Malone again with "disturbing news" about a report he had seen in the *Amsterdam News*, the black-owned newspaper in New York City. Far from being a flop, the Chase-Riboud novel had apparently sold thirty thousand copies in hardcover, and a paperback edition was on the way. "I have seen an ad for the Avon paperback," Dabney bridled, "and it is lurid in the extreme." The publisher promised to promote the book "with a 30-second TV commercial to be seen by thousands of viewers in major markets, backed by print advertising in the June issue of *Cosmopolitan*." Meanwhile, another television network revived plans for a miniseries based on the novel. "All they are interested in is making money, and who cares about the facts?" Dabney wrote. "CBS was talked out of the plan they had, and possibly this can be done with ABC." Dabney said he would ask McCarthy "for advice on how best to proceed."

McCarthy confirmed that another network, NBC, had plans to develop a miniseries based on the Chase-Riboud novel. He suggested that Malone enlist a member of the University of Virginia Board of Visitors to write a letter to the president of NBC. Dabney pleaded for Malone to continue the fight. "I am sure that you are the most important person of all to write the letter of protest because of your great prestige and the respect in which your views are held; and I should think Merrill Peterson should be enlisted for the duration." Malone cringed at the thought of another letter-writing campaign: "Let me say in the first place that I have no assurance that it would ever reach the president of NBC or be read by him. I never had the slightest acknowledgment to the letters I wrote to the CBS people."[28]

At eighty-three years old, Malone had grown weary of the Hemings controversy, both physically and professionally. In a letter to Dabney he admitted, "I must confess that I am completely worn out with this particular controversy and want to pass the buck if I can possibly do so." Malone asked Frank L. Hereford Jr., the president of the University of Virginia, and Frederick Nolting if they would be willing to write official letters of protest, but both declined. Hereford explained,

> I am as appalled as you at the prospect of what a national television network might do to the Hemings story but I am a little reluctant to get in touch with anyone at NBC myself as President of the University. While we ought to encourage sound scholarship and scrupulous attention to the facts, in a case such as this, it worries me that any representation I might make would be taken to mean that the University is trying to act as a censor.

Nolting, likewise, wanted to keep Monticello out of the controversy. "He is trying to find the name of somebody close to the president of NBC whom he can approach on a personal ground. The point is that he does not want to involve the Foundation," Malone informed Dabney.[29]

While Malone was eager to pass the baton, Dabney was determined to wage the fight to the end. He informed Malone that he was writing a 35,000-word book on the Hemings controversy. "Of course this will be no effective rebuttal to Brodie's Book of the Month and Chase-Riboud's Literary Guild selection and the vast amounts of publicity both works have received. But it seems desirable to have something on the record in hard covers."

Published in 1981, *The Jefferson Scandals: A Rebuttal* allowed Dabney to repeat many of the points he had already made in newspaper and magazine articles. It took issue with Brodie's claim that Malone and Peterson were members of a Jefferson establishment, dedicated to the "canonization" of Jefferson. Dabney pointed out the diverse backgrounds of the two historians, who were both born, raised, and educated outside Virginia. He explained that Malone and Peterson had come to the University of Virginia for "the superb collection of Jefferson materials in the university's Alderman Library and at Monticello," not out of their devotion to Virginia or Jefferson. Far from uncritical, they both had written "scathingly" of Jefferson's conduct "in connection with the trial of Aaron Burr for treason and in ramming the embargo legislation through Congress." Malone and Peterson were united in their rejection of the Hemings story, Dabney acknowledged, but they were hardly canonizers.[30]

Reviews of *The Jefferson Scandals* were mixed. The *New Yorker* called Dabney a "well-known journalist and historian" who "courteously yet firmly" presented the verifiable facts. The *New York Times* called him "a respected journalist with a long and strong record as a civil rights advocate," who "despite a slight tone of protesting too much, is reasonable in his research." Others were more critical. *Commentary* reviewer Peter Shaw complained that Dabney "approached the subject as an apologist rather than a disinterested historian." In his zeal to defend Jefferson against the charge of miscegenation, Dabney missed "the broader implications of Sally Hemings's presence at Monticello, a matter of far greater import than the titillating question of her relationship to Jefferson."[31]

In 1984, two years before his death, Malone made his only concession to the controversy in an interview with the *New York Times*. "Gesturing with his big hands, Dr. Malone said that what struck him as most speculative and unhistorical in the Brodie version was not that Jefferson might have slept with Hemings but rather that he had carried on the affair with her in Paris and later as President for years on end. A sexual encounter, on the other hand, could neither be proved nor disproved, he conceded, adding, 'it might have happened once or twice.'"[32]

Long after Malone died, Monticello officially accepted the Sally Hemings story, and embraced it in their report in 2000 analyzing the DNA evidence. Malone may have taken some solace, however, when columnist George Will named Thomas Jefferson the "Person of the Millennium," declaring that Jefferson "is what a free person looks like, confident, serene, rational, disciplined, temperate, tolerant, curious." Jefferson, Will proclaimed, expressed the "American idea," not "only in stirring cadences, but also in the way he lived, as statesman, scientist, architect, educator." Will did not mention Sally Hemings, sex, or slaveholding.[33]

17   The Pulitzer Prize

*Each time that a volume of your Jefferson has appeared I
expected it to win a Pulitzer Prize, and any of the
volumes would have deserved. But now that you have so
splendidly rounded off Jefferson's public career, it is
especially fitting that what is truly a monumental work
of American scholarship be so recognized.*

—HISTORIAN DAVID HERBERT DONALD[1]

*Malone had been the premier interpreter of the premier
philosopher of American freedom. His Jefferson
biography, the labor of his last four decades, sets a
standard for the form.*

—EDWIN YODER, 1986[2]

A telegram from the White House arrived in Dumas Malone's office on
October 4, 1981. It read simply, "The President and Mrs. Reagan
request the pleasure of your company at a luncheon in recognition of the
National Endowment of the Arts and the National Endowment of the
Humanities on Wednesday, October 14, 1981 at 11:45 AM. Entrance
southwest gate. Formal invitation follows. RSVP, giving date of birth and
Social Security number—*The social secretary. The White House.*"[3]

It was certainly not the first or the last correspondence Malone had with
White House occupants. He had personally met and corresponded with
FDR, as well as Presidents John F. Kennedy, Jimmy Carter, and Lyndon

Johnson. He corresponded with Harry Truman about the McCarthy hearings as well as Thomas Jefferson:

Dear Mr. Truman:

You may have forgotten that when I saw you at the Woodward's several weeks ago I promised to send you information about the McCarthy record. . . . As I remember I also told you that I was going to give you precise information about a book. It is Merrill D. Peterson's *The Jefferson Image in the American Mind.* . . . It is a most excellent book and one which you, as a student of history and public affairs, will find extremely interesting. . . . It was the greatest pleasure to my wife and me to meet you when you were here. On all sides I heard extremely favorable and friendly comments on your visit to the University.[4]

Truman responded, "I read it with a lot of interest and I am looking forward to your further report." The letterhead read, "Harry S. Truman, Independence, Missouri."[5]

Malone received many more distinguished invitations after he won the Pulitzer Prize in 1975. For example, on a hot July afternoon in 1981 he was at Scribner's bookstore on the Duke of Gloucester Street in Williamsburg, Virginia. He and Elisabeth were surrounded by an enthusiastic group of faculty and staff members and students from William and Mary's Department of History and the Institute of Early American History. The Malones had traveled there for a book signing for the final volume of his biography, *The Sage of Monticello*, and their audience greeted them with graciousness and warmth.

On several occasions at William and Mary, the overwhelming reception Malone received from colleagues, friends, and admirers had reflected the depth of gratitude that Virginians held for "this special Virginia gentleman." In fact, Malone had received the honorary degree of doctor of literature from the College of William and Mary in May 1977 and had given a speech titled "Prelude to Independence" at the colonial capital. In his toast to Malone at the dinner in his honor, Thomas Graves said, "Dumas Malone, through his own superb writings, especially through his crowning and monumental achievement of *Jefferson and His Time* has followed in his footsteps. These two men, in the quality of their lives, have epitomized the greatest gift a teacher can offer his students—a love of learning, through the reading of great books."[6]

This was just one of many honorary dinners held for Malone in 1981 on publication of the final volume. After his Pulitzer win, he was a coveted speaker and turned down many more invitations than he accepted. Steve Hochman remembered that Malone never wrote out his speeches but had some bullet points to prompt him. This practice was in large part a product of his family upbringing. Malone's father, a minister, was an extemporaneous speaker, and Malone learned from him. He never gave a speech from a written text because he thought it superior to speak without notes. Malone's speeches, as well as his class lectures, were often unrehearsed.

Like most men who make tremendous impressions, Malone gave himself no airs. When strangers were introduced to him, he customarily responded as if they were wise and he could learn from them. Malone reminded occasional reporters of Socrates, largely because of his measured sober way of talking and also because of his humor and his acceptance of those much younger and less experienced than himself. He was a grand conversationalist, so it was disagreeable to have to leave as long as he could converse. "People often felt like that golden Alcibiades," one reporter wrote, "who was tempted to ask Socrates to shut up, lest one should grow old sitting at his feet. Few of those who liked him so much entered at all into the world that was most important to him, the world of careful, documented scholarship, but it seemed to make no difference."[7]

William Abbot, editor of the Washington papers at the University of Virginia, shared office space with Malone. Abbot recalled one of his most impressive memories was the day Malone addressed a gathering of university presidents at Charlottesville and spoke (without notes, as usual) of the joy of his work. His fascination with humanity in general lay at the root of his enthusiasm for history, Abbott said, and this is doubtless why so many who knew virtually nothing of history were strongly attracted to him.

The summer before he won the Pulitzer, the Malone family had repaired to Cape Cod, as they did almost every summer. Malone wrote many of his volumes on Jefferson in his attic, and from there, in the distance, he could see Buzzards Bay, which was not yet obscured by trees. This was another "move for Mr. Jefferson," he later said, as "Jefferson was no more sea-going than I was."[8] Malone noted, however, that Jefferson had become a student of the whaling and fishing industries and wrote classic papers on them. There was a time when the president had had many admirers at New Bedford and on the island of Nantucket, Malone explained.

"I was to keep company with him on Cape Cod many another summer," Malone said. Gifford would often find his father stretched out on a couch after a long day of writing, listening to a Red Sox game on the radio. When Malone lived in Washington, he was an avid Washington Senators fan, and back at Columbia, he would always pop into someone's office to ask the score of the Yankees game. On occasion he would take Gifford to a baseball game at Fenway or to a college football game at Harvard Square.

The summer house, however, also posed some logistical issues for Malone. Because his study was in the attic, the family complained that "they could not get me down from the eighteenth century" to participate in normal human activities, such as going for a swim or eating lunch. Eventually Malone moved down to what had been his woodshed. With the help of the family handyman, John Wyatt, Malone lined the shelves and rough walls with knotty pine, installed bookshelves, and turned his new space into a pleasant rustic study. On the wall opposite his desk, the historian hung a print of the Rembrandt Peale portrait of Jefferson, circa 1801. "I had my back to it most of the time, and it could be said that Mr. Jefferson looked over my shoulder as I was writing. Undoubtedly he sometimes shook his head, but I hope he generally nodded his approval."[9]

Malone seemed most at ease supervising the house near Cape Cod. For example, in a letter to one of the handymen, he instructed, "The enclosed check is for your services in keeping an eye on the house. I learned from August Clough that he has shingled the front of the house. I have asked the Ten Acre Bottle Shop to hold a case of beer for you. Mrs. Malone and Pam join me in Christmas wishes for you."[10]

Medals, commendations, and honorary degrees multiplied yearly. When Malone received the Pulitzer Prize in history, he was the oldest recipient of that coveted award.[11] "I'm sure that's a mistake," he said wryly of his winning the coveted prize. In 1971 Malone had been nominated for a National

Book Award but did not win. Instead James MacGregor Burns won for his *Roosevelt: The Soldier of Freedom.* Malone was again nominated in 1982. David McCullough won for *Mornings on Horseback* that year.

In addition to his Pulitzer, Malone received numerous other prizes, awards, and accolades. Among them was the John F. Kennedy Medal, which was accompanied by a letter on June 7, 1972: "It is my privilege to inform you that you have been chosen by a very distinguished committee of Members of the Massachusetts Historical Society as the recipient of the Kennedy Medal. . . . The Kennedy Medal is the highest honor the Massachusetts Historical Society [MHS] can confer."[12] Malone responded in kind, saying this was a "delightful surprise" and "a great honor. The prospect fills me with pleasure and pride."[13]

In 1964, shortly after President Kennedy's death, the Council of the Massachusetts Historical Society had created the Kennedy Medal, which would be awarded to individuals who had done something outstanding in the field of history. By that time, the society had received several gifts designated for use in any appropriate way to perpetuate the memory of the president, who was an active member of the society and a great friend of historical scholarship. The MHS commissioned eminent artist and MHS fellow Rudolph Ruzicka to design the medal, which has since been presented to eleven honorees. Before Malone received the medal, it had been awarded only once before: to Samuel Morison for his *Dissent in Three American Wars.* The eleven historians who have received the medal are Samuel Eliot Morison (1967), Dumas Malone (1972), Thomas Boylston Adams (1976), Oscar Handlin (1991), Edmund S. Morgan (2002), Alfred DuPont Chandler Jr. (2003), Bernard Bailyn (2004), John Hope Franklin (2005), Arthur M. Schlesinger Jr. (2006), Laurel Thatcher Ulrich (2009), and Gordon S. Wood (2012).

Malone also received the Bruce Catton Prize, given by the Society of American Historians. The $5,000 award was presented for lifetime achievement in the writing of American history. The award, which was given biennially under terms of a grant to the society from the American Heritage Publishing Company, was named for Bruce Catton, the historian and first editor of *American Heritage Magazine.*[14]

Malone received the Southeastern Library Association's outstanding author award, although he was not able to accept in person. He did write to the committee saying, "No award could give me more pleasure, than one from the librarians of my native region. I want to take this opportunity to congratulate them on the great progress they have made. . . . I shall always cherish the honor you and your colleagues have paid me. I salute you as keepers of our treasure houses of literature and learning and as guardians of our civilization."[15]

In 1969 Malone was made a Knight of Mark Twain by the *Mark Twain Journal*, "in recognition of your outstanding contribution to world peace." Malone's amusing response read, "I am bowled over by your letter of January 3 stating that I had been elected [a] Knight of Mark Twain. I am not aware that I have made any outstanding contribution to world peace . . . to deserve this honor. I shall be interested to learn anything further you may have to say about it, but in the meantime I am insisting that all my friends address me as 'Sir.'"[16]

In 1982 Malone was nominated for the National Book Critics Circle (NBCC) Award for his last volume, *The Sage of Monticello*. The nominating committee wrote to Malone, "As you know, *The Sage of Monticello* was chosen by the NBCC committee as one of the 20 most distinguished American works in the field of non-fiction. Congratulations and best wishes."[17]

In the same year Malone was the recipient of the Medal for Distinguished Services to the Humanities presented by University of Virginia president Edgar F. Shannon. At the award dinner Malone told the audience, "This is one of the nicest things that ever happened to me and I am deeply grateful to Senators of Phi Beta Kappa for nominating me for this award. As for president Shannon, [I] have long been in debt to him for his kind acts and generous words. He has now made the debt overwhelming. I will merely say here that I wish Mr. Jefferson could know him."[18]

In 1964 President Lyndon Johnson invited Malone to be a part of the "Historic Documents Bill and archive." Special Assistant to the President Lawrence F. O'Brien (whose office was later burglarized in the Watergate break-in) wrote Malone to thank him for participating in historic documents preservation: "The President has asked me to send you the enclosed pen used when he signed H.R. 6237, the Historic Documents bill."[19]

Malone received one of his most prestigious awards at the celebration of the fifteenth birthday of the National Endowments for the Arts and Humanities, held in the East Room at the White House on September 30, 1980. President and Mrs. Carter selected him to give the keynote address,

"On the Humanities." His speech was followed by a concert by Mstislav Rostropovich, who played "Happy Birthday."

"I assume that the honor of representing the humanities on this occasion has been granted me on ground of seniority," Malone said. "If I am not the oldest beneficiary of the national endowment for the humanities, I am certainly one of the oldest. I cannot do justice to the achievements of this great organization. Therefore I will speak briefly of my personal reflections with it, and of its main purposes, as I understand."[20] Malone went on to reminisce about his experience writing the history of Thomas Jefferson. He recalled that a distinguished historian, Carl Becker, had predicted that if anyone should be so foolhardy as to attempt a comprehensive biography of Thomas Jefferson, he "would enter the labyrinth and never emerge. I was in the middle of the labyrinth when I approached the endowment and, with their help, I have been slowly making my way through ever since." Malone quoted Jefferson, who at the end of his life "said to a friend that he had one foot in the grave and the other was uplifted to follow. The best explanation I can think of is that Mr. Jefferson is all but the perfect symbol of what the national endowment for the humanities is all about. . . . [Jefferson] was very nearly that."[21]

Malone later received a congratulatory note and photograph from Mrs. Carter, as well as Vice President Walter Mondale, who wrote, "Thank you so much for sending along your autographed book—we're so pleased to have it in the library and I was delighted to see you at the White House."[22] Mondale also requested an autographed copy of *Jefferson and the Ordeal of Liberty*: "It was such a pleasure to see and to listen to you last night at the anniversary celebration of the Humanities and Art Endowment. The Vice-President and Mrs. Mondale would be most grateful if you would inscribe a copy . . . for the library at the Vice-President's House."[23] Malone wrote back, saying that it "was a very great pleasure to do this and that I particularly enjoyed meeting [Mrs. Mondale] at the White House last week."[24]

Malone's Pulitzer Prize was well deserved and somewhat overdue. In the slew of congratulatory letters he received from colleagues, scholars, and celebrities, "overdue" seemed a common theme, as were congratulations from former students, who themselves were now professors. Arthur Schlesinger Jr.

wrote simply, "Warmest congratulations. There never was a Pulitzer Prize more merited."[25] Malone replied, "As I recall you were the youngest or nearly the youngest person ever to receive the Pulitzer Prize, while the papers are stating all too correctly that I am the oldest. I'm not claiming even now that I have caught up with you but I'm glad to know that I have approached this much closer. Thank you so much for your note. I shall cherish it always."[26]

A decade earlier Malone had written a plaintive note to Schlesinger on the death of his father, Arthur Sr., whom Malone had known while at Harvard:

> I am shocked and inexpressibly saddened by the passing of a very old and very dear friend. One of the wisest and best men, he was an unfailing champion of truth, justice and humanity. I shall ever honor his achievements and cherish his memory. I first met him when teaching in the Harvard Summer School the year after I was married, and I then enjoyed for the first time his characteristic hospitality. . . . Fine sanity and unobtrusive wisdom distinguished him and also reminded [me] of what his friendship of forty years has meant to me. [He] was a wise and understanding friend who could be implicitly trusted. Think of me as one of those who will miss him the most.[27]

Arthur Schlesinger Jr. replied, "Your words about my father brought comfort at a time of great sorrow, and I am deeply grateful to you for writing."[28]

Another colleague wrote, "No one more greatly deserved this prize for many years than you, for your extraordinary scholarship mixed with unflagging industry and plain good sense. May I join in honoring you . . . the sixth volume, which we all await."[29] A former student, Francis Lowenheim, wrote to Malone,

> A little over 25 years ago at Columbia University, I had the incomparable privilege of hearing your great lectures on Thomas Jefferson and the study of his life and times. I shall never forget these lectures and along with your countless friends and admirers throughout the country I send to you now my heart[felt] congratulations on receiving the Pulitzer Prize in history. Never was a prize more richly deserved. You may be sure that your masterful volumes on Thomas Jefferson will be read and admired as long as America's past itself is studied.[30]

A professor from Columbia wrote, "Your friends here are just delighted that the Pulitzer has finally come to you—deserved and long overdue."

Daniel Boorstin, the librarian of Congress, gave his "congratulations on your Pulitzer which has just been announced. There never was an award so thoroughly over-earned and over-deserved. The Pulitzer committee has given Ruth and me great pleasure by recognizing [your] scholarship and has added luster to the Pulitzer prizes."[31] Milton Konvitz of Cornell wrote, "I do not see why the Pulitzer committee had to wait to see all five volumes; in a less imperfect world, they would now have awarded you the prize once again, as if to say that they really meant it the first time."[32] A former Columbia colleague echoed the sentiment: "It goes without saying how delighted I am that Pulitzer people have finally gotten around to recognizing your great book. All of us in the history department rejoice."[33] James Bear of the Thomas Jefferson Memorial Foundation wrote, "As Mr. Jefferson might say on such a signal occasion as one's being the recipient of a Pulitzer Prize—I salute you with highest personal esteem."[34] William Fishback, the UVA's director of public affairs, summed it up best when he wrote, "That you should win the Pulitzer Prize is of course long overdue. Certainly those who were fortunate to have you as a teacher in the classroom or at the lunch table in the colonnade club applaud this special recognition. We all hope however that this distraction will not delay completion of the sixth volume of Jefferson."[35] Julian P. Boyd of Princeton penned a note saying, "I was delighted when the Pulitzer jury recognized the importance and distinction of your work. This choice honors the awards—something the Pulitzer lists in general have long needed."[36]

Virginia governor Mills Godwin also praised Malone's grand prize: "I was delighted to read that a friend had been honored with the Pulitzer Prize. This is an honor not to be taken lightly. It marks excellence of a high degree. I know you must be proud, and certainly Virginia is proud of you."[37] Former governor Linwood Holton, an old friend of Malone's, also weighed in with praise: "I can think of no better crowning touch to your magnificent biography of Mr. Jefferson than for you to have been selected for the Pulitzer in acknowledgement of your work."[38] Malone replied, "It is a satisfaction to have this degree of recognition of my work, although the regard in which it is held by my friends is even more pleasing. I am plugging away on the last volume, and make progress by inches."[39]

In addition to being one of his good friends, Linwood Holton was one of Malone's staunchest supporters. Over the years, Holton and Malone had a close relationship, and while Holton was governor, he would visit Malone four or five times a year in Charlottesville. Before his visits, he would famously ask Malone if he had a good supply of "Virginia Gentleman and Mr. Malone would reply, 'The ice will be out when you get here governor.'"[40]

Holton remembered that Malone was "flattered and pleased" when the governor had his official portrait painted with him holding *Jefferson and the Rights of Man*. Malone was present at the unveiling of the official portrait, which still hangs on the third floor of the Capitol in Richmond.[41] The historian wrote in his memoir, "The second volume received a tribute which may be properly described as unique. According to custom, each governor of Virginia has his portrait painted before retirement. This is hung in the state capitol with those of his predecessors. Governor Linwood Holton had himself portrayed holding a copy of *Jefferson and the Rights of Man*. By that time [Holton] had all the volumes of my series but the last, and liked the second one best."[42]

On more than one occasion their discussions turned to the Sally Hemings controversy. "Malone discounted it," Holton reported. "His rationale was that Jefferson was much too shy to have an affair in front of his entire family."[43]

Among the many congratulatory letters Malone received, none touched him more than one written by the daughter of Douglas Southall Freeman. Malone wrote, "Among the many letters of congratulations I have received none will be more cherished than yours. You speak from inside knowledge of the difficulties involved in this sort of work. Thank you so much."[44]

One of the Pulitzer panelists described the actual process of awarding Malone's Pulitzer in 1975. Malone had no idea of the politics that took place behind the scenes:

> After many letters and with many books still to be sent to us, on October 19, 1974, I listed my first five choices among the books I had read so far. My squibs summarized former discussions. I ranked Bernard Bailyn's Ordeal of Thomas Hutchinson first. ("This one stands out above all oth-

ers. For me it has no faults.") Then came Wallace Stegner's *Uneasy Chair* ("Love it as I do, DeVoto seems not important enough"); Dumas Malone's *Jefferson the President* ("Apologetics"). . . . Malone's fifth volume caused us much soul-searching. Dangerfield agreed that it was apologetic and dense too. We did not know that the history jury was also considering Malone's work, and we debated at length whether to recommend the five-volume work, which had been submitted to us, for a special citation. I got the impression from the Pulitzer office that the advisory board might not welcome a special citation, though clearly we could have made the recommendation if we chose and we were deeply tempted. The five-volume set, which the publisher submitted to both the history and biography juries, won the history prize; we did not think the fifth volume alone, the one published in our year of decision, deserved a prize from us.[45]

The Biography Jury for 1975 unanimously recommended Robert A. Caro's *The Power Broker: Robert Moses and the Fall of New York* for the Pulitzer. The jury felt that *The Power Broker* was "gargantuan in theme and impact as well as size. It is shattering, enormously vital, and original in a sense that no other book is." There were several conventional biographies that year, the jury noted, that were seriously considered. The best of these were Roper's *FLO*, Bailyn's, "and Malone's fifth volume of his *Jefferson*. Each may be 'definitive,' yet each is original only in the usual scholarly sense of being based on research in the primary sources." But the jury still ultimately favored Caro over Malone. "Although a journalist writing on a man who is alive, Caro has also done everything a scholar should to get at his subject; his research exhausted virginal manuscript collections, municipal records, personal files of political leaders, and other rarely used sources, and he conducted over 500 interviews. The research is as impressive, prodigious, and thorough as it could be."[46]

Caro's achievement, the Pulitzer jury felt, went well beyond that of Malone's and "the other comparatively conventional biographies." The jury felt that Caro had excelled at the interpretative level by brilliantly analyzing the role of a master urban planner and builder who worked outside the normal democratic process and used the "public authority" device as a force in the growth and management of the city. "For Caro's unique achievement, the jury believes that despite extravagances, he deserves the Pulitzer Prize for Biography. Unanimous verdict."[47]

Malone's winning the Pulitzer for History was bittersweet. The final volume, published on July 4, 1981, the 155th anniversary of Jefferson's death, came after a tremendous physical and emotional effort. It had been written in longhand, five hundred words a day, with the help of assistants and an enlarging machine that enabled Malone to see what he wrote. At the time, he conceded he had doubts about finishing the series. "I never, never knew for sure but I was determined to do it if I lived," he admitted.[48]

18   Fame and the Famous

*I must confess that after years of association with Thomas
Jefferson, George Washington, John Adams and other
giants of our early history, I am relatively indifferent to
contemporary celebrities.*

—DUMAS MALONE[1]

*It has been my inestimable privilege to journey through a
momentous period of history with an extraordinary man,
and my account of the journey cannot hope to match the
richness of the experience.*

—DUMAS MALONE, 1981[2]

Even before he won the Pulitzer, Malone's fame grew nationally and
internationally, and he corresponded with and met many famous peo-
ple, including John F. Kennedy, FDR, Harry Truman, Jimmy Carter, Walter
Mondale, Felix Frankfurter, Queen Elizabeth II, Arthur Schlesinger Sr. and
Jr., Barbara Tuchman, and Senators Huey Long, Harry F. Byrd, and John
Warner.

In 1957 Senator John F. Kennedy wrote to Malone, asking for a list of
distinguished past senators:

The United States Senate has determined to place in its reception room
in the Capitol portraits of those five deceased members, since the foundation of the government, [that] have attained the highest distinction as

statesmen. As chairman of the special committee entrusted with the choice, I recently requested the members of our advisory committee to suggest a list of individuals of high standing well acquainted with the work in history of the Senate to assist us with their best judgment. I am happy to inform you that you have been named as a member of the panel. My colleagues and I appreciate your cooperation. With every good wish, Sincerely Yours, John F. Kennedy.[3]

Malone responded to Kennedy with an alphabetical list of five past senators he considered to be the most distinguished: John Calhoun of South Carolina, Henry Clay of Kentucky, Stephen Douglas of Illinois, Robert La Follette of Wisconsin, and Daniel Webster of Massachusetts. He also included George W. Norris of Nebraska and Arthur Vandenberg of Michigan as other possible candidates. In his letter to Kennedy, Malone wrote,

It seems to me that the three giants of the Senate during its golden age— Webster, Clay, and Calhoun—are practically inescapable choices. All three performed their most famous services in the Senate. . . . Douglas seems to be another "must," despite the fact that he also falls in the antebellum era. Since four of my five suggestions fall within the first half of our national history, I attach two more names from the most recent period. Norris stands out because of his single-minded devotion to the highest public standards and for his genuinely constructive policies. . . . Vandenberg is not suggested because of his domestic record, but because of his conspicuous contributions to bipartisanship and foreign affairs. On that ground both parties and the entire nation can fittingly honor him.[4]

Malone went on to tell Kennedy that "it is a great pleasure to comply with your request, that I send suggestions regarding distinguished Senators of the past. I hope that the list and comments which I enclose may be of help to your committee in deciding whom to honor with portraits. As you'll see, my suggestions fall chiefly in the first half of our national history, but I could see no way of leaving out the giants of the Senate's golden age."[5]

On September 29, 1965, President Lyndon Johnson invited Malone to the White House for the signing of the National Foundation on the Arts and the Humanities Act into law. The act called for the creation of the

National Endowment for the Humanities (NEH) and the National Endowment for the Arts (NEA) as separate, independent agencies. The *Washington Post* called the creation of the endowments "a momentous step." More than two hundred people filled the Rose Garden for the bill-signing ceremony. The guest list included actor Gregory Peck, photographer Ansel Adams, writer Ralph Ellison, architect Walter Gropius, and philanthropist Paul Mellon. The ceremony marked the highpoint of a day devoted to celebrating culture. Vice President Hubert Humphrey hosted a reception in the Rose Garden, and the Harkness Ballet performed that evening in the East Room of the White House.

The bill they gathered to celebrate was the culmination of a movement calling for the federal government to invest in culture, just as it had with science. As Glenn Seaborg, the head of the Atomic Energy Commission, told a Senate committee, "We cannot afford to drift physically, morally, or esthetically in a world in which the current moves so rapidly perhaps toward an abyss. Science and technology are providing us with the means to travel swiftly. But what course do we take? This is the question that no computer can answer."[6]

Among his many encounters with the rich and famous, Malone recalled the time in the early 1970s, during the Watergate scandal, when Justice Lewis Powell sent word to him that he wanted to read his then unpublished chapters on the conspiracy trial of Aaron Burr in 1807. Malone told Powell that the court had ruled that President Jefferson and his papers were subject to subpoenas.

"Thanks very much for your letter of November fourth and for the reprint of your article on Jefferson as President," wrote Senator George McGovern in 1969. "I am eager to read it. Likewise, I will be delighted to read your book because Jefferson is my favorite political figure and so your treatment of his presidency will have special appeal for me. I will look forward to continued pleasant associations with you. *With kindest personal regards. George McGovern.*"[7]

Merrill Peterson, perhaps the second most knowledgeable person about Jefferson after Malone, even bowed to Malone in some of his letters. In 1969, he wrote that when he compared his books to Malone's biography of Jefferson, he felt "rather like a cockboat in the wake of a battleship."[8] Malone was always modest in his replies and sought to give credit to others. For example, a 1969 letter to Professor Lester Cappon in Williamsburg read, "For the revival of interest in early American history, which is now so obvious, you deserve very large credit."[9]

Malone received many letters from various Virginia dignitaries, including Governor Linwood Holton: "That the citizens of Virginia are proud of your accomplishments which have distinguished you and brought distinction to the Commonwealth. We would like to honor a representative group of distinguished Virginians at a reception at the executive mansion in Richmond on September 23, 1972. Mrs. Holton and I look forward to offering our congratulations to you in person."[10] On August 2, 1972, in response to the governor's invitation, Malone wrote, "Since I ceased driving a car I have something of a problem in going places. Chances are that either my daughter or my research assistant will drive me down and see me safely in your portals."[11]

Malone collected numerous letters from librarians across the country, none more cherished than from Librarian of Congress Daniel Boorstin. On June 3, 1976, he wrote to Malone,

> It was a delight to see you and Elizabeth at the opening of 'the eye of Jefferson' and have you visit the library this morning. We are delighted and I see no difficulties in permitting the library to publish a chapter or chapters on Jefferson's library, and Jefferson as a librarian. It will not only be a splendid contribution to the Library of Congress history but will be a valued keepsake for many and a resource for study for others.[12]

Malone's correspondence with Supreme Court Justice Felix Frankfurter was numerous and friendly. In January 1941 Frankfurter wrote Malone, "Now that I have read your T. Jefferson letter I can understand through actual knowledge and not merely on faith, the enthusiasm of the examiners for not the least of our intellectual difficulties is the lack of historical perspective of such arrogant ignoramuses as Joe Kennedy and Lindberg."[13] Malone responded that he missed Frankfurter "much more than I can say" and "in connection with the effort to interpret Jefferson to our own days is that I am in correspondence with *LIFE* about their doing a Jefferson piece sometime in the spring. However I do not believe I told you that I'm returning to my biography of Jefferson and am finding that it is giving me a new lease on life. If you have any suggestions about the letter or about anything else, please do not hesitate to send them on."[14]

Malone, even though a preeminent scholar in his own right, was never afraid to seek help from prominent scholars in areas that were unfamiliar to him. For example, in a 1969 letter to Julian Boyd, Malone wrote, "In Jefferson's letter of June 19, 1807 to George Hay he says that he is enclosing a copy of a letter just received and which obviously relates to Luther Martin. . . . I have been unable to find the enclosure in this letter and am wondering if you have found it. Your records are complete that I assume you can answer this question without much trouble. Any help you can give me in this connection will be most welcome."[15]

Malone's sterling reputation as a historian and biographer parlayed into a film titled *Dumas Malone: A Journey with Mr. Jefferson* in 1982. The film included a series of interviews of Malone by Marc Pachter, the historian for the National Portrait Gallery and scholar in residence at the International Communication Agency. The U.S. Information Agency (USIA) produced the movie, which centered on three themes: the first and principal framework dealt with Thomas Jefferson as an international figure, the second was to be Jefferson's later years, and the last theme was Malone's own relationship with Jefferson during his forty years of writing.

Producer Larry Ott seemed pleased on the outcome of the film and wrote to Malone, "It was an honor and a great pleasure to meet you in Charlottesville this week. . . . Your patience and good humor during the rather long and tedious two days helped to make it an even more pleasant and productive experience for us all."[16]

The film received a warm reception. In fact, when it was shown at the USIA, the auditorium sold out. Pachter introduced the film and recalled that the "evening was a great success and the audience seemed to enjoy your interview immensely."[17] The film was also screened at the Museum of American History at the Smithsonian Institution's Resident Scholars Program and drew more than 270 people, who completely filled the auditorium. Ott wrote to Malone that the film "was one of the productions with which I am most proud to have associated during my nearly 16 years at the Agency."[18]

It was so well received that UVA president Frank Hereford urged Congress to allow the film to be shown domestically as well as oversees. In a letter to then senator John Warner, Hereford wrote, "Last spring the USIA completed a videotaped interview with our renowned Jefferson scholar, Dumas Malone. . . . Under present regulations, the tape is not to be shown in the United States, but I'm advised that Congress can, and frequently does, make exceptions to the regulations."[19]

Senator Warner responded to Hereford, "I am pleased to honor your request. Enclosed you will find a copy of the measure, said to be 3073, as well as my floor statement upon the introduction of the bill on Friday, December 3, 1982."[20] Warner introduced legislation to allow the domestic release of the USIA documentary about Malone. Congressman J. Kenneth Robinson joined Warner in sponsoring the bill. Warner gave an enthusiastic speech on the Senate floor introducing the legislation:

> This recording is an interview with Dumas Malone, [the] renowned biographer of our third president Thomas Jefferson. [We are] seeking congressional consideration of these matters. . . . The Smithsonian and the Thomas Jefferson Memorial Foundation are planning exhibits of Gilbert Stuart's Edgehill portrait earlier this spring. Filmed on location at the University of Virginia and Monticello in November 1981, the program concentrates on Jefferson's personality and career. Release of this work in the United States would enable people all across the country and especially those viewing the actual exhibit at the Smithsonian and Monticello this spring to gain richer insights into our . . . president by the man who knows him best. Mr. President, I ask unanimous consent that the bill be printed in the record.[21]

Congress approved the measure, and it became part of the congressional record and Public Law 97-388 of the Ninety-seventh Congress on December 23, 1982: "The director of the United States Information Agency shall make available to the administrator of General services a master copy of the film titled 'Dumas Malone: Journey with Mr. Jefferson' and the administrator shall reimburse the director for any expenses of the agency in making that master copy available. 96 STAT 1948."[22]

Perhaps Malone's most distinguished encounter, however, was with the Queen of England, Elizabeth II, who visited the United States for the bicentennial in 1976. Indeed, the queen had a little known affiliation with Virginia. She was a direct descendant of Col. Augustine Warner (1611–74) of Warner Hall, Gloucester County, Virginia. Queen Elizabeth's mother, the wife of King George VI, was the daughter of Claude Bowes-Lyon, fourteenth Earl of Strathmore, who was a direct descendant of Augustine

Warner through John Smith of Purton, Gloucester County, Virginia. In fact, the Warner family had another distinction. Mildred Warner was the grandmother of George Washington.[23]

The University of Virginia and the governor of Virginia invited Malone to a luncheon reception with the queen. In the invitation, the governor's assistant, Sandy Gilliam, outlined for Malone the royal protocol:

> I forgot to say that the British Embassy has decreed that Americans are not expected to bow or courtesy; a slight inclination of the head when you're presented in and a bob from Mrs. Malone would be most satisfactory, though not obligatory. One other thing, the Embassy says gloves will not be worn by ladies, hats are optional and dresses are short.
>
> The governor would like to present you and Mrs. Malone to the Queen and Prince Philip just before lunch. . . . As each guest is presented to the Queen and Prince go on to the next person in line. . . . Guests will peel off and head for the tables. The reason for this is that once the Queen has met everyone in this group she will go to her table in the dome room and Bishop Hall will begin grace. All of this sounds complicated as the dickens, and I apologize. We have to answer to many different masters and working out all of these plans. Not the least of whom is the Secret Service with their rather stringent security requirements.[24]

On July 10, 1976, at precisely 12:30, in the Rotunda at the University of Virginia, the queen of England dined on a southern luncheon of chilled cream of asparagus soup, baked Virginia ham, watermelon pickles, and hot biscuits (Malone's favorite). Afterward, the queen and Prince Philip were presented with a special five-volume set of Malone's biography. Each of the volumes was hand-bound in Colonial Williamsburg in the eighteenth-century printing office. The books were covered with red Nigerian goatskin, traditionally used on the finest books in the world. The edges had been decorated by a technique called "marbling," developed in Japan in the twelfth century and commercially employed in Europe in the seventeenth and eighteenth centuries. The pattern chosen for the decorative volumes was red for the endpapers and an English peacock design of the eighteenth century. The twenty-four-carat-gold decorative tooling on the cover of each volume was a traditional English Cambridge design. Master bookbinder Eugene N. Crane undertook the decorative tooling in Williamsburg.

Governor Godwin signed each dedication page with the inscription, "Presented to her Majesty Queen Elizabeth, her Royal highness, and Prince Philip on the occasion of their visit to Charlottesville, Virginia during America's Independence celebration of July 10, 1976."

Among the two hundred guests and dignitaries seated at the queen's table, which was decorated with simple arrangements of garden roses, were the Reverend Robert P. Hall, bishop of the Episcopal diocese of Virginia, who said grace; Anthony Crossland, British secretary of state for foreign Commonwealth affairs; Peter Ramsbotham, British ambassador to the United States; Ann Armstrong, U.S. ambassador to Great Britain; and Henry Catto Jr., chief of protocol of the United States.

After lunch, the queen "rested" at Pavilion I on the West Lawn and then visited Monticello. The precise sequence of events was laid out in a memorandum by the governor's office, the British embassy, and the Secret Service:

> The motorcade of the Queen and the Duke of Edinburgh is set to arrive at Monticello at 3 PM Saturday, 10 July 1976. The motorcade will enter at the entrance gate on state road 53. This route will be via the exit road that leads past the graveyard. The Queen will ride with Governor Godwin. The Duke of Edinburgh will ride with Mrs. Godwin. At the midpoint of their walkabout the Queen and the Duke of Edinburgh will proceed to a small circle in the center of the lawn where Mr. Nolting will make the presentation of the foundation's gift to the Queen.[25]

Years later Malone sent the queen his final volume, which he had completed in 1981. The queen's office wrote Malone on March 15, 1982, and said, "The Queen has asked me to write to you to say how delighted she is to have the sixth and last volume of your book on Jefferson to add to the five volumes of which were presented to her Majesty at the time of her Bicentennial visit to Virginia in 1976. It is splendid that you have been able to complete the work which will make a notable addition to the Royal Library at Windsor."[26]

When he worked with the National Association of Educational Broadcasters to produce a series of radio programs titled *The Jeffersonian Heritage*, Malone met a famous Broadway producer and actor: "My role was that of consultant. I well remember meeting representatives of the Association at the Cape in the late summer of 1951. This was in my study in what had been the woodshed in our old house at West Falmouth. As best I can recall, I was visited by William O. Harley, the coordinator of the programs, George Probst, chairman of the committee and the producer of the series, Frank Papp, was also there." The purpose of these programs was to present historic ideas in dramatic form. Malone was impressed by the radio personnel's sincerity, and "I embarked on this enterprise with considerable enthusiasm, along with some trepidation."[27]

At the radio program's request, he drew up a list of topics, including obvious ones such as freedom of religion, freedom of speech, and public education. Programs were written by scriptwriters, who were selected by Frank Papp. "I had many conferences with him, as I did with them," wrote Malone. All the scripts were subject to approval, and a good many of them had to be revised. One of the writers told Malone that he could not make a living if he confined himself to this sort of writing. "It was much too fussy and took too much time," Malone revealed. "On the whole, however, the script writers and I got along very well. I truly realized that if I was pedantic, the programs were likely to be dull. Some dramatic license had to be granted."[28]

The programs contained a great many quotations from Jefferson, but "I did not insist that these be in their own setting of time and place, though I was insistent on this in my own writing. I finally agreed to the statement that these programs were authentic in spirit while imaginative in form. I tried to make sure that Jefferson and the other major figures were always in character." The scriptwriters, in their effort to be dramatic, sometimes exaggerated conflict, and sometimes it seemed to Malone that they were unfair to Jefferson's opponents. Malone wrote,

> The only contribution of my own that I remember was in the matter of local pronunciation. I saw to it that the name of Jefferson's great law teacher, George Wythe, was pronounced to rhyme with Smith, though one would not suspect that from the spelling. The part of Jefferson was played very effectively by Claude Rains. His soft voice may even have resembled Jefferson's, but he did not need to look like him because this was radio. This imaginative medium offered us many advantages.[29]

Brushes with fame, however, did not bring great fortune to Malone. Throughout his life, the state of his finances were a constant concern. Although

Malone made a decent living teaching and writing, financial matters worried him in his professional life, as reflected in his memoir: "The first stage of my long journey with Mr. Jefferson had been pretty expensive. It was richly rewarding, of course, but certainly not in money."[30]

The tone of his application for a third Guggenheim Fellowship bordered on professional pleading:

> As I told you then I am now proceeding on a grant from the national endowment for the humanities. This was made for only one year, but on the basis of a three-year project which was expected to continue. Shortly before seeing you, I learned that the NEH was undisposed to grant renewals. Besides the disadvantages arising from my dubious age and the fact that I have already had two Guggenheim Fellowships, there are a couple of other questions that disturb me.[31]

In a severe blow, Gordon Rey, the president of the Guggenheim Foundation, denied Malone, who had received two previous fellowships for his biography, the fellowship money: "Having carefully considered all the factors that you describe, I am inclined to advise you not to apply for a third Guggenheim Fellowship this year. Such an application would necessarily be a long shot at best, particularly since the virtual disappearance of other fellowship programs is sure to make our selection procedures even more stringent. I am sorry to have to reply in this sense."[32]

By necessity, Malone became frugal when it came to money, as evidenced by his letter to Shirley Fewell about work on his Charlottesville house:

> I am staggered by the bill you have just sent me which, it seems to me, is about twice as big as it ought to be. There was no need for you to bring three men to do the ordered jobs on my house, and I am quite unwilling to pay this much for what they did. . . . After talking with my friends last year, I became convinced that you considerably overcharged me for the work you did on the tool house and fence, but I let that go because of my genuine regard for you.[33]

Writing to August Clough, a handyman for his Cape Code home, Malone requested, "For my own records I would like a receipt for this payment divided between the house and the Barn. Also, I would appreciate a somewhat more detailed break-down, if you can give it without too much trouble—that is, I would like to be able to distinguish repairs, such as those of broken-window-panes, from more permanent improvements like the shingling of the roof."[34]

Malone was so concerned about his finances that he obtained a second mortgage on his house. "In fact," Malone later wrote, "my new house had cost considerably more than I had intended or could afford. The bank had been too generous in extending credit, even at an increased salary from the University. I might have had difficulty meeting the payments." He wrote to attorney Fred Landess, "Please pardon my delay in acknowledging your letter of March 23 and the original deed of trust, securing the second mortgage on my house at 2000 Lewis Mountain Road."[35]

Perhaps Malone's views about money projected into his biography. Although no one could argue that Jefferson was frugal, Malone argued in an interview in 1981 that Jefferson would be dismayed by the "commercialization" of today's society:

> The society in which Jefferson lived was an economy of things rather than money. A sack of flour was something to be eaten—not just something to be sold. We've gotten to the point where the dollar is really the measure of everything, the most obvious example being the world of sport. You have Bud Collins reporting a tennis match—and we are very fond of Bud Collins—and three or four times in the course of his reporting, he'll tell you how much money is involved.

In other words, Malone declared, the monetary concern has to win. The human consideration was secondary. "It seems to me a fatal thing," he lamented.[36]

19 Blindness

Apart from my blindness and deafness I am in excellent shape and hope to live until July 4.
　　　　　　　　　—DUMAS MALONE, 1981[1]

At my age of life little is left but memory.
　　　　　　　　　—DUMAS MALONE, 1982[2]

Aging was not just decay to Dumas Malone. It was growing and persevering to his stated goal. He understood this as he moved more slowly through the years. "You must be tolerant of an old man's fading memory," he often warned.[3] Robust though he was, he had finished his last volume with the help of a vision machine that enabled him to read by magnifying his text. He was a survivor, "triumphantly healthy, a wise, marvelous gentleman," one reporter noted.[4] Dumas Malone won his race with time. In 1981, when the final volume was published, Malone was in his ninetieth year—and almost totally blind.

Edmund Berkeley, a good friend and curator of manuscripts and archivist at UVA, noticed Malone's determination to carry on with exacting work despite overwhelming physical troubles: "He had a study on the fifth floor of the library, and when it became hard for him to come and go unaided, he'd come to the back door, and some of the editors of the Madison papers would go down and get him up to his office. It's remarkable the way he trained himself to listen so carefully to what was read to him that he could go on with his work from that."[5]

Malone had suffered from age-related macular degeneration (AMD) for years and endured a series of operations on his eyes beginning in the 1960s. The first signs of this macular degeneration began when Malone was in his fifties. The ailment progressed to a gradual loss of central vision. He hardly complained to his doctors of the gradual dimming of his sight, even though it was worse when he read. He experienced distorted vision, and straight lines appeared wavy to him. Dark, blurry areas or white often appeared in the center of his vision, and he had problems for decades with color perception.

Malone's AMD was caused by the deterioration of his retina, and eventually it severely impaired his vision. Dr. Ken Wallenborn, one of the historian's general doctors who also urged him to give up smoking (he gave up cigarettes but not pipe smoking), told him there was no cure for macular degeneration, but it could be treated with vitamins, medication, and vision aids. Laser therapy had not been invented by the time Malone contracted the disease. Reduced central vision from AMD made it difficult for him to work and manage many of the activities of his daily life. He gave up driving a car and had to learn to adapt to severely low vision. For a writer, editor, and author, this was a devastating physical and emotional blow.

Wallenborn treated Malone for years, and after their medical appointments, the two men often talked at length about their mutual interest, Thomas Jefferson. Dr. Wallenborn, a slight man with wire-rimmed glasses, complemented by a short, stylish haircut, recalled finishing a high-tech examination of Malone's eyes one time. He had to give his patient bad news. Malone had grade-4 posterior subscapular cataracts and signs of macular degeneration. He told Malone that the cataracts could be removed with little or no damage to his cornea, but the macular degeneration was incurable. The disease would act like a curtain covering the window of sight.

Malone's first operation for cataracts was in 1966. Multiple operations followed, including a major procedure by ophthalmologist and chairman of the department, Dr. Marion K. "Slug" Humphries on October 23, 1972, at the University of Virginia Hospital in the Barringer Wing. "I remember this well," Steve Hochman related, "because he stayed in the hospital for quite a few days. It was only after the 1972 surgery that [he] began wearing the extremely thick lenses worn in that era by everyone. After the surgery [his] eyesight improved, but at some point the deterioration from the macular degeneration made it extremely difficult for him to read."[6]

As his eyesight deteriorated, he pressed on. Malone's vision was worsening quickly as he researched and wrote the last two volumes of his work. When he started the final volume of his biography in 1976, he had to rely on thick glasses, a vision machine for writing, and two hearing aids for his near deafness. He wrote to Daniel Boorstin on June 9, 1976, "I am sorry that I have reached such a state of decrepitude that I cannot be trusted to make long trips alone, but that does seem to be the case."[7]

Malone corresponded with his doctor in West Falmouth, Paul Magnusson, concerning his hearing problems and a prescription for glycerol. He asked Magnusson if this "was a safe and effective thing to use to prevent the sort of thing that I have suffered from. What I am doing now is going to a doctor every month . . . which is rather troublesome and expensive."[8] In fact, Malone was so meticulous he wrote to Frank Bracken about his two hearing aids and their specific batteries: "I was a little surprised to discover that these batteries were made by Zenith. My hearing aid, as you will remember, is an Oticon. I assume that there was no mistake about this because the batteries seem to work, although they have not lasted as long as I expected. . . . I am not sure I am getting much benefit out of the left one."[9]

Malone related the state of his health to Governor Holton: "Perhaps I should report that I am probably going to be out of commission for a week or so, since I am having an operation on my eye next week."[10] In more than one procedure, cups attached to wires sat over Malone's eyes. An electroretinogram emitted an irritating tone, and the operating room was dimly lit. Malone's doctor adjusted an intensity dial on the machine, and a series of flashing lights hit Malone's eyes. The nurse jotted down a reading; she then spun the machine away from Malone's face and pushed a button that prompted it to print a detailed report.

In 1980 Malone expressed cautious, perhaps unrealistic, optimism about his sight. He wrote to a colleague, "I hope I haven't given a false impression about my own physical condition. I am not blind and have been told that I shall never be. But my eyesight is dim, and I need a lot of help in getting around. So I shall have to content myself with staying home."[11]

Hochman became invaluable to Malone. In all probability, if not for Hochman, Malone would not have completed the last two volumes of the biography.

Steve Hochman, six feet tall, with short brown hair, was only twenty-three when he first started to work for Professor Malone.[12] He had been born and raised in St. Joseph, Missouri. His father, Julius, was a roofing contractor and volunteer director of St. Joseph's boys baseball league. Hochman had a younger brother, attended local public schools, and graduated from Central High School in June 1963. The editor of the school newspaper, he had always had an interest in reading and writing. He had spent his summers working for the baseball league and the sports section of the *St. Joseph Gazette*. As a high school and college student, he was interested in music and stage productions.

Hochman had earned his bachelor degree with honors in June 1967 at the University of Missouri. He had considered pursuing journalism at Missouri, but courses he took about the American Revolution and the early national period convinced him to major in history instead. He achieved departmental honors in history and was listed in *Who's Who among Students in American Universities and Colleges*. When the time came to apply for graduate school, Hochman applied to the University of Virginia, which had an almost palpable Jefferson presence, he recalled.

When Malone met him, Hochman was a first-year graduate student at the university and a Thomas Jefferson Memorial Foundation fellow. He had written a paper that later became his master's thesis on the topic "Republicanism in Virginia and the Constitution of 1776." University professors Merrill Peterson and William Abbot recommended him to Malone. When Malone hired Hochman in September 1968, his rate of pay was $225 per month. Malone would not let his new assistant start work, however, until his draft status was determined. Ultimately, Hochman was not drafted to serve in Vietnam, and he worked with Malone for the next thirteen years.

"I took a course on Jefferson the first year," Hochman said. "I was certainly not a Jeffersonian when I arrived there, but you are turned into one living at a University with Monticello up on a mountain."[13] Hochman was thrilled when he received the job offer from Malone: "I certainly am looking forward to working for you," he wrote to Malone in the summer of 1968. "I have been rereading *Jefferson the Virginian* and I plan to have acquired the necessary background for doing intelligent research. My parents are even enthused over our plans."[14]

Hochman had embarked on an extended Jeffersonian voyage. When he began working with Malone, the historian was serving as Jefferson biographer in residence at UVA, following his formal retirement from the history faculty. He hired Hochman as a graduate assistant after receiving the National Endowment for the Humanities grant to work on the Jefferson volumes. Hochman's work with Malone would extend to the summer of 1981, when *The Sage of Monticello* was released. "Actually most of my time working with Professor Malone was spent on the sixth volume, which is about the 17 years after the presidency up to Jefferson's death in 1826," Hochman explained. "Professor Malone's eyesight deteriorated dramatically during this period, so I began working full time at that point."[15]

Malone and Hochman conferred on what should be researched, and then Hochman would record the material on audiotape for Malone to digest. Sometimes they would do a "live recording," during which Malone often interrupted the tape to discuss material or request additional research. "Steve would read things I needed," Malone remembered. "Minutes of the trustees of the University, copies of *The Richmond Enquirer* for legislative news. Then he would record them on tape and index the important parts. That way I became more familiar with the material than if I'd read it. I could play the tape back four or five times. I might not have read it that often."[16]

Then Malone would write with the aid of a video screen that magnified his script forty times. Half a word filled up the whole screen. "It never crossed my mind to stop. If I'd gone completely blind, I probably would have dictated, but I don't dictate very well. In the last three volumes I was getting pretty old, and you never know how long you're going to live. So I made a point of cleaning up each chapter as I went along, leaving it in publishable form."[17]

One by one the pages on his legal pad filled up, each marking another step in Malone's journey with Jefferson. "The procedure since my eyesight failed has been very different. While working on the last volume I would write in the morning with the help of my reading machine, then I would bring in what I'd written to the office, and it would be typed and read back to me," Malone said. "After we got enough material to make a chapter or a large part of a chapter, it would be read again, and be read many times. The text was probably read to me four or five times."[18]

Malone explained that all of his writings had been triple spaced so there would be room for corrections. After two or three drafts, his secretary would put a chapter in final form. But before she sent it off to the publisher, his secretary would proofread it again. Malone was always shocked to see how many changes had to be made. "You can always improve it a little," he clarified, "the challenge is [trying] to figure out when the law of diminishing returns begins to operate, not [making it] worth the time that you put in on it. But you keep at it forever. I should have said earlier that I have come to rely less and less on detailed outlines and have relied increasingly on chronology."[19]

Kay Sargeant, his loyal secretary for more than fourteen years, typed almost everything Malone and Hochman gave her. In fact, she would often go down to the collections for Malone and take handwritten notes. "I also took shorthand for Mr. Malone's dictation."[20]

Perhaps, no one worked more closely with Malone than Sargeant, who started to work for him in 1967. She remembered Malone's work schedule and would often pick him up from his home after lunch and take him to the office. He would work with Hochman, writing and dictating, until about 4:30 in the afternoon, and then he'd take some work home.

She recalled Malone had extensive correspondence with famous figures, but she was most impressed when Senator John Warner came to visit Malone in his office. In 1976, when he was still married to Elizabeth Taylor, Warner was "the best looking man I had ever seen," she said.

Professor Malone was "amiable and jovial," Sargeant remembered, and always wore a coat and tie in the office. "On occasion he would smoke his pipe, but had to give that up for health years later." One anecdote she told spoke volumes of Malone's upbringing and his sense of southern manners. A young man came up to Malone's office and asked if he could speak with him about Thomas Jefferson. Malone had graciously agreed to see him even though he did not have an appointment. The young man was wearing a hat and did not take it off when he entered Malone's office. After a few minutes, Malone asked him to remove his hat. The young man refused, and Malone terminated the interview. Somewhat bewildered by the turn of events, the young man left.[21]

Hochman read about a machine, called the Visualtek, that magnified printed materials and compensated for fading eyesight in a Richmond newspaper. With the aid of Ray Frantz, the librarian of the University of

Virginia, he ordered two of these readers for Malone, one for his office and one for his home. The machines, as well as tape recorders, proved indispensable in preparation of the last two volumes. To quote from Hochman's personal account,

> The new system required my conducting all the research, organizing the materials, and reading them on tape for Mr. Malone to listen to and study. I developed chronological indexes to the tapes, which Mrs. Sargeant would type and Mr. Malone could read with his machine. Reading for him was a very tedious process. Only one or two words appeared at a time on the screen. He used the machine most effectively for his writing. He wrote by hand, the text was typed by Mrs. Sargeant, and he could revise it under the camera. Most revision, however, was done by ear. That is, Mrs. Sargeant or I would read to him and he would tell us what changes needed to be made.[22]

Malone's use of the Visualtek drew considerable publicity, both for the company and from others wishing to learn about the machine. He received numerous letters from other people with similar eye problems, inquiring about the use of the Visualtek. "I've recently fallen victim to macular degeneration of my eyes and I read an article that you use some equipment that magnifies the printed page. Could you tell me who makes this equipment," read a typical letter.[23]

Malone always viewed himself first as a teacher, a result of his mother's influence, but he also relished the written word. Even though he found writing more difficult with the passing years, he became more demanding even as his eyesight failed him. In his last years, visitors to Malone's spacious book-lined study in the Alderman Library were greeted by a white-haired, old man with a slow gait but a lively countenance; he was eager to talk and laughed heartily over his situation. "I can't imagine anything more absurd," he once remarked to a visiting reporter. "Here's a man 85 years old, who can hardly see, writing a book!"[24]

Jean Holliday, who lived across the street from the Malones for some years, once said, "How many times have I seen him walking down this street, almost blind, but invariably cheery with his greetings to people on the way." Staige Blackford, editor of the *Virginia Quarterly Review*, remembered, "Once I took him home from a seminar and got his mail, which included a recording for the blind. I said, 'It's Oliver Twist,' and he said, 'Oh, excellent. I haven't read that in more than 70 years.'"

As his eyes deteriorated, Malone depended more and more on audiobooks for reading the classics. He wrote in a speech to Phi Beta Kappa, "In my old age I have had the pleasure of renewing and deepening my [interest] with the Greeks, whom I too long neglected. My reading has to be through the ear, not the eye. But thanks to the tape recorder and a generous young woman who reads to me every day during the summer, I have been having a wonderful time with the Greeks. I got a fitting motto from Solon, the Athenian law giver, who said, 'Each day I grow older and learn something new.'"[25]

Malone's reading list of audiobooks included Charles Dickens's *David Copperfield*, George Eliot's *Middlemarch*, and Antonia Fraser's *Mary Queen of Scots*. When his own volumes 1 and 2 were recorded on tape, Malone discussed the taping with Charlottesville Unit Studio director Margaret Anderson. He told her that he used the tapes of his earlier books for reference as he completed the final volume of his biography. Eventually, all six of Malone's volumes were recorded on tape for him and the general public.

Malone kept active by ordering audiobooks through various libraries, including the Virginia State Library for the Visually and Physically Handicapped. He also received many tapes through Recording for the Blind, which offered free taped educational books to the "print-handicapped." In February 1981 he received a letter from Carl Chadsy, the associate director of this organization: "The most impressive thing of all about Recording for the Blind is the unbelievable accomplishments of people like yourself who have overcome a difficult handicap to join the mainstream of life."[26] Malone replied, "If it will be of any help to you, you can report that I have received very valuable services from recording for the blind. These have been of great help to us in my work. I am not totally blind but read with much difficulty." Ever the perfectionist, Malone commented on the recordings in his letter and corrected several of the pronunciations in the tapes: "Since comments on the tapes are requested I will make one criticism of the recording of my book, *Jefferson the Virginian*. Among the mispronounced names that I noted in the first few chapters were *Wythe, Eppes, Henrico, Rivanna and Fluvanna*. . . . My own first name is pronounced three ways in the tapes I have heard thus far."[27]

"I have had an assistant for many years, and he has read everything and put it on tape," Malone explained in an interview with the *New York Times*.

Having to rely on tapes was a problem at first, but there were compensations. "No chapter would get through without being read to me a half-dozen times, and you can get by ear what the eye sometimes misses," he explained. "But organization is still a problem, and you should see me trying to sign my name without the machine."[28]

Near the end of his life, Malone said he had two regrets: he could no longer read a newspaper and he did not continue his hobbies. "I used to play tennis, but I quit that some time ago," he confessed. "Now I listen to Mozart and Chopin. I'm very old-fashioned, I don't get much beyond the 19th century. I proceeded on the assumption that there are many things I don't know much about, so I stay with the tried and the true."[29] Malone did not give up book reviewing, however, "until I became virtually blind at the age of 85."[30]

The year before he died he seemed to face reality and the tragedy of his condition. "Being nearly 94 years old and nearly blind, I have had to forgo all reading."[31]

It was fitting that Malone dedicated the final volume, *The Sage of Monticello*, to Steve Hochman and Kay Sargeant: "This work as a whole is for ELISABETH GIFFORD MALONE. This volume is for my devoted co-workers STEVEN HAROLD HOCHMAN and KATHERINE MOON SARGEANT."[32]

20   Death on the Mountain

The earth belongs always to the living generation.
                                        —THOMAS JEFFERSON[1]

*If I were living life all over again, I would make the
funeral oration of Pericles required reading in all my
history classes.*

                              —DUMAS MALONE, SPEECH TO
                                PHI BETA KAPPA (1982)

Biographer, Historian.
        —EPITAPH ON DUMAS MALONE'S HEADSTONE, 1986

Earl Warren died of what they said was old age at eighty-three, Malone
told Elisabeth. He went on to say, "Walter Lippmann just died of 'old
age' at 85. I said to my wife, 'This doesn't sound good.'" Malone believed
that "it is a wonderful thing for an old man when he can be productive."[2]

Helen Cripe described the scene of Malone's eighty-first birthday. Helen
was living in Charlottesville and preparing her dissertation for publication
with Bob Rutland, editor of the James Madison papers. "I saw Mr. Malone
frequently, as his office was just down the hall. The year before there had
been a big celebration for his 80th birthday," she recalled.

His 81st birthday came around and nobody seemed to notice except for
Bob. Bob went down to the snack bar late in the afternoon and bought a

plate of rather tatty-looking cupcakes, which is all they had left. We all took the plate down to Mr. Malone's office and told him we thought an 81st birthday was far more significant than an 80th. He roared with laughter, thanked us, and said that for his birthday dinner at home he was requesting fried chicken, in which he apparently was not supposed to indulge too often.[3]

Through near blindness, deafness, a fractured hip, and various other physical ailments, Dumas Malone clearly enjoyed the celebrations occasioned by finishing his great work in his last years on earth. Little did he know that on Christmas Day he would suffer a heart attack at the Tides Inn in Irvington, Virginia. Fortunately, he recovered and lived several more years.

In celebration of the publication of *The Sage of Monticello* in 1981, a luncheon was held in Malone's honor at New York's 21 Club in June. It was attended by fellow historians Richard Morris, Arthur Schlesinger Jr., Bruce Bliven Jr., and Barbara Tuchman. On the Fourth of July weekend, Malone attended a dinner in his honor in the Rotunda at the University of Virginia. This dinner was followed by a reception at Monticello. At eighty-nine, Malone was still the best possible company, a funny raconteur with a relaxed southern style, a genuinely friendly man who talked about his close friend, Thomas Jefferson, with a lifetime's knowledge and unabated liking.[4]

At the dinner, Malone quoted his often-used line, "It was reported that President William Howard Taft after he had lectured at the University of Virginia said, 'They still talked of Mr. Jefferson as though he were in the next room.'" The quotation was one of Malone's favorites, and when he himself spoke of Jefferson in the book-filled study of his modest Lewis Mountain Road bungalow, Jefferson's presence, if not precisely located in the next room, could indeed be felt emanating from the nearby summit of his "little mountain."

Volume 6 of Jefferson's biography was published on the Fourth of July 1981. *The Sage of Monticello*, the fulfillment of thirty-eight years of work, chronicled the last seventeen years of Jefferson's life, which were spent mostly at his home at Monticello. When *The Sage of Monticello* was published, Malone's name had long since become inseparable from that of the third president. Historian C. Vann Woodward, reviewing Malone's final volume in the *New York Times Book Review* wrote, "The work that this volume completes stands as a masterly achievement of scholarship, the finest biography of Jefferson we have or are likely to have and a monumental triumph of the senior American historian."[5]

In fact, the reviews of Malone's last volume were more effusive than those for any other volume. A *Christian Science Monitor* reviewer described "Professor Malone as modest; his accomplishments are commendable. His deep scholarship, genuine understanding, and good common sense are apparent throughout. His style is clear, forceful, and interesting." H. J. Laski of the *New Republic* contended, "We . . . have, at last, a biography that not only takes account of the greatness of material so admirably organized in recent years, but one that is worthy of its exciting subject." A critic from the *American Historical Review* simply called it "American historical scholarship at its very best."[6]

Malone, showing off his crinkling charm and zest for conversation, was in good form during one of his last interviews in early June 1985. He was ninety-three but talked a blue streak and had forgotten nothing he ever learned about American history.[7] Once Malone had told a journalist that Jefferson was most able to be the kind of man he wanted to be during the years he lived in France. But what about Malone? Had he been the kind of man he wanted to be? "Well . . . I've been more remote from life than I would have liked," he answered.

> I've been a little more in the cloister and the ivory tower than I ever expected to be, and I don't feel I've participated quite enough in life as it was going on. But I think I've always been conscious of life, and I hope it's evident in my writing. My life has been richer in experience than I ever had any reason to expect. How could I have ever known that I would have the experience of living all these years in company with a man like Jefferson? It's been an enormous privilege, and in that way my life's been much richer . . . than I had any reason to expect. I've dealt with great things and great people. Sometimes people ask me what I do, and I say I live through great events with great men. To associate with men like Jefferson and George Washington

and John Adams and to go through the things they went through, in that sense, life has been very rich. But you always wonder. It's been good for me. But how good has it been for others? You never know.[8]

Malone spoke in short bursts now, inhaling air, exhaling words. His voice was still strong, but sometimes raspy. He sensed his long journey with Mr. Jefferson was coming to an end.

Ravaged by complications from pneumonia, Dumas Malone died in his home on December 27, 1986, two weeks short of his ninety-fifth birthday. He was surrounded by family members and his nurse on the bitterly cold Saturday morning when he took his last breath. "My wife, Margaret, and my daughter, Elizabeth, and I had been there on the previous day," Gifford recalled, "and each of us had had a chance to see him. No one knew, of course, how much time he had left, although we all knew that it would not be much longer."[9]

The obituary in *The New York Times* read that Malone had died "after a brief illness."[10] He was buried that Tuesday at the University Cemetery in a private ceremony, attended by a small gathering of family and colleagues, and handled by the Hill and Wood Funeral Home. Founded in 1828 at the corner of Alderman and McCormack roads, the University Cemetery is rich with history. Nowhere else in Virginia can one encounter this many accomplished professors, a world-renowned physicist (Jesse Beams), and a literary compiler (William McGuffey) whose nineteenth-century works, *The McGuffey Readers*, sold better than any book but the Bible. The cemetery also holds three University of Virginia presidents, including Edwin Alderman. Among other notables buried there are Harry Clemons and Richard Heath Dabney. Not far from Malone's gravesite sits the Confederate cemetery, a peaceful glen that holds the remains of 1,097 Confederate soldiers from regiments representing eleven southern states, most of whom died during the war at the Charlottesville General Hospital.

This sense of poetry and history sets the University Cemetery apart as a special place for repose and reflection. Its wonder is realized in the embracing stillness one senses within moments of entering the cemetery. Interred at UVA's serene cemetery are 937 distinguished faculty members, but none are more famous than Dumas Malone. Robert M. O'Neil, former president of the University of Virginia, eulogized Malone: "The passing of Dumas Malone marks the close of an era in Virginia's and the university's history. It was through him that most of us came to know and understand—and revere—Thomas Jefferson."

"The things about him that were so distinctive were his gentility and his scholarship," Rutland recalled. "He was one of the finest men I ever knew. His death is an irreplaceable loss to the community."[11]

When Malone died, Frank Hereford, another former president of the University of Virginia, commented,

> After he won the Pulitzer Prize in 1975 for the biography, I said to him that the honor of the prize had just been raised enormously, and it had. He was a wonderful gentleman. That comes to mind first with all who knew him. He called the university the "old place," and used to phone before he left for Cape Cod in the summer to say he was going, then again when he got back to say he was reporting back "for duty." I heard somebody ask him at a cocktail party how he was and he said he was just fine, never felt better. He saw me and grinned. "That's rubbish, of course. I've been in the hospital three days this week and never felt worse. But who wants to hear that?"[12]

In the last year of his life, Malone still conveyed a sense of intellectual and physical vigor. Yet he was troubled in his old age by admirers who seemed to imagine he was Mr. Jefferson reincarnate.

> People often ask, "How could you devote yourself so long to one person?" Well, they have a false impression. I consider that I have made a journey through history in the company of Mr. Jefferson. Think of going through the period of the French Revolution, the American Revolution, the Napoleonic Wars and the beginning of the Republic in the presence of the man who was in touch with all of it. . . . I have probably known him longer than any living person has, and I have known him as a friend.[13]

Dumas and Elisabeth Malone (who died in October 1992) are buried in the section of the University of Virginia's cemetery closest to Lewis Mountain Road, within sight of his home and Monticello. When the sun eased up over the eastern horizon and touched Malone's gravestone, two dozen chilled students from the University of Virginia clustered around his grave and raised their voices and overflowing cups for a rousing cheer. This day, April 13, 1987, was the anniversary of the birth of Thomas Jefferson, a day of considerable pomp and ceremony coined "Founder's Day." A gravestone near the Malones reads prophetically, "Sun behind the mountains, pausing at the crest—waiting for his tired feet coming home to rest."[14]

Afterword

Greatness is not found in possessions, power, position, or prestige. It is discovered in goodness, humility, service, and character.

—**William Arthur Ward**[1]

I myself have found history a perennially challenging and inexhaustible subject.

—**Dumas Malone**[2]

Malone has heroically resisted the urge to defend rather than describe the man.

—**Garry Wills**[3]

History is haunted by the preoccupations and crises of the age in which it is written. And so it was with Dumas Malone and *Jefferson and His Time*. He began his long journey in 1943, during World War II. In the intervening decades, the country experienced McCarthy's "red baiting," the Korean War, the Cuban missile crisis, a presidential assassination and two other presidential assassination attempts, the war in Vietnam, the emergence of counterculture, the Watergate scandal, and the collapse of Soviet communism. By the time he was born, the car had not yet been invented. The year he died, the space shuttle Challenger exploded.

The debate over Jefferson's legacy has become increasingly complex since 1943, when Americans proudly celebrated the two hundredth anniversary of his birth. Ambivalence and qualification now surround most writings on Jefferson; the innocence of the 1940s and 1950s has yielded to skepticism and cynicism since the alleged DNA match in 1998. Yet, Malone never believed his quest of forty years would render any kind of moral symmetry on Jefferson or reconcile the Virginian's views on slavery or freedom. Malone's singular purpose was to tell us about Thomas Jefferson in his time. "To get the facts right was my first concern," he explained. "I'm sure that some people can take the very facts that I have presented and reach different conclusions from those I have reached. That's . . . bound to happen with a man like Jefferson, who has so many sides, and who is, in many respects, a controversial figure."[4]

Malone regarded his biography of Jefferson as merely an aspect of history, and in the course of his life, he viewed both biography and history from as many angles as he possibly could. "In order to understand any historic figure," he remarked, "or any past age one needs to live with the person and in the age as best he can. This is not merely escape but also professional necessity."[5]

Malone witnessed his own profession change radically during his lifetime and he commented frequently on this change:

> I never liked the word "objective" because that implies a certain indifference. Of course you're terribly involved with the person you're writing about, you're terribly interested in him. And certainly it's often hard to be that. But I don't like the idea of the adversary system in connection with scholarship of any sort. I don't regard myself as a counsel for the defense, not at all. I'm trying to portray Jefferson a man, trying to explain him. Again and again I encounter controversial questions and things for which people have criticized Jefferson. I tried to explain them and to show why he acted as he did. But that doesn't necessarily mean that I'm defending him, you see, I'm perfectly sure that somebody's going to say that I am.[6]

Malone realized that "sometimes you stand up so straight, you lean backwards. But fairness and honesty are my goals. Although nobody's completely fair, and nobody's completely honest, some are more so than others. Of course, you can never wholly divest yourself of your own personality, your own convictions, your own prejudices."[7]

What would Malone think of what some critics have termed "revision-ist history" and "advocacy scholarship"?

I think historical writing has improved. Now there are more good writers than there were in my day. I am sure of that. For example, my old profes-sor Charles M. Andrews was a great scholar and a good writer, but he was suspicious of anyone trying to be popular. The profession counted it against a scholar if he was popular. That's gone entirely now. No one minds scholars' books being read. There are far more books with wide acceptance that have been written by scholars in recent years than when I started out.[8]

Malone acknowledged that in every decade

there are fads and fashions, of course. Some people say you are out of date if you don't go along with the current fashion. I pay no attention to fash-ion. In writing the history of the Civil War or the Revolution, I don't think of myself as a prosecutor or as . . . an advocate. The adversary system has come into scholarship to a certain extent. In the student uprisings of the 1960s they said you had to take a stand. Historians must be careful, how-ever, not to take a stand as advocates. This is a noisy world, and you can't be heard unless you yell. Maybe that is what they do: take a strong posi-tion and everybody pays attention. But that is not my idea of the way scholarship is done. It should be cooperative, not competitive. In a sense you are a rival to other scholars, but most of all you help each other. I don't like this antagonistic spirit.[9]

Malone thought a great deal about the relationship between history and biography but considered himself a historian first and foremost. "History is greater than biography," he explained. "The sort of biography I do, deal-ing with the relatively distant past is a part of history. You use the same cri-teria as with history. Although you have to see history from as many angles as you can, when you go to write something, you can't look [at it] from all the angles. I happened to get into biography, and I happened to like it."[10]

Malone reiterated that he was going through history with Jefferson. "But you can't be content with biography. You have to read a lot of other things," he wrote. "I used it in my teaching only incidentally. Bernard Mayo used to give an excellent course in biography here, but I'd rather not. That is a personal thing. I write biography because I'm interested in people. Biography has to be a narrative. People like that."[11]

Malone viewed history through his life experience: "The more experience you have, the better you ought to be able to do it," he explained. "I am sure I couldn't possibly have written Jefferson's life at 40 as well as I did at 70. I just understood things better. You aren't necessarily wiser because you are older, but you should be. You are certainly more experienced."[12]

Malone described the purpose of the study of history as finding the truth in so far as a scholar is able to, and he often quoted Montaigne in this context: "'I do not understand. I pause. I examine.' I've tried very hard to understand. I've always been a foe of pedantry. I think that knowledge without understanding is a barren thing."[13]

Malone seemed quite aware that subjectivity seeped into all historical writing. But any historian should apply to his work the same sort of values that he applied to his own life. With that in mind, Malone never read "secondary accounts on Jefferson. . . . The main reason for this is that I do not want to be influenced by other people but to reach my own conclusions on the basis of study or original sources."[14]

When Malone died, his generous colleague, Professor Merrill Peterson, wrote a moving tribute to him in the *Virginia Quarterly Review* titled "Dumas Malone: An Appreciation." Peterson observed that while the present generation of historians cannot think of Thomas Jefferson without thinking of his biographer, Dumas Malone's rise to national eminence came through other means. People learned early in Malone's career that he had the gift of communicating to a general audience. Malone, however, "can be honored for more than his volumes on Thomas Jefferson. His contributions to humanistic scholarship have been matched by few."[15]

To write history, Thomas Jefferson said, "requires a whole life of observation, of labor and correction." Truly Jefferson was fortunate in gaining as a biographer a many-sided man, a man of style and character. All of which is prelude to celebrating "the career of Dumas Malone, the man whose six-volume biography of Jefferson taught us how consummately true reverence—*pietas*, as the ancients called it—can be combined with a responsible realism," Peterson wrote. "Until his death at 94, Malone had been the premier interpreter of the premier philosopher of American freedom. His Jefferson biography, the labor of his last four decades, sets a standard for the form."[16]

How did Malone strike a balance between candor and the nurturing of those values exemplified in Jefferson that bind society together?[17] His answer was simple: while a biographer will have his prejudices, his primary role is explanation, not pleading. This point was evident in his response to Fawn Brodie's book. Malone's work enjoyed a great windfall of attention when Brodie published her one-volume "intimate portrait" of Jefferson. Brodie's book gave Malone the opportunity to explain Jefferson to a wider audience. He tried to distinguish between our longing for heroes and our thirst for their salacious secrets. In this realm, Malone spoke with unrivaled authority. "I think I understand him a bit," the old man would say of Jefferson with a twinkle in the eyes behind the thick lenses, as if speaking of a brilliant but eccentric neighbor. "So spoke, with typical modesty, the man who knew more about Jefferson than anyone ever had," Peterson eulogized, "probably including Jefferson himself."[18]

Malone's contribution to historical writing has been extensive. He combined excellent scholarship with a readable style. He has left no source untouched in his desire to learn all about his subjects, whether Thomas Jefferson, Thomas Cooper, or Edwin A. Alderman. His editing of the *Dictionary of American Biography* established the methods and standards for short, definitive biography. The multivolume work, *Jefferson and His Time*, will be definitive for decades, if not a generation. It is difficult to see any better work ever being written on Jefferson. One of Malone's colleagues said it quite simply: "Dumas Malone's contributions to historical writing will be enduring."[19]

Malone was a historian before he was anything else, and this philosophy shaped his perspective on Jefferson. It is true that virtually all his scholarship, beginning with his first book in 1926, through his editorship at the DAB, and culminating in his monumental work, was biographical. But Malone always conceived of biography as a species of history, that species wherein the story of the past is drawn around the life of a single personage. Historical biography in the hands of "a master like Malone," Merrill Peterson observed, "may be imaginative, it may be literature, but it was founded upon deep research and deep knowledge of the past. It has its beginnings in the stacks of libraries, dusty archives, attics, and newspaper morgues. It was never the work of a mere man of letters. It demanded unceasing sweat and toil in the historical footsteps of the subject."[20]

Malone followed Jefferson's footsteps through eighty-three tumultuous years. He managed to accomplish the long journey in half the time it took Jefferson. Given the scale of the work, this pace was remarkable by "Woodrow Wilson's standard that it should not take a man longer to write history than it took the actors to make it."[21]

Malone adhered to one philosophy: "My main purposes for this work are that it shall be comprehensive, that it shall relate Jefferson's career to his age, and that it shall be true to his own chronology."[22] Seldom has an author so well fulfilled his intentions. *Jefferson and His Time* was comprehensive, not only in fullness and detail, but in Malone's specific goal: treating the whole of a many-sided man. It always related Jefferson to his time, and that is what makes it a work of history as well as biography. And it was timed to Jefferson's own chronology. This, in fact, may be Malone's greatest achievement. To most previous scholars, Jefferson seemed an enigma. But Malone viewed Jefferson as a living, growing, changing man, and in this dynamic context Jefferson's life assumed a clarity and consistency scarcely written before.[23]

"Jefferson still lives," the reputed last utterance of John Adams, was the patriotic theme of the Jefferson bicentennial. Among Malone's contributions to the commemoration was an imaginary letter, "Mr. Jefferson to Mr. Roosevelt," published in the *Virginia Quarterly Review*. "This remarkable epistle," one historian wrote, "is an eloquent testimonial of the continuing relevance of Jefferson, of the vital link, as Malone saw it, between the liberalism of Jefferson and his own sense of historical scholarship as a living artifact of the culture."[24]

Here, too, was the mirror of Thomas Jefferson in the mind of Dumas Malone, who had always been guided by the Jeffersonian axiom, "Nothing is unchangeable but the inherent and inalienable rights of man."[25] If we think of modern biography as a telescope for looking at the past, our eyepiece is the present. The biographer is part of his time, and we must draw lines of reference between their time and ours. No doubt Malone would have agreed with his UVA colleague that "the biographer's realization of the nature of his task and the technique he brings to it are as illuminating about the age in which he lives as they are about the age he recreates."[26]

Malone thought that the biographer's role "was not to prettify or deflate but to portray character plausibly, in the round." Anyone who was fortunate enough to know him soon reached a conclusion about Dumas Malone.

One ingredient of heroic biography is a heroic biographer, one in whom the subject's virtues find radiant reflection.[27] Malone well knew that "the greatest obstacle to achievement was a fixed and dogmatic state of mind." Thankfully, he did not suffer this foible. In that sense, Thomas Jefferson has been lucky indeed. Excellence in life and statecraft, in art and intellect, became Jefferson's legacy to our nation. Excellence in biography is Malone's legacy to Thomas Jefferson—and to us. In life and now in death, Malone has already achieved much more than most humans do in two lifetimes. His achievement is not biography, it is a man.[28]

EPILOGUE
Jefferson's DNA

Ideally, the scholar should welcome light from any quarter.
> —DUMAS MALONE, *VIRGINIA QUARTERLY REVIEW*[1]

With the exception of one member . . . our individual conclusions range from serious skepticism about the [Sally Hemings] charge to a conviction that it is almost certainly untrue.
> —SCHOLARS REPORT, 2011[2]

In 2008 author Annette Gordon-Reed published *The Hemingses of Monticello: An American Family*. The book won a National Book Award and the Pulitzer Prize. The narrative explores the lives of Sally Hemings and the other members of the Hemings family in elaborate detail. Yet, it provided little new information about Sally. From the first page, Gordon-Reed assumes, as did Fawn Brodie, that Jefferson was the father of all Sally's children and had a four-decade-long relationship with her.

Malone was not alive to see this book published or the erosion of Jefferson's image in the American mind. Indeed, what would Malone have thought of the 1998 DNA test allegedly linking Jefferson to Sally Hemings? What would he think of the slew of books, subsequent to his own biography, focusing on Jefferson's views of slavery and the possible paternity to a slave girl? Most probably he would have closely analyzed the facts and circumstances surrounding the apparent DNA match. No doubt, he would have contributed to and been satisfied with the Scholars Commission Report published in 2011, which factually analyzed the controversy in a biographical time line and, basically, debunked the entire Sally Hemings myth.[3]

Malone would have studied the following conclusions from the thirteen-member, blue-ribbon panel of prominent historians and scientists (white, black, male, female) named to analyze the DNA test results. They evaluated all the evidence in the controversy, including the DNA, and concluded that what was presented as historical fact was based on a singular misleading headline in a 1998 science journal: "Jefferson Fathered Slave's Last Child." Rumored for centuries, the affair was allegedly "confirmed" when a retired pathologist named Eugene Foster collected DNA samples from Jefferson's and Hemings's descendants, including Field Jefferson, his uncle.

Malone would have applauded the factual approach of the Scholars Commission. In fact, had he been alive, Malone probably would have chaired the panel. After a year of investigating history's most famous paternity case, the independent historians tamped down the simmering allegation: "Our conclusions range from serious skepticism about the charge to a conviction that it is almost certainly false."[4]

"Thomas Jefferson was simply not guilty of the charge," said the preeminent historian Professor Forrest McDonald, who served on the panel. McDonald and other panel members believe the new evidence indicates a different suspect—Jefferson's brother, Randolph, who was unmarried in his early fifties and known for socializing with the Monticello slaves. Randolph, unlike his accomplished brother, was easily influenced by others. An old militia list revealed connections between Randolph and white men with black mistresses—in two cases, those mistresses were Hemingses.

The Scholars Commission concluded that Randolph Jefferson and the Carr brothers were more likely Sally's sexual partners. Against this historical backdrop Randolph entered the controversy. Unfortunately, Malone and other scholars of his time had scant information about Jefferson's brother, and neither a portrait nor a physical description of Randolph exists. The following is Jefferson's description of Randolph after his death in an 1815: "That he considered his said brother as not possessing skill for the judicious management of his affairs, and that in all occasions of life a diffidence in his own opinions . . . and an easy pliancy to the wishes and urgency of others made him very susceptible of influence from those who had any views upon him."[5]

Randolph was born on October 1, 1755, about thirteen years after Jefferson. He was a "very amiable man" who "never amounted to anything much," even though the brothers were similarly educated and reared. They even took violin lessons from the same tutor.[6]

Randolph served in the Revolutionary War and was commissioned a captain in the Buckingham militia in 1794. He served with Captain Wingfield's Company in the Albemarle Militia in 1776 along with William Fosset, Stephen Hughes, Joseph Nielson, and Thomas West, all of whom were involved in interracial sexual relationships. Fosset and Nielson became hired workers at Monticello and specifically cohabitated with members of the Hemings family. Mary Hemings (Sally's sister) was Fosset's mistress, and Nielson fathered a child with Betty Hemings, Sally's mother.[7]

The 1998 DNA study of the Y chromosome found a link between descendants of Eston Hemings (Sally's son) and descendants of some male Jefferson, the Scholars Commission noted. In fact, the DNA tests indicated that any one of seven Jeffersons could have been Eston's father: Thomas Jefferson, Randolph, one of Randolph's four sons, or their cousin George.

According to Robert Turner, University of Virginia law professor and chairman of the Scholars Commission, Randolph fathered children by his own slaves and reportedly spent time with slaves at Monticello.[8] Randolph is a far more likely suspect than Jefferson, the panel concluded, because he visited Monticello often and his years as a widower corresponded with the years in which Hemings had children. "We know that Randolph had a habit of socializing at night with the slaves," Turner added, and he "would fiddle and dance in slave quarters." According to former Monticello slave Isaac Jefferson, "Old Master's brother, Mass Randall, was a mighty simple man: used to come out among black people, play the fiddle and dance half the night; hadn't much more sense than Isaac."[9] McDonald described Randolph more bluntly as a "half wit."[10]

Additional research by the Scholars Commission provided a number of compelling reasons why they considered Randolph to be the probable father of Sally's son Eston:[11]

- Randolph was expected at Monticello to visit his family during Eston's conception period; his twin sister, Lucy, and her family, who lived near Monticello, were preparing to move west that fall, so Randolph would have visited before they left.

- Randolph had the same Jefferson Y chromosome as his older brother Thomas Jefferson and other Jefferson males. Randolph had the same parents as Thomas and carried the same genes that determine appearance.
- Randolph had a reputation for socializing with Jefferson's slaves and was counseled about his use of alcohol.
- Randolph lived less than twenty miles from Monticello and had a pattern of visiting his brother in the spring and late summer. Randolph and his sons owned more than enough horses for them to visit Monticello.
- Randolph was fifty-one years old and a widower in 1807, whereas his brother Thomas was sixty-four years old, frail, and in declining health. All Sally's children were born between 1795 and 1808, when Randolph was single.
- Randolph made his will at Monticello six days following Eston's birth. He left his estate to his five legitimate sons, apparently to prevent any future paternity claims.
- Randolph was rumored among descendants of former slaves to have fathered "colored children." Until 1976 the oral history of Eston's heirs maintained that they descended from a Jefferson "uncle." Randolph was known at Monticello as Uncle Randolph.[12]
- Most important, Randolph had six legitimate male children; Jefferson, in contrast, had all girls, except for a nonviable infant son. The DNA match was to a son.[13]

The evidence seemed clear, according to the Scholars Commission Report, that Randolph was present at Monticello at the time of Eston's conception. In fact, Thomas Jefferson wrote an invitation to his brother dated August 12, 1807, approximately nine months before Sally gave birth:

Dear brother

I did not recieve your letter of July 9 till the 8th. inst. and now, by the first post inclose you 20.D. to pay for the clover and greenswerd seed; which goes by post to Warren. The greenswerd seed I wish to have here; but the white clover seed is to go to Bedford. I must therefore get you to make interest with Mr. Crouch to have it conveyed to the care of Mr. Brown mercht. of Lynchhburg for Burgess Griffin at Poplar Forest. This he can do I expect by his batteaux which go to Lynchburg. Our sister Marks arrived here last night and we shall be happy to see you also. I salute you affectionately.

Th. Jefferson[14]

Thus, documentary evidence placed Randolph, with his sons most probably, at Monticello to see his sister before she departed. Since the trip to Monticello was less than a day's ride, this was an easy journey in good weather.

"The commission agrees unanimously that the allegation is by no means proven," the summary of the report reads, "and we find it regrettable that public confusion about the 1998 DNA testing and other evidence has misled many people." With the exception of one low-key dissent, the scholars' conclusions "range from serious skepticism about the charge to a conviction that it is almost certainly false."[15] One of the historians on the Scholars Commission was Alf J. Mapp, author of two books that discounted the possibility of Jefferson having had a sexual relationship with Hemings. Previously, McDonald and at least three other panel members had believed the story was true, said Turner.[16] Turner also noted that none of the scholars were paid for investigating the controversy.

"Regarding the relations that existed between Thomas Jefferson and his slave Sally Hemings, lies were told long ago, and today, even with the help of DNA analysis, we still cannot be certain as to who told the truth," Professor Rahe, the lone dissenter, argued in the report.[17]

Turner agreed with Dumas Malone's assessment from years before. He believed it would have been out of character for Jefferson to have risked entering into a sexual relationship with Sally, who was thirty years younger and served as maid to one of his daughters. McDonald concluded from his own look at the DNA evidence and his knowledge of Jefferson that the father had to be someone else, most probably Randolph. "It's going to be as devastating a critique as you're likely to see," McDonald suggested prior to the release of the report. "I'm a Hamiltonian," he said, referring to Alexander Hamilton, with whom Jefferson was at odds politically. "I'm always delighted to hear the worst about Thomas Jefferson. It's just that this particular thing won't wash."[18]

After more than a year of independent research, it is worth noting the commission's verbatim conclusion, the same conclusion Dumas Malone came to in the 1950s:

> The question of whether Thomas Jefferson fathered one or more children by his slave Sally Hemings is an issue about which honorable people can and do disagree. After a careful review of all of the evidence, the commission agrees unanimously that the allegation is by no means proven; and we find it regrettable that public confusion about the 1998 DNA testing and other evidence has misled many people. . . .

Conclusions:
We do not pretend that this is the final word on the issue. We understand that useable DNA might be obtained from the grave of William Beverly Hemings, son of Madison Hemings, which could provide new information of relevance to this inquiry. If his Y chromosome did not match that of Eston Hemings and the descendants of Field Jefferson, that would confirm that Sally Hemings could not have been monogamous. A match with the Carr family would also be significant. A match with Eston might strengthen the case for Sally's monogamy, but would not conclusively establish even which Jefferson male was the father of either child. Our thoughts here are further tempered by our concerns about the ethical propriety of disturbing the remains of the dead in the interest of historical curiosity. It may also prove useful to search for evidence concerning the whereabouts of Sally Hemings over the years. This could prove decisive, but we are not optimistic about the existence of additional records of this nature at this point in history.

In the end, after roughly one year of examining the issues, we find the question of whether Thomas Jefferson fathered one or more children by his slave Sally Hemings to be one about which honorable people can and do disagree. . . . With the exception of one member . . . our individual conclusions range from serious skepticism about the charge to a conviction that it is almost certainly untrue.[19]

Appendix A
Jefferson Letter to Roosevelt

In 1943 the Jefferson Memorial was dedicated. Dumas Malone was an invited guest. He later penned a famous imaginary letter from Thomas Jefferson to President Roosevelt:

Mr. Jefferson to Mr. Roosevelt
An Imaginary Letter

The President of the United States:

Dear Sir,—This letter is being written midway in your third term and somewhat in advance of my own birthday, when I should be two hundred years old had I continued on earth. To you it may seem unnatural for me to speak now, but the times are strange. On April 13 there may be some celebrations in my honor, as there have been in the past, and at one of these you may speak, if the onerous burdens of your high office will permit. I do not presume to suggest that you read these words of mine in public, but if you should do this, you would do it much better than I ever could. My voice was never as good as yours and I always preferred a written message to a speech. That is one reason why I abandoned the custom of addressing the Congress in person, though there were some other motives in my mind a hundred and forty-two years ago. I had a horror of seeming to dictate to anyone, and I generally tried to make my thoughts and wishes known in informal ways.

Next to unhurried conversation with understanding friends I always liked letters best. A large number of those I wrote in years long past have been preserved, I believe. One that I sent to a French friend in 1793 comes to mind just now. In this I said: "I continue eternally attached to the principles of your Revolution. I hope it will end in the establishment of some firm government, friendly to liberty, and capable of maintaining it. If it does, the world will become inevitably free." I understand that, after a century and a half, a revolution of another sort is raging on earth and that our own Republic is one of the few remaining governments friendly to liberty and capable of maintaining it. For this reason I am constrained to speak.

Your times are strikingly like and strikingly unlike my own. I also lived in a momentous age of change. As you know, I began my career by participating actively in the struggle for American independence. This was a relatively mild upheaval as revolutions go, but it served to stimulate the far-reaching movement which spread from France. I was in that country when the storm began to gather there; I heard of its later fury from personal friends after I had returned home; and I lived to read of Bonaparte's rise and fall. There was no real peace until after I had retired to my hilltop in Virginia and become old.

You have lived in an even more cataclysmic period. You have witnessed a transformation in the mechanics of civilization, and of destruction, the like of which I never dreamed of, though I was an enthusiastic votary of natural philosophy, which, in its maturity, men now call science. You have witnessed the rise of Hitler, who seems more powerful and more dangerous than Bonaparte, just as the reign of terror which he has imposed far surpasses anything that ever occurred in France; and you have seen emerge from Pacific islands war lords more treacherous than anyone I knew. Having survived one world war, you have been cast into the midst of another that is even more crucial and more terrible. The difference between the two eras, however, is not merely one of degree: it is a difference in kind. The violence of my day was an incident in the struggle for new freedoms; in your day it seems to have begun with the design to make men slaves.

Throughout the early part of my career, when my major immediate concern was the winning of human liberty, I was deeply sympathetic with the revolutionary movements of the age, for they were directed toward the ends to which my own life was dedicated. I was by no means averse to the use of violence in such a cause. You may recall a saying of mine that has been often quoted in this connection: "The tree of liberty must be refreshed from time to time with the blood of patriots and tyrants. It is their natural manure." This was at the dawn of the French Revolution. In later years my utterances were more restrained. One reason for this, besides my advancing age, was that, as a responsible public official, I was confronted with the problem of preserving the measure of freedom that this country had already gained. In your case, the chronological order is reversed. Your immediate problem, in a time of worldwide conflict, is the preservation of the Republic and its existing liberties, insufficient though these may seem; but you have expressed the strong desire to extend them as you can, at home and in other lands. You must first check a revolution aimed at the overthrow of freedom, but you must remain ever mindful of the necessity that the revolution of freedom shall be resumed.

My comrades and I, as we struggled for the overthrow of ancient tyrannies and the establishment of a government that should be more just, thought of ourselves as living in an era of beginnings, and our faith was fresh as the light of dawn. To you it must often have seemed that you have labored through the pitiless heat of noonday and that you are now witnessing the setting of some sun. I will not pretend to claim that the unrolling of the nineteenth century, with all its splendors and triumphs, has fully satisfied the hopes of one who saw the new era born, for new tyrannies have appeared to replace the old and against these I should have struggled had I lived on. Some of the methods that I used in my own time may now seem as antiquated as the clothes I wore and the coaches I rode in, but the spirit of liberty which burned within my breast is, I believe, an undying flame. So I will voice to you my faith that what seems to you an end will prove to be another beginning, and that those peoples who have the will to struggle are destined to see the dawn of a better day.

In this perpetually recurring battle to win, to maintain, and to extend human liberty, I venture to hope that my countrymen can gain some inspiration and guidance from the things I did and said. I deem it important, however, that they see me as I was, and not merely as I have been reported and described. Accordingly, with your consent, I will present certain mature reflections upon my own career. Rarely have I been so subjective.

At the outset I want to state frankly that I am glad that I am not now the President of the United States. This is not primarily because, in my own time, I thought that two terms were enough for anybody, for, much as I always feared the perpetuation of political power, I abide by the principle stated in my first inaugural: absolute acquiescence in the decisions of the majority is the vital principle of republics. This, I hope, no American will ever forget.

The most important reason for being glad that I am not President instead of you is that I never was temperamentally suited to executive office, and least of all in time of military crisis. I was governor of Virginia in the American Revolution, when Tarleton's raiders drove the legislators and me from Richmond, and then forced me to flee from Monticello to Poplar Forest, another plantation of mine. My enemies were unjust in seeing any personal cowardice in this or any dereliction of duty, but my contemporaries were right in believing that in such stormy times the helm of state required another hand. I had been much happier and more useful as a legislator, designing a new government for the Commonwealth or drafting papers for the Continental Congress, such as the Declaration of Independence, of which doubtless you sometimes speak.

When I was first nominated for the presidency a couple of decades later, by the informal methods which then prevailed, I told one of my friends that my private gratifications would be most indulged by that issue which would leave me most at home. When my old friend John Adams was declared the victor and, according to the laws then in operation, I became vice-president, many people did not believe me when I said that I was glad. The government was then in Philadelphia and the unexacting duties of the second office left me ample leisure to engage in scientific conversations at the American Philosophical Society with the successors of the great Dr. Franklin. Then and afterward the first magistracy seemed to me but splendid misery.

When I was elected four years later, at the dawn of the nineteenth century, I was less reluctant, for more vital issues were at stake. My election didn't constitute a political revolution exactly, as my friends and I sometimes claimed, but it seemed to us that the victory of our party was a significant event. The Federalists had become aristocratic and intolerant while we spoke for a larger group; they looked backward but we looked ahead.

We called ourselves Republicans because we thought our opponents monarchists. They tell me that on the eve of your Civil War the name was revived by another party, in the effort to restore doctrines of human equality and freedom such as had been advocated by me. I am sure that one of their standard bearers, Mr. Lincoln, understood these principles, whether or not all of his successors did. The doctrines of popular rule which people were also so kind as to identify with me were perpetuated in the name of the other party, the Democratic, though at a later time many Democrats actively identified themselves with the institution of human slavery, to which I was consistently opposed. At the outset both parties declared their loyalty to me, so I may be pardoned the hope that both of them will remember the principles with which they began.

My reelection was generally attributed at the time to the Louisiana Purchase, which was undoubtedly the most momentous event of my presidency, though I could not claim that the credit was solely mine. This relieved the young Republic immeasurably by removing the menace of Bonaparte from our shores. I detested that unprincipled tyrant and shudder to think that in your own day new despots have arisen to invoke his name. The acquisition of the imperial domain of Louisiana also provided room in which republican government could spread. Like the vast majority of our people, I believed profoundly in the spread of our political institutions, and I attributed the opposition of the Federalists in this instance to narrowness, provincialism, and complacency. If they had had their way they would have confined and insulated republicanism and thus insured its decline and death. If I were living in your day I should doubtless be opposed to further territorial expansion if this should involve any considerable degree of human exploitation; but it is not inappropriate to remind you that in my time we believed that our institutions deserved adoption elsewhere, and that the spread of them constituted the fullest guarantee of their persistence here.

Unfortunately, the purchase of Louisiana was accompanied by disturbing circumstances. We could not consult the Congress at the crucial point in the negotiations, and in acquiring this territory I had to go beyond the letter of the Constitution by which the actions of the federal government were restricted and restrained. The natural charge of inconsistency was deeply embarrassing to me, even though it was raised chiefly by men who opposed me on other grounds.

In form, this action was not compatible with certain things that I had previously said, but who can now doubt that by means of it the empire of freedom was extended.

During my second term the government, in the sincere effort to secure the country against foreign dangers, adopted certain restrictions on private commerce in the form of an Embargo. On the one hand, these seemed preferable to war, and, on the other, to abject submission to the contending banditti of the time, the English and the French, who were so flagrantly infringing on our neutral rights. Unfortunately, however, events proved this law to be the most embarrassing one we were called upon to enforce. Many citizens seemed to set their private gain above the peace and honor of the Republic and were openly defiant. The processes of enforcement involved greater infringements upon the liberty of individuals than I had anticipated, and the cost of safe abstention from the affairs of Europe proved greater than certain vocal elements in our society were willing to endure. From the moment that this became apparent I could see no system which would keep us entirely free from the European agents of destruction. In the end the Embargo had to be repealed, much to my chagrin.

It was then, on the eve of my return to Monticello, where throughout life all my wishes ended, that I wrote to my friend Du Pont de Nemours: "Nature intended me for the tranquil pursuits of science, by rendering them my supreme delight." I had said some years before that no man would ever bring out of the presidency the reputation which carried him into it. Since my temperament was sanguine, the mood of depression did not linger; and in the perspective of history the temporary decline in my personal reputation seems unimportant; but, in my own final judgment, my most valuable services were performed, not as an administrator, but as a herald of freedom and enlightenment.

I was convinced that if misfortunes should befall the country under my successor, Mr. Madison, it would be because no human wisdom could avert them. Actually, he suffered from foreign invasion. From the turmoil of world war we did not escape, much as we had wanted to. It was ironical that such a fate should have befallen him, for he was as un-suited to military leadership as I was. He had shared with me and others the struggle against the Colossus of the Federalists, Mr. Hamilton, but that brilliant statesman found greater joy in battle for its own sake. Had we lived in your day, it is entirely possible that neither Mr. Madison nor I would have been in political life at all. I should have loved to experiment in one of your wonderful laboratories, though I shouldn't have wanted to do only that, and he would have been supremely happy in the library of one of your schools of law. As I said with entire sincerity in my old age, "No man ever had less desire of entering into public offices than myself." During my extended tour of duty I often longed for my books, my friends, my farms; but there was a tradition then which I fear grew weaker at a later time, when men were more absorbed in the pursuit of wealth, that a good citizen owed a debt of public service, in whatever line he could be useful.

I also served my country as a party leader, but I was never a politician in the full modern sense. I was a Patriot against the Loyalists, and a Democratic-Republican against the Federalists; but politics was not my profession any more than it was the profession of General Washington, and I hated the bickerings of partisan strife. But a man of my position could not afford to resist the challenge of public life at the dawn of our national history when there were so many great things to be done.

To all those who have described me as a political philosopher, spinning fine theories in the rarefied air of Monticello, I should like to state that such I never had the opportunity to become. I had thought and studied much about the principles of human government before I became a member of the House of Burgesses of Virginia, and I continued to muse upon them throughout my long life, but I never wrote anything approaching a treatise on political philosophy. Indeed, except for my "Notes on the State of Virginia," I never wrote a book and I didn't really intend to publish that. I drafted state papers in great number, I drew up party manifestoes, and I wrote hundreds of letters to my associates and to correspondents in other lands. It is these writings that friends and enemies have quoted in succeeding years, and it is from these that my political philosophy has been deduced.

Without retracting anything, let me issue to you and to my countrymen a word of warning about the use of these sayings and writings of mine, which were so generally directed toward some specific situation and designed to meet some specific end. I hope that I had the power, which has been attributed to me, of discerning the universal in the particular, as in the Declaration of Independence; but I must insist that my words be judged in the light of the conditions that called them forth and that my philosophy be perceived, not in isolated sayings, many of which are inconsistent, but in the trend of my policies as a whole. Human nature being what it is, I could hardly be expected to speak just the same way about newspapers when I was trying to encourage them as instruments against Alexander Hamilton, as when they were maliciously attacking me as President of the United States. My emphasis could not be exactly the same when I was leading the opposition against the Alien and Sedition Acts, as when, in the capacity of President, I was trying to enforce the Embargo. Anyone who reads the letters that I wrote during those years ought to use his common sense in separating immediate opinions from abiding convictions. I am fully aware of the fact that since my death careless and unscrupulous men have quoted me for their own particular purposes, without regard to the major trends of my thought and life.

Let me illustrate from the history of the doctrine of state rights, which has been so often identified with me. For a long generation after my death my southern compatriots regarded my emphasis on the importance of the individual states in the Federal Union as the outstanding feature of my political philosophy. Some of them went so far as to trace the doctrine of secession straight back to me, despite my just claim to be one of the founders of the Republic. The War between the States may be presumed to have settled this particular question for all time, and it may now seem to be of only academic interest. None the less, there are abiding issues here and I want to set the record straight. I don't care to be quoted in defense of positions to which I was opposed.

On close examination it will appear that my strongest utterances in favor of the states, and in opposition to the increasing power of the federal government, grew out of my struggle against the Federalists when they were in power. The one most often quoted, perhaps, was in the Kentucky Resolutions, when I was protesting against the notorious Alien and Sedition Acts. As the spokesman of the opposition, I rightly condemned the tyranny of the ruling majority; and I hope that under similar conditions men will continue to protest until the end of time. The doctrine of state rights, as I invoked it then, was designed to safeguard the minority and to uphold eternal principles of individual freedom. It is not surprising that the New England Federalists reversed themselves by using similar arguments when Mr. Madison and I were in power and seemed to be encroaching upon the states. On both sides there was unquestionable inconsistency, though this seems to have bothered them less than it did me. It would appear that the doctrine of state rights has generally been invoked in behalf of minority groups and that, in itself, it is an incomplete philosophy of government. In its nature it is negative, and I myself discovered as President that it constituted a distinct embarrassment when positive action was required.

I do not mean to deny that the doctrine was characteristic of me, for few men have been so attached to their locality as I was. My heart was always in Albemarle County and even in old age I sometimes referred to Virginia as "my country." Local institutions always seemed important to me. In the main, however, I emphasized the state as the best available means of combatting the political tyranny that I always feared. I never thought of setting up a shield for inequality and injustice.

At a later time many of my southern compatriots adopted part of my doctrines, in their outward form. They ignored the fact that I had opposed slavery and its extension into the West, and some of them characterized the egalitarian phrases of the Declaration of Independence as glittering generalities. Convinced that they were falling into the minority, they emphasized the rights of the state against the federal government. What they were really attempting to do was to buttress the social system in which they lived. Of their surpassingly difficult social problem I was and am fully aware, but it is hard for me to forgive those among them who viewed slavery and a system of social caste, not as evils to be gradually overcome, but as positive goods to be safeguarded and extended. As you know, the doctrine of state rights proved a serious handicap when they themselves set up a government. The President of the ill-fated Confederacy was hampered throughout his tragic career as an executive by the selfish bickering of the states he sought to unite in a common cause.

Long before the secession of the southern states, however, the political and social philosophy of the slave-owners had crystallized into a rigidity which never characterized my thought. It assumed classic form in the syllogisms of Calhoun, whose powerful but gloomy mind looked backward, not forward. My enthusiasm was ever for the future and, however I may have emphasized the states against the encroachments of the federal government when protests seemed to be required, as a responsible statesman I was forced to adjust myself to circumstances, and I always tried to put the interests of the entire country first. If I were living now, I am sure that I should not forget the importance of the smaller local units of government, but, as a practical man, I should certainly be foolish if I failed to recast my thinking in terms of the extraordinary changes that have taken place. In my time it took three days to drive the hundred-odd miles from Washington to Monticello, and we had no telegraph or telephone. It would be absurd to talk as though there had been no change.

I hope I shall be remembered most, not as an advocate of particular measures, which may be ill adapted to another age, but as a lifelong devotee of human liberty. An oft-quoted sentence from one of my letters to Dr. Benjamin Rush sums up my essential philosophy as few of my sayings do: "I have sworn upon the altar of God eternal hostility against every form of tyranny over the mind of man." My efforts were naturally and properly directed against those tyrannies which seemed most menacing in my own time. Thus, when I wrote the Declaration of Independence I was thinking of the despotism of kings. In your day there is little to be feared from crowned monarchs, but the principle remains that government should rest upon the consent of the governed and not be imposed upon men against their will. In my struggle against the established church in Virginia I was particularly aware of the tyranny of clergymen and priests. I understand that the danger of this has lessened with the years, but the truth remains that in conscience men are free.

I was prejudiced against political rulers in general and feared the encroachments of governmental power on the freedom of the individual, which I always valued most. It seemed to me that the natural tendency is for liberty to yield and for government to gain ground. I suspected my rival Mr. Hamilton, of valuing governmental power for itself, and not merely as a means to human happiness and well-being. To those persons in the world today who value force and power for their own sake, I should be unalterably opposed.

One danger was less obvious in my time than it has been in yours. There was nothing in my lifelong insistence on minority rights which can be held to justify the dominance of a powerful minority against the interests of the country as a whole. Some have pointed out that I was suspicious of a group which has come to be termed capitalistic and which, it is held, Mr. Hamilton favored. At the beginning of our government under the Constitution there were men who speculated in securities and lined their nests with paper, and for these men I had scant respect; but the enormous growth of financial power in this country came along afterward. To use language which is more common now than it was then, I feared capitalists, dreaded industrialization, and distrusted the urban working class as I had observed it in Europe. My hopes were centered on the tillers of the soil. But I sought to limit the privileges of the landed aristocrats of Virginia and for this some of them never forgave me. My preference for a land of small, independent farmers is an index of my distrust of the concentration of private wealth and power. The growth of industry has been greater and more rapid than I even dreamed and certain of my fears have been more than realized. What measures should now be taken to correct the ills to which industrialism has given rise I am not prepared to say, but the logic of my entire career points to an emphasis, not on machines or on money, but on men.

In individuals I always believed and to them I always sought to give opportunity. It is not correct to say that I believed all men to be alike or intrinsically equal, for no one realized more than I that gifts and natural endowments vary. It was my thought to remove all artificial obstacles, such as inherited privilege, and thus to free men to win such positions as they deserved. If, since my day, there has been any crystallization of economic classes, serving to impede the free movement of talent, this I should deplore.

Besides removing obstacles, I favored the granting of opportunities, in proportion to natural abilities and individual desert. My plans for public education in Virginia were not carried out in my time, but the development of public schools of all grades, the establishment of libraries, the development of science and the arts, were second in my thought only to the overthrow of tyranny itself. These represented my program in its most positive form.

If I were living now, you may be sure that I should oppose with all the force at my command whatever should seem to be the greatest tyrannies of the age, the chief obstacles to the free life of the human spirit; and I should favor what seem to be the most effective means of bringing appropriate opportunity within the reach of all, regardless of race or economic status. If there are those who quote me in regard to the limitations of government and the dangers of its power, proper inquiry may be made about the objects they have in mind. If they are sincerely concerned for the well-being of the individual citizen, however humble he may be, and are not disposed to buttress some existing inequality, their judgment about the means to be employed should be listened to with respect. But I must protest against the use of my name in defense of purposes that are alien to my spirit. If there is anything eternal about me it is the purposes that I voiced and the spirit that I showed. So far as methods are concerned, the supreme law of life is the law of change. It must not be forgotten that I was regarded in my day as a revolutionary. I was never a defender of an imperfect and unjust status quo. The road to human perfection has proved longer than I thought and men have employed the language of individualism as a cloak for selfishness and greed, but never has it seemed more important than it does now to reassert faith in the dignity of human personality and in the power of the human mind.

Since I was so deeply concerned during so much of my life with the problems of foreign affairs, perhaps I may add a final word about the world setting in which the American experiment of democratic government was carried on in my day and is being carried on in yours. The two great powers and rivals of my time were England and France. I have often been described as opposing the one and favoring the other, but my policy never was anything but pro-American. At the outset of my career, when we were struggling to rid ourselves of the British yoke, naturally I was against King George III and his minions. For aid in this conflict we were and should have been grateful to the French. Both governments seemed to me corrupt, and, as I wrote one of my friends, the English required to be kicked into common good manners.

However, I also said that the English would never find any political passion in me either for them or against them, but that whenever they should be prepared to meet us halfway I should meet them with satisfaction. I could not overlook the fact that, after the Revolution, they sought to hold us in commercial subjection and refused to carry out fully the terms of peace. There were individual Americans of the time who were willing to disregard these offenses against the Republic because of hopes of immediate financial gain. And, somewhat later, there were those who feared the explosive power of French democratic ideas and preferred a degree of subjection to the British to any sort of dealings with the unholy Jacobins. If you change the labels and speak of Fascists and Communists, you can undoubtedly find men of the same sort in the United States today.

To begin with, as a nation we had little to fear from France because there was no real conflict of interest. Indeed, the Spanish, established on our southern border, constituted a far greater menace. As the American minister, I lived for several years among the French, sipping their wines, listening to their music, and talking with their savants. They seemed to me the most agreeable of Europeans; and, at that time, almost every civilized human being saw in their lovely country his second home. At the outset their Revolution seemed closely akin to our own, and, despite the excesses into which they fell, I continued to maintain faith in them until their government appeared to crystallize in despotic form. Their subsequent depredations on our commerce I deplored, and when Bonaparte threatened to acquire Louisiana he became a direct menace which had to be removed. Few rejoiced more than I in his ultimate overthrow, though, in the course of the conflict, the British, as a maritime power strongly established in our own continent, had seemed to imperil us the more.

With the downfall of this despot and the appearance of a more conciliatory spirit on the part of the British, now that their own grave danger was past, my attitude toward these traditional enemies of ours greatly changed. In the course of time the hope that I had voiced to John Adams has been largely realized. "Were the English people under a government which should treat us with justice and equity," I said, "I should myself feel with great strength the ties which bind us together, of origin, language, laws, and manners; and I am persuaded the two people would become in the future, as it was with the ancient Greeks, among whom it was reproachful for Greek to be found fighting against Greek in a foreign army." Subsequently, after Mr. Monroe announced the doctrine which was destined to become famous, I went so far as to say: "These two nations, holding cordially together, have nothing to fear from the united world." In the year 1943, when new and even more sinister forces than Bonaparte are threatening the world, I respectfully commend this remark of my old age to the consideration of my countrymen, without implying, however, that additional allies are not needed.

It was at the height of the conflict between the French robbers and the British pirates, shortly after my presidency, when this young Republic seemed to have no choice but to oppose the immediate offender, that I wrote the following: "When we reflect that the eyes of the virtuous all over the world are turned with anxiety on us, as the only depositories of the sacred fire of liberty, and that our falling into anarchy would decide forever the destinies of mankind, and seal the political heresy that man is incapable of self-government, the only contest between divided friends should be who will dare farthest into the ranks of the common enemy."

At this moment, in your administration, our spiritual isolation is less complete, for those countries where the language of freedom and democracy is still spoken and still understood are our friends, even though the mists of ancient prejudice may still divide us. At such a time I beg of you and all my countrymen not to think of me as an apostle of negation, but as a sworn enemy of tyranny, ready to join forces actively with every friend of liberty, wherever he may be.

My best wishes for your felicity attend you, and believe me to be assuredly

Your humble servant, Th. Jefferson.[1]

APPENDIX **B**
Prizes, Awards, and Writings

PRIZES AND AWARDS

The fifth volume of *Jefferson and His Time* received a Pulitzer Prize in 1975. Malone received the John Addison Porter Prize from Yale University for *The Public Life of Thomas Cooper* in 1923; the Guggenheim fellowship in 1951–52 and 1958–59; and the Thomas Jefferson Award from the University of Virginia in 1964; and the John F. Kennedy Medal from the Massachusetts Historical Society and the Wilbur L. Cross Medal from Yale University in 1972. Malone was the first recipient of the Bruce Catton Prize (1984), named for the former editor of *American Heritage* and awarded every two years for outstanding history writing. Given the Presidential Medal of Freedom in 1983, he also was awarded an honorary degree by the College of William and Mary (1977). He held memberships in the American Historical Association, the American Academy of Arts and Sciences, the American Antiquarian Society, the Southern Historical Association, the Massachusetts Historical Society, Phi Beta Kappa, Omicron Delta Kappa, the Century Club in New York, and the Cosmos Club in Washington, D.C.

WRITINGS

The American Economy: Keystone of World Prosperity. New York: Academy of
  Political Science, 1954.
*Correspondence between Thomas Jefferson and Pierre Samuel du Pont de Nemours:
  1798–1817*. Boston: Houghton, 1930. Reprint, Da Capo Press, 1970.
  (Editor and author of introduction.)
Edwin A. Alderman: A Biography. New York: Doubleday, Doran, 1940.
Emerging Problems: Domestic and International. New York: Academy of
  Political Science, 1957.

Empire for Liberty: The Genesis and Growth of the United States of America, 2 vols. With Basil Rauch. New York: Appleton, 1960. Enlarged edition with six parts published in 1964–65.

Europe and Asia: The Cases of Germany and Japan. New York: Academy of Political Science, 1955.

International Economic Outlook. New York: Academy of Political Science, 1953.

The Interpretation of History. Edited by J. R. Strayer. Princeton, NJ: Princeton University Press, 1943. (Contributor.)

Jefferson and His Time, 6 vols. Boston: Little, Brown, 1948–81.

The Jeffersonian Heritage (radio program). Boston: Beacon Press, 1953.

Malone and Jefferson: The Biographer and the Sage. Charlottesville: University of Virginia Library, 1981.

An Outline of the Life of Thomas Jefferson. Charlottesville: University of Virginia, 1924.

An Outline of United States History. With Ralph Henry Gabriel and Frederick J. Manning. New Haven, CT: Yale University Press, 1921.

Political Science Quarterly, 1953–58. (Editor.)

The Public Life of Thomas Cooper: 1783–1839. New Haven, CT: Yale University Press, 1926. Reprint, University of South Carolina Press, 1961.

Rhetoric and the Founders. With Arthur Schlesinger Jr. and Norman Graebner. Lanham, MD: University Press of America, 1987.

Right to Work. New York: Academy of Political Science, 1954.

Saints in Action. New York: Abingdon, 1939. Reprint, Books for Libraries, 1971.

The Story of the Declaration of Independence. New York: Oxford University Press, 1954. Bicentennial edition, 1976.

Thomas Jefferson as Political Leader. Berkeley: University of California Press, 1963. Reprint, Greenwood Press, 1979.

Notes

Preface

1   Mitch Albom, *Tuesdays with Morrie* (New York: Broadway Books, 1997), 79.

2   William G. Hyland, *In Defense of Thomas Jefferson: The Sally Hemings Sex Scandal* (New York: Thomas Dunne Books, 2009).

3   Walter Clemons, "A Monument to Jefferson," review of *Jefferson and His Time: The Sage of Monticello*, by Dumas Malone, *Newsweek*, July 27, 1981.

4   Ann Freudenberg, preface to *Malone and Jefferson: The Biographer and the Sage* by Dumas Malone (Charlottesville: University of Virginia Library, 1981).

5   Dumas Malone, *Jefferson and His Time*, 6 vols. (Boston: Little, Brown, 1948–81). The six volumes are as follows: volume 1, *Jefferson the Virginian* (1948); volume 2, *Jefferson and the Rights of Man* (1951); volume 3, *Jefferson and the Ordeal of Liberty* (1962); volume 4, *Jefferson the President: First Term, 1801–1805* (1970); volume 5, *Jefferson the President: Second Term, 1805–1809* (1974); and volume 6, *The Sage of Monticello* (1981).

6   James Macgregor Burns and Susan Dunn, *George Washington* (New York: Time Books, 2004), xi.

7   Malone's unfinished and unpublished memoir at the time of his death was titled "My Long Journey with Mr. Jefferson" (MSS 12807, Box 18, Merrill Peterson Papers, Albert and Shirley Small Special Collections Library, Alderman Library, University of Virginia, Charlottesville, VA). The manuscript was written when Malone was ninety-two years old in 1983. I have drawn heavily upon it as a primary source for Malone's quotes, remembrances, and thoughts. Although the page numbers are not in order, I have tried to reference the various sections that I quote from Malone's manuscript.

8   Jeffrey Smith, "In the Autumn of His Years, Dumas Malone Reaps a Rich Harvest," *Emory Magazine* 58 (December 1981): 8–12.

9 M. E. Bradford, "The Long Shadow of Thomas Jefferson," *National Review*, October 2, 1981, 1146–47.

10 Merrill D. Peterson, "Dumas Malone: An Appreciation," *William and Mary Quarterly*, 3rd ser., 45, no. 2 (April 1988), 237–52.

11 Smith, "In the Autumn of His Years," 8–12; Paul A. Horne Jr., "Dumas Malone (10 January 1892–)," in *Dictionary of Literary Biography*, vol. 17, *Twentieth-Century American Historians*, ed. Clyde N. Wilson (Detroit: Gale Research, 1983), 250–57.

12 Betty L. Mitchell, "Biography," Library of Southern Literature (Chapel Hill: University of North Carolina at Chapel Hill, 2004), http://docsouth.unc.edu/southlit/biography.html.

13 Peterson, "Dumas Malone," 237–52.

14 "Jefferson Scholar Dumas Malone Dies," *Richmond Times-Dispatch*, December 28, 1986.

15 "Dumas Malone: 1892–1986," *Virginia Magazine of History and Biography* 95, no. 2 (April 1987): 243–44.

Chapter 1. The White House

1 Mary Ellen Phelps, "Jefferson Biographer Wins Freedom Medal," *Cavalier Daily*, January 21, 1983.

2 Garry Wills, "Prodigious Life, The Sage of Monticello," review of *Jefferson and His Time: The Sage of Monticello*, by Dumas Malone, *The New Republic*, August 1 and 8, 1981, 32–34.

3 White House, telegram to Dumas Malone, February 17, 1983, Dumas Malone Papers, Special Collections MSS 12712-b, SC-STKS, Albert and Shirley Small Special Collections Library, Alderman Library, University of Virginia, Charlottesville, VA. Hereafter cited as Malone Papers.

4 Personal interview with Gifford Malone, Vienna, Virginia, March 2011.

5 James A. Bear, letter to Dumas Malone, February 28, 1983, Malone Papers.

Chapter 2. Reflections

1 Julian P. Boyd, letter to Douglas Southall Freeman, January 6, 1945, Douglas Southall Freeman Papers, Box 59, Library of Congress Manuscripts Division, Washington, LCD. Boyd was curator of the Jefferson papers at Princeton University.

2 Rouhollah K. Ramz, letter to Dumas Malone, May 16, 1975, Malone Papers. Ramz, of Kings College in Cambridge, was acknowledging Malone's Pulitzer Prize in 1975.

3 This chapter is an amalgam of personal remembrances and interviews with Steven Hochman; Katherine Sargeant, Malone's personal secretary for fourteen years; and Gifford Malone. I am grateful for their personal reminiscences. See also Virginius Dabney, *Across the Years: Memories of a Virginian* (Garden City, NY: Doubleday, 1978), 4; and "My Long Journey."

4 Reid Beddow, "Dumas Malone, The Sage of Charlottesville," *Washington Post Book World* 11, no. 27, July 5, 1981.

5 Ibid.

6 Smith, "In the Autumn of His Years," 8–12.

Chapter 3. The Deep South

1 "My Long Journey."

2 Dabney, *Across the Years*, 2.

3 Lisa Grunwald and Stephen J. Adler, eds., *Letters of the Century: America, 1900–1999* (New York: Dial Press, 1999), 9.

4 Malone's siblings were Raiford Kemp Malone, Miles Malone, Lillian Malone, Elizabeth Malone, Sarah Malone, and Virginia Malone.

5 "Before 1929," in "My Long Journey," 1.

6 Arthur Schlesinger Jr., *Life in the 20th Century* (Boston: Houghton Mifflin, 2000), 62.

7 "My Long Journey," 17.

8 Dumas Malone, "The Riddle of Greatness" (speech, October 20, 1937), Malone Papers.

9 Palmer, "Coldwater, MS," *Born and Raised in the South* (blog), September 28, 2008, http://ltc4940.blogspot.com/2008/09/coldwater-ms.html.

10 Smith, "In the Autumn of His Years," 9; see also Malone, *Malone and Jefferson*, 3; "My Long Journey."

11 Malone, *Malone and Jefferson*, 3. See, in general, "My Long Journey" and Smith, "In the Autumn of His Years, " 8–12.

12 Smith, "In the Autumn of His Years," 8–12.

13 "How and Why I Became an Historian," in "My Long Journey."

14 Ibid.

15 Dumas Malone, "The Scholar's Way: Then and Now," *Virginia Quarterly Review* 51, no. 2 (Spring 1975): 200.

16 Smith, "In the Autumn of His Years," 8–12.

17 James Harvey Young, "Emory College, a Brief History," 1982, Malone Papers.

18 Smith, "In the Autumn of His Years," 8–12.

19 Prologue to "My Long Journey," 2.

20 Dumas Malone, "Reflections," *Virginia Magazine of History and Biography* 93, no. 1 (January 1985): 3–13.

21 Smith, "In the Autumn of His Years," 8–12.

22 Ibid.

23 Ibid.

24 Ibid.

25 Ibid.

26 Ibid.

27 Henry Mitchell, "The Gentleman Historian: Dumas Malone, Sage of Charlottesville," *Washington Post*, January 4, 1987.

28 Dumas Malone, Phi Beta Kappa speech, August 21, 1982, Malone Papers.

29 Malone, "Reflections," 3–13.

30 Prologue to "My Long Journey," 3.

31 Dumas Malone, letter to Emory University, Malone Papers.

Chapter 4. A Marine

1 Edward A. Leake, correspondence with the author, December 9, 2011.

2 W. Thomas Smith Jr., "A Rite of Passage Unlike Any Other: S.C. Boot Camp Readies Marine Recruits for War," *Washington Times*, October 10, 2005.

3 Peterson, "Dumas Malone," 237–52.

4 Ibid.

5 Smith, "In the Autumn of His Years," 8–12.

6 Ibid.

7 Ibid.

8 Malone, "Reflections," 3–13.

9 Ibid.

10 Ibid.

11 Prologue to "My Long Journey," 7.

12 Barbara Tuchman, *The Guns of August: The Proud Tower*, ed. Margaret MacMillan (New York: Library of America, 2012), 71. Tuchman noted, "The assassination of the Austrian heir apparent, Archduke Franz Ferdinand, by Serbia nationalist on June 28, 1914, satisfied his condition."

13 "My Long Journey," prologue, 7–9.

14 Smith, "Rite of Passage."

15 Kate Wiltrout, "What Would Make Someone Sign Up for This?" *Virginian-Pilot*, December 12, 2004.

16 Ibid.

17 Ibid.

18 Ibid.

19 "Camp Upton: U.S. Army Reception Center," *Long Island during World War II: True Tales of Nazi Saboteurs, U-Boat Hunting, and More*, Skylighters: The Web Site of 225th AAA Searchlight Battalion, http://www.skylighters.org/longisland/upton.html.

20 Burke Davis, *Marine! The Life of Chesty Pullers* (New York: Bantam Books, 1988), 16–17.

21 Wiltrout, "What Would Make Someone Sign Up for This?"

22 "Boot Camp Letters: Sgt. Walter H. Lockard," World War I Letters, http://www.wwiletters.com/boot_camp.htm.

23 "My Long Journey."

24 Edward Leake, correspondence with the author, August 2, 2011.

25 "My Long Journey."

26 Ibid.

27 Ibid.

28 Ibid.

29 Ralph Fuller, "Thomas Jefferson's 'Alter Ego' Lives," *Washington Post*, July 1, 1976.

30 "My Long Journey," prologue, 7–8.

31 Ibid.

32 Ibid., 10.

Chapter 5. Brothers

1 Dumas Malone, letter to Professor Harry Ammon, October 11, 1963, Malone Papers.

2 Thomas Pyles, "In Memoriam, Kemp Malone Onomatologist," *Journal of the American Names Society* 21, no. 3 (September 1973): 131–32.

3 Albert C. Baugh, "Kemp Malone 1889–1971," reprinted in *Year Book—The American Philosophical Society* (Philadelphia: American Philosophical Society, 1972), 230–34.

4 Gifford Malone, correspondence with the author, May 13, 2011.

5 Dumas Malone, letter to Thomas Pyles, November 13, 1973, Malone Papers.

6 Gifford Malone, correspondence with the author, May 13, 2011.

7 Gifford Malone, interview by and correspondence with the author, Vienna, Virginia, March 2011.

8 Gifford Malone, correspondence with the author, May 13, 2011.

9 Ibid.

10 "My Long Journey."

11 Ibid.

12 Jesse Slingluff, letter to Dumas Malone, October 22, 1971, Malone Papers.

13 Charles Davis, letter to the editor, *Baltimore Sun*, October 26, 1971, Malone Papers.

14 H. Prentice Miller, letter to Inez Malone, April 17, 1975, Malone Papers.

15 Judson Ward, letter to Dumas Malone, April 4, 1977, Malone Papers.

16 Dumas Malone, letter to Judson Ward, April 11, 1977, Malone Papers.

17 Dumas Malone, letter to Inez Malone, March 31, 1977, Malone Papers.

18 "University Receives Extensive Library of Alumnus Malone," *Emory Magazine*, no. 5 (June 1974), Malone Papers.

19 Gifford Malone (as told to him by his Aunt Inez), interview with the author, March 2011.

Chapter 6. Yale

1 Dumas Malone, letter to Mary Elizabeth Johnston, March 18, 1963, Malone Papers.

2 Letter to Malone from student in 1958, Malone Papers, University of Viriginia Special Collections.

3 Presentation of the Wilbur Lucius Cross Medal to Malone at Yale, June 12, 1972, Malone Papers.

4 "About Yale/History," Yale University website, http://www.yale.edu/about /history.html.

5 Ibid.

6 See, in general, "My Long Journey."

7   "My Long Journey."

8   Ibid.

9   Ibid.

10   Dumas Malone, letter to Russell Stroup, February 1963, Malone Papers.

11   "My Long Journey."

12   Malone, "Reflections," 3–13.

13   "My Long Journey," 2–3.

14   Ibid.

15   Malone, "Reflections," 3–13.

16   Ibid.

17   Ibid.

18   Horne, "Dumas Malone."

19   "My Long Journey," 3.

20   Horne, "Dumas Malone."

21   Ibid.

22   "My Long Journey," prologue, 11–12; "Before 1929," in ibid., 5.

Chapter 7. Along the Lawn

1   "My Long Journey."

2   David Maurer, "Set in Stone," *UVA Magazine*, Spring 2008, http://uvamagazine.org/features/article/set_in_stone/#.UGTI47KPUa8.

3   "My Long Journey," 6.

4   Ibid.

5   Malone, "Reflections," 3–13.

6   Marble Inscription, Alderman Library, Charlottesville, VA.

7   Dabney, *Across the Years*, 73.

8   Ibid.; see also University of Virginia website.

9   Ibid.

10   William Dodd, letter to Dumas Malone, June 19, 1923, Malone Papers.

11   The Dabneys were a famous and distinguished Virginia family. Virginius Dabney's great-great-grandmother was the granddaughter of Dabney Carr and Martha Jefferson, sister of Thomas Jefferson. Virginius Dabney's great-great-grandfather, John A. G. Davis, purchased for the Dabney home furniture from the original Monticello when it was auctioned off following Jefferson's death. The two chairs

had graced the Tuileres palace in Paris during the reign of Marie Antoinette. They were purchased in the French capital by James Monroe for Thomas Jefferson.

12 Malone, "Reflections," 3–13.

13 Dabney, *Across the Years*, 38.

14 Malone, "Reflections," 3–13.

15 Dabney, *Across the Years*, 31–32.

16 Ibid.

17 Ibid., 51.

18 Malone, "Reflections," 3–13.

19 Malone, "Scholar's Way," 200.

20 "Edwin A. Alderman (1905–1931)," Carr's Hill: A Centennial Celebration, University of Virginia, April 12, 2011, http://www.virginia.edu/carrshill /alderman.html.

21 Ibid.

22 Ibid.

23 Ibid.

24 Dabney, *Across the Years*, 86.

25 Ibid.

26 "My Long Journey."

27 Ibid.

28 Ibid.

29 Ibid.

30 Ibid.

31 Ibid., 16.

32 Ibid., 19.

33 Ibid.

34 Malone, *Malone and Jefferson*, 4.

35 "My Long Journey," 5–6.

36 Ibid.

37 Ibid.

38 Malone, "Reflections," 3–13.

39 "My Long Journey."

40 Ibid.

41 Ibid.

42 Ibid.

Chapter 8. Elisabeth

1 Gifford Malone, correspondence with the author via e-mail, November, 14, 2011.

2 "Professional Correspondence," Malone Papers; Professional Correspondence January 1986–March 1987 Box: 20, 2 folders; Professional Correspondence 1979–1985 Box: 21, 6 folders; Professional Correspondence August 1975–1978 Box: 22, 6 folders; Professional Correspondence 1971–July 1975 Box: 23, 6 folders; Professional Correspondence 1923–1970 Box: 24, 6 folders.

3 Gifford Malone, interview by the author, December 20, 2011.

4 "My Long Journey."

5 Dumas Malone, letter to Dr. John Henderson, October 21, 1974, Malone Papers.

6 Dumas Malone, letter to Paul Barringer, October 2, 1964, Malone Papers.

7 Dumas Malone, letter to Arthur Thompson, November 21, 1963, Malone Papers.

8 Malone, *Malone and Jefferson*, 8.

9 Elisabeth Malone, letter to Head of Domestic, 1974, Malone Papers; Personal Correspondence 1947–1982 Box:18, 5 folders.

10 Dumas Malone, letter to John Wyatt, 1974, Malone Papers; Personal Correspondence 1947–1982 Box: 18, 5 folders.

11 Gifford Malone, correspondence with the author, May 30, 2012.

12 Gifford Malone, interview by the author, March 2010.

13 Malone e-mail correspondence with the author.

14 Ibid.

15 Ibid.

16 Katherine Sargeant, telephone interview by the author, November 30, 2011.

17 Malone e-mail correspondence with the author.

18 Ibid.

19 Ibid.

Chapter 9. The *Dictionary*

1 Dumas Malone, *The Virginia Magazine of History and Biography* 93, no. 1 (January 1985), 5, Virginia Historical Society, http://www.jstor.org/stable /4248774.

2 "Driver of Auto That Killed Johnson," *New York Times*, January 21, 1931.

3 "My Long Journey."

4 Ibid.

5 Ibid.

6 Ibid.

7 Malone memoir, Alderman Library.

8 Clyde W. Barrow. "Johnson, Allen," *American National Biography* (New York: Oxford University Press, February 2000), http://www.anb.org/articles/14/14 -00322.html.

9 Ibid.

10 "Scholars Eulogize Dr. Allen Johnson," *New York Times*, February 1, 1931.

11 Malone, "Reflections," 3–13.

12 "Dr. Malone Named Biography Editor," *New York Times*, February 3, 1931.

13 Malone, "Reflections," 3–13.

14 Ibid.

15 Speeches 1938, Malone Papers; Professional Correspondence 1923–1970 Box: 24, 6 folders; Speaking Engagements and Projects 1968–1969 Box: 28.

16 Dumas Malone, interview in *Johnson County Democrat and Oxford Leader*, Malone Papers; Professional Correspondence 1923–1970 Box: 24, 6 folders; Interviews with Dumas Malone and Related Material 1954–1982 Box: 37, 2 folders.

17 Ibid.

18 Ibid.

19 Ibid.

20 "My Long Journey," 7–12.

21 Ibid.

22 Gifford Malone, interview by the author, September 22, 2010.

23 "My Long Journey," revision, ch. 11, "The Dictionary of American Biography."

24 "My Long Journey," 18–20.

25 Ibid., 19.

26 Ibid., 20.

27 Ibid., 20–23.

28 Ibid., 21.

29 Ibid., ch. 3, 1.

30 Ibid.

31 Ibid., 2.

32 Ibid., 3.

33 Dabney, *Across the Years*, 137.

34 Harry F. Byrd, letter to Dumas Malone, February 7, 1963, Malone Papers.

35 "My Long Journey," ch. 3, 3.

36 Ibid.

37 Ibid.

38 "Reminiscences—Justice Brandeis," in "My Long Journey."

39 Ibid.

40 Ibid.

41 "Reminiscences—F. D. R.," in "My Long Journey."

42 Ibid., 11–12.

43 Ibid.

44 Ibid.

45 Ibid.

46 Ibid., 13.

47 Ibid., 14.

48 Ibid., 14.

49 Ibid., ch. 3, 11.

Chapter 10. Harvard University Press

1 Malone, "Reflections," 3–13.

2 "History of Harvard University," Harvard University website, 2012, http://www.news.harvard.edu/guide/content/history-harvard-university.

3 "A Brief History of Harvard University Press," Harvard University Press website, 2012, http://www.hup.harvard.edu/about/history.html.

4 Malone, "Reflections," 3–13.

5 Quoted in Max Hall, *Harvard University Press: A History* (Cambridge, MA: Harvard University Press, 1986), 64–104.

6 Quoted in ibid.

7 "My Long Journey."

8 Hall, *Harvard University Press*, 66.

9   Ibid., 68.

10   Ibid., 68, 69.

11   "My Long Journey," ch. 4, 6.

12   Ibid.

13   Quoted in Hall, *Harvard University Press*, 68.

14   Ibid.

15   Ibid., 69.

16   Ibid.

17   Ibid., 68, 69.

18   "My Long Journey," ch. 4, 9.

19   Hall, *Harvard University Press*, 64–104.

20   Ibid., 70.

21   Ibid.

22   Ibid.

23   "My Long Journey."

24   Ibid.

25   Ibid.

26   Hall, *Harvard University Press*, 72.

27   Ibid., 74.

28   Ibid., 72, 74, and 76.

29   Ibid., 77; Schlesinger, *Life in the 20th Century*, 243.

30   Ibid., 85.

31   Ibid.

32   Ibid., 86.

33   Ibid., 85, 86, 90.

34   Schlesinger, *Life in the 20th Century*, 243.

35   Hall, *Harvard University Press*, 90.

36   "My Long Journey," 15; Hall, *Harvard University Press*, 91.

37   "My Long Journey."

38   Hall, *Harvard University Press*, 94.

39   "My Long Journey," ch. 4, 2.

40   Ibid., 14.

41   Ibid., 2, 14, 15.

42 Hall, *Harvard University Press*, 103.

43 Ibid., 103–4.

44 See in general Malone, "Reflections"; and "My Long Journey," revision, ch. 11, "The Dictionary of American Biography."

45 Dumas Malone, letter to Mark Carroll, June 17, 1970, Malone Papers.

46 Hall, *Harvard University Press*, 104.

47 "My Long Journey."

Chapter 11. Columbia

1 Quoted in Sid Moody, "After 40 Years as Jefferson's Best Friend, Dumas Malone Is Ready to Lay Down His Pen," *Alton Telegraph*, July 3, 1981.

2 Dumas Malone, "The Great Generation Revisited" (speech, Symposium of the Miracle of Virginia: The Role of American Leadership 1765–1789, 1959), Malone Papers.

3 Dumas Malone, letter to Roger Scaife, May 20, 1938, Malone Papers.

4 Ibid.

5 Roger Scaife, letter to Dumas Malone, May 23, 1938, Malone Papers.

6 "My Long Journey."

7 Roger Scaife, letter to Dumas Malone, December 5, 1940, Malone Papers.

8 Dumas Malone, letter to Larned G. Bradford, April 19, 1966, Malone Papers.

9 "My Long Journey," "Long Journey," chapter 7, 4.

10 Ibid., ch. 6.

11 Ibid., 2.

12 Ibid., 13. See appendix A for full text of letter.

13 Ibid., 31 A Insert.

14 Ibid., 15–16.

15 Ibid., 5–85.

16 Ibid.

17 Frank Monaghan, letter to Dumas Malone, June 28, 1945, Malone Papers.

18 "My Long Journey," "Long Journey," chapter 6.

19 Ibid.

20 Ibid., 8

21 Ibid., 10

22 Ibid., 12.

23 Ibid., 8, 10, 11, 12.

24 Dumas Malone, letter to John A. Krout, April 17, 1945, Malone Papers.

25 John A. Krout, letter to Dumas Malone, April 26, 1945, Malone Papers.

26 John A. Krout, letter to Dumas Malone, May 2, 1945, Malone Papers. Malone later wrote about professor salaries in general, commenting, "There is no university in America where Professors are overpaid, and in the South the scale of salaries is still so low as to be distressing" (Dumas Malone, "The University of Tomorrow," *Emory Alumnus*, March–April 1932, Malone Papers).

27 John A. Krout, letter to Dumas Malone, June 28, 1945, Malone Papers.

28 Ralph Gabriel, letter to Dumas Malone, 1945, Professional Correspondence 1923–1970, Box: 24, 6 folders, Malone Papers.

29 Dumas Malone, "A Scholar in Winter," *UVA Alumni News*, September–October 1971.

30 "My Long Journey."

Chapter 12. On Writing and Politics

1 Dumas Malone, "Reflections," *The Virginia Magazine of History and Biography* 93, no. 1 (January 1985): 5, published by Virginia Historical Society, http://www.jstor.org/stable/4248774.

2 "My Long Journey."

3 Malone, *Malone and Jefferson*, 3.

4 "My Long Journey," "Long Journey," chapter 6, 11.

5 Ibid., 16.

6 Ibid., "Long Journey," chapter 7, 8.

7 Ibid., 9.

8 Ibid.

9 Ibid.

10 Ibid., 11–13.

11 Ibid.

12 Ibid.

13 Ibid.

14 Ibid., 8, 9, 11–13, 16.

15 Ibid., 4

16 Ibid., 5.

17 Ibid.

18 Ibid.

19 Ibid.

20 Ibid., 4, 5.

21 Gifford Malone, interview by the author, September 22, 2010.

22 Dumas Malone, letter to John Oakes, July 19, 1964, Malone Papers.

23 "My Long Journey."

24 Malone memoir, "Long Journey with Mr. Jefferson," ch. 10, 14–17; see also Ron Chernow, *Washington: A Life* (New York: Penguin, 2010), 290.

25 "My Long Journey," 10.

26 Dumas Malone, "The Great Generation Revisited," symposium of the miracle of Virginia: the role of American leadership 1765–1789, (1959, Malone Papers; Speaking Engagements and Projects 1968–1969 Box: 28).

27 "My Long Journey," ch. 7.

28 Ibid.

29 Ibid.

30 Ibid.

31 Ibid.

32 Ibid.

33 Ibid.

34 Ibid.

35 Ibid.

36 Ibid.

37 Ibid.

38 Ibid.

39 Ibid.

40 Ibid.

Chapter 13. Jefferson, the Virginian

1 Malone, *Jefferson the Virginian*, x.

2 Quoted in Hamilton W. Pierson, ed., *Jefferson at Monticello: The Private Life of Thomas Jefferson* (New York: Charles Scribner, 1862), Rare Book Collection, Library of Congress, Washington, DC. Captain Bacon was Jefferson's overseer at Monticello.

3 "J Papers and M Circle," in "My Long Journey," 14.

4   Ibid.

5   Dumas Malone, address at rededication of the Alderman Memorial Library, UVA, Charlottesville, VA, June 13, 1938, Malone Papers; and "My Long Journey," 4.

6   Dumas Malone, letter to Anita Waddington Rice, December 17, 1974, Malone Papers.

7   Dumas Malone, interview by Marc Pachter, USIA film titled "Dumas Malone: A Journey with Mr. Jefferson," 1981.

8   Malone, *Jefferson the Virginian*, introduction.

9   Moody, "After 40 Years as Jefferson's Best Friend."

10 Ibid.

11 "My Long Journey."

12 Richard Leopold, *The Nation*, May 1, 1948, 481–83.

13 Ibid.

14 Ibid.

15 Malone, *Jefferson the Virginian*, xi.

16 See, in general, Malone, *Jefferson the Virginian*.

17 Malone, foreword to ibid.

18 Malone, introduction to ibid.

19 Malone, *Malone and Jefferson*, 13–14.

20 "My Long Journey," "Long Journey," chapter 6, 7.

21 Joseph Story, letter to Samuel P. P. Fay, May 30, 1807, Malone Papers.

22 Lamberts' Travels Description of Jefferson, p. 353, Malone Papers.

23 John D. Battle Jr., "The 'Periodical Head-achs' of Thomas Jefferson," *Cleveland Clinic Quarterly* 51 (1983): 531–39.

24 Malone, introduction to *Jefferson the Virginian*.

25 Thomas Graves, speech in honor of Dumas Malone, Charlottesville, VA, October 21, 1981, Malone Papers.

26 Ibid.

27 Mark R. Wenger, "Thomas Jefferson, the College of William and Mary, and the University of Virginia," *Virginia Magazine of History and Biography* 103, no. 3 (July 1995): 339–74.

28 Ibid.

29 Ibid.

30 Wenger, "Thomas Jefferson," 342; also see William Dawson, letter to Edmund Gibson, August 11, 1732, in "Unpublished Letters at Fulham," *William and Mary Quarterly*, 1st ser., 9 (1901): 220; Marcus Whiffen, *The Public Buildings of Williamsburg: Colonial Capital of Virginia: An Architectural History* (Williamsburg, VA: Colonial Williamsburg, 1958), 96–112, 118–30; James D. Kornwolf, *So Good a Design: The Colonial Campus of the College of William and Mary: Its History, Background, and Legacy* (Williamsburg, VA: College of William and Mary, Joseph and Margaret Muscarelle Museum of Art, 1989), 32–73.

31 Wenger, "Thomas Jefferson," 344.

32 William Dawson, letter to Edmund Gibson, August 11, 1732, in "Unpublished Letters at Fulham," 220; "Journal of the Meetings of the Faculty of William and Mary College," April 9, 1770; "Specification of the losses of Samuel Henley"; Dell Upton, *Holy Things and Profane: Anglican Parish Churches in Colonial Virginia* (New York: Architectural History Foundation, 1986), 9–10; George M. Brydon, *Virginia's Mother Church and the Political Conditions under Which It Grew* (Richmond: Virginia Historical Society, 1947), 1:383–85, 459–60, 465–66. Prayer books for lay readers or "clerks" were provided by the parishes, and privately owned copies show up in many inventories of the period.

33 J. E. Morpurgo, *Their Majesties' Royall Colledge: William and Mary in the Seventeenth and Eighteenth Centuries* (Williamsburg, VA: College of William and Mary, 1976), 115–26; John M. Hemphill, "Parsons and Patrons, Governors and Visitors: Struggles for Control of the College of William and Mary, 1690–1780" (unpublished research paper, 1988), 13–24, ViWC; Malone, *Jefferson the Virginian*, 37 (quotation).

34 Malone, *Jefferson the Virginian*, 55–58; Thomas Jefferson, letter to Vine Utley, March 21, 1819, in *The Writings of Thomas Jefferson*, ed. Andrew A. Lipscomb and Albert Ellery Bergh (Washington, DC, Issued under the auspices of the Thomas Jefferson Memorial Association of the United States, 1904–1905), 15:187; "Governor Page," *Virginia Historical Register and Literary Note Book* 3 (1850): 151.

35 Only Dawson and Indian master Emmanuel Jones were left. See "Journal of the Meetings of the Faculty of William and Mary College," September 25, 1760; Thomas Jefferson, letter to L. H. Girardin, January 15, 1815, in *Writings of Jefferson*, 14:231; Thomas Jefferson, "Autobiography," in *The Life and Selected Writings of Thomas Jefferson*, ed. Adrienne Koch and William Peden (New York: Modern Library, 1944), 4–5. For the evolution of Jefferson's views on religion, see Paul K. Conkin, "The Religious Pilgrimage of Thomas Jefferson," in *Jeffersonian Legacies*, ed. Peter S. Onuf (Charlottesville: University Press of Virginia, 1993), 19–49.

36 Malone, *Malone and Jefferson*, 15.

37 Ibid.

38 Dumas Malone, "The First Fourth of July," *Parade Magazine*, July 3, 1955, 2.

39 Ibid.

40 Ibid.

41 Ibid.

42 Ibid.

43 Ibid.

44 Ibid.

45 Ibid.

Chapter 14. Douglas Southall Freeman

1 Mary Tyler Freeman Cheek McClenahan, "Reflections," *Virginia Magazine of History and Biography* 94, no. 1 (January 1986): 25–39.

2 "My Long Journey," 14; Malone, "The Great Generation Revisited."

3 "My Long Journey."

4 "Before 1929," in "My Long Journey," 1.

5 Malone, "Reflections," 3–13.

6 "My Long Journey," "Long Journey," chapter 6, 9.

7 Ibid.

8 Ibid.

9 See, in general, David E. Johnson, *Douglas Southall Freeman* (Gretna, LA: Pelican Press, 2002).

10 "My Long Journey."

11 See, in general, Dumas Malone, "The Pen of Douglas Southall Freeman," afterword to *George Washington: A Biography*, by Douglas Southall Freeman (New York: Collier Books, 1993), 755–66.

12 Ibid.

13 Ibid.

14 Cheek, "Reflections," 25–39.

15 Malone, "Pen of Douglas Southall Freeman," 755–66.

16 Ibid.

17 Ibid.

18 Ibid.

19 Ibid.

20 Ibid.

21 Ibid.

22 Ibid.

23 Ibid.

24 Ibid.

25 Malone, "Reflections," 3–13.

26 Ibid.

27 Malone, "Pen of Douglas Southall Freeman," 755–66.

28 Ibid.

29 Ibid.

Chapter 15. Sally Hemings

1 George Will, "The Last Word," *Newsweek*, August 11, 2008, 64.

2 Douglass Adair, "The Jefferson Scandals," in *Fame and the Founding Fathers: Essays by Douglass Adair*, ed. Trevor Colbourn (New York: Norton, 1974; reprint, Liberty Fund, 1998), 227–73.

3 The major books in the recent debate between Jefferson and Sally Hemings include Annette Gordon-Reed, *Thomas Jefferson and Sally Hemings: An American Controversy* (Charlottesville: University Press of Virginia, 1997); Annette Gordon-Reed, *The Hemingses of Monticello: An American Family* (New York: Norton, 2008); Hyland, *In Defense of Thomas Jefferson*; Robert F. Turner, ed., *The Jefferson-Hemings Controversy: Report of the Scholars Commission* (Durham, NC: Carolina Academic Press, 2011); Virginia Scharff, *The Women Jefferson Loved* (New York: Harper, 2010); Jon Kukla, *Mr. Jefferson's Women* (New York: Knopf, 2007); Andrew Burstein, *Jefferson's Secrets: Death and Desire at Monticello* (New York: Basic Books, 2005); Thomas Jefferson Memorial Foundation, *Report of the Research Committee on Thomas Jefferson and Sally Hemings*, Charlottesville, VA, January 2000, http://www.monticello.org/site/plantation-and-slavery/report-research-committee-thomas-jefferson-and-sally-hemings; "Thomas Jefferson and Sally Hemings Redux," *William and Mary Quarterly*, 3rd ser., 57 (January 2000): 121–210; Helen F. M. Leary, "Sally Hemings's Children: A Genealogical Analysis of the Evidence," *National Genealogical Society Quarterly* 89, no. 3 (September 2001): 165–207; "An Evaluation by Genealogical Proof Standards," *William and Mary Quarterly*, 3rd ser., 57 (January 2000): 208–18; Jan Ellen Lewis and Peter S. Onuf, eds., *Sally Hemings and Thomas Jefferson: History, Memory, and Civic Culture* (Charlottesville: University Press of Virginia, 1999); Eyler Robert Coates, ed., *The Jefferson-Hemings Myth: An American Travesty* (Charlottesville, VA: Jefferson Editions, 2001); Cynthia H. Burton, *Jefferson Vindicated: Fallacies, Omissions,*

and Contradictions in the Hemings Genealogical Search (Keswick, VA: Cynthia H.
Burton, 2005); Scot A. French and Edward L. Ayers, "The Strange Career of
Thomas Jefferson: Race and Slavery in American Memory, 1943–1993," in
Jeffersonian Legacies, ed. Peter S. Onuf (Charlottesville: University Press of
Virginia, 1993), 418–56; Colbourn, ed., *Fame and the Founding Fathers*, 160–
91; Fawn M. Brodie, *Thomas Jefferson: An Intimate History* (New York: Norton,
1974); Virginius Dabney and Jon Kukla, "The Monticello Scandals: History
and Fiction," *Virginia Cavalcade* 29 (Autumn 1979): 52–61; Barbara Chase-
Riboud, *Sally Hemings: A Novel* (New York: Viking Press, 1979); Virginius
Dabney, *The Jefferson Scandals: A Rebuttal* (New York: Dodd, Mead, 1981);
Sloan R. Williams, "Genetic Genealogy: The Woodson Family's Experience,"
Culture, Medicine and Psychiatry 29 (2005): 225–52; Byron W. Woodson, *A
President in the Family: Thomas Jefferson, Sally Hemings, and Thomas Woodson*
(Westport, CT: Praeger, 2001); Shannon Lanier and Jane Feldman, *Jefferson's
Children: The Story of One American Family* (New York: Random House, 2000).

4   Malone, letter to Rickie Asby, November 7, 1974, Malone Papers. *The Jefferson-
Hemings Controversy: Report of the Scholars Commission*, edited by Turner,
presented the findings of fourteen independent scholars, all of whom agreed
with Malone—their conclusion about the Sally Hemings allegation "was deep
skepticism and a belief that [it] is most certainly not true." See also Hyland, *In
Defense of Thomas Jefferson*.

5   Schlesinger, *Life in the 20th Century*, 449.

6   Malone, of course, did not have the advantage of knowing that a DNA test
conducted in 1998 would scientifically rule out either of the Carr brothers as
the father of Sally's child Eston Hemings. See the epilogue for a detailed
discussion of the DNA test results. The DNA test is also covered in Hyland, *In
Defense of Thomas Jefferson*; Turner, *Jefferson-Hemings Controversy*; and Thomas
Jefferson Memorial Foundation, *Report of the Research Committee*. According to
Dr. Eugene Foster, the retired UVA pathologist who performed the DNA tests
in 1998, the results were threefold: (1) The analysis found no match between
the DNA of Jefferson and the Woodson descendants. Thus, Woodson was not
fathered by a Jefferson. This result debunked any gossip that Jefferson and Sally
had a sexual relationship in Paris. (2) No match was found between the Carrs'
DNA and that of Hemings's descendants. Thus, neither of the Carr brothers
was the father of Eston Hemings (but either one could have been the father of
Sally's other children). (3) The Y-chromosome haplotypes of the descendants of
Field Jefferson (Thomas's uncle) and Eston Hemings did match. This implicates
a male Jefferson (though not necessarily Thomas Jefferson, as the public was led
to believe) as Eston's father. The misleading and sensationalized headline in
Nature, however, pronounced Jefferson guilty: "Jefferson Fathered Slave's Last
Child." The headline "A Male Jefferson Fathered Slave's Last Child" would have
been more accurate. Although some early reports in the press conveyed the

speculative and limited nature of the DNA study, the subtleties were gradually lost. Matters were complicated by solipsistic revisionists spreading the word that Jefferson's paternity was scientific fact.

7 French and Ayers, "Strange Career of Thomas Jefferson," 453, n. 14.

8 Burton, *Jefferson Vindicated*, 40. Burton has covered Jefferson's health in explicit detail through correspondence and Jefferson's own health records; see pp. 40–46.

9 John T. Morse Jr., *Thomas Jefferson* (Nashville, TN: Cumberland House, 2004), 5. The most thorough discussion of Jefferson's health can be found in Burton, *Jefferson Vindicated.*

10 Sarah N. Randolph, *The Domestic Life of Thomas Jefferson* (Charlottesville: University Press of Virginia, 1978), 232, transcript of Jefferson to James Madison, April 27, 1795; Jefferson, letter to Thomas Mann Randolph, January 31, 1796, Library of Congress.

11 Hyland, *In Defense of Thomas Jefferson.*

12 Malone, *Jefferson the President*, 212.

13 Burstein, *Jefferson's Secrets*, 160.

14 Hyland, *In Defense of Thomas Jefferson*, 3.

15 Ibid., 23; Miller is quoted in Dabney, *Jefferson Scandals*, 120. See, in general, Gordon-Reed, *Hemingses of Monticello* and *Thomas Jefferson and Sally Hemings.*

16 Isaac Jefferson, "Memoir of a Monticello Slave," in *Jefferson at Monticello*, ed. James A. Bear Jr. (Charlottesville: University Press of Virginia, 1967), 3, 4; Burton, *Jefferson Vindicated*, 134–36.

17 Jefferson, "Memoir of a Monticello Slave," 4.

18 Lucia C. Stanton, *Free Some Day: The African-American Families of Monticello* (Charlottesville, VA: Thomas Jefferson Foundation, 2000), 106; Elizabeth Langhorne, *Monticello: A Family Story* (Chapel Hill, NC: Algonquin Books of Chapel Hill, 1989), 182. John Hemings, Betty's son, had been apprenticed to Jefferson's principal builder, James Dinsmore, and became a master builder and cabinet maker. Joe Fossett, son of Mary Hemings, was Monticello's blacksmith and had learned his trade from William Stewart (see Langhorne, *Monticello*, 182).

19 Donald Jackson, *A Year at Monticello, 1795* (Golden, CO: Fulcrum, 1989), 91–92.

20 Kukla, *Mr. Jefferson's Women*, 121; see also, Hyland, *In Defense of Thomas Jefferson*, ch. 11, "Secret Rooms and other Hollywood Legends."

21 Gordon-Reed, *Thomas Jefferson and Sally Hemings*, 209, 240.

22 Newell G. Bringhurst, "Fawn M. Brodie: Her Biographies as Autobiography," *Pacific Historical Review* 59, no. 2 (May 1990): 203–29; Fawn Brodie's

experiences at the University of Utah are vividly described in her "It Happened Very Quietly," in *Remembering: The University of Utah*, Elizabeth Haglund, ed. (Salt Lake City: University of Utah Press, 1981), 85–95.

23 Ibid.

24 Fawn M. Brodie, "Jefferson Biographers and the Psychology of Canonization," *Journal of Interdisciplinary History* 2, no. 1 (Summer 1971): 155–71.

25 See, in general, French and Ayers, "Strange Career of Thomas Jefferson," 418–56.

26 Brodie, "Jefferson Biographers," 155–71.

27 Ibid. See, in general, French and Ayers, "Strange Career of Thomas Jefferson," 418–56.

28 Quoted in French and Ayers, "Strange Career of Thomas Jefferson," 418–56.

29 Fawn Brodie, letter to James A. Bear, December 18, 1975, Malone Papers.

30 Fawn Brodie, letter to Dumas Malone, March 10, 1969, #12717-6, Box 24, Professional Correspondence, Malone Papers.

31 Ibid.

32 Ibid.

33 See, in general, French and Ayers, "Strange Career of Thomas Jefferson," 418–56; and Virginius Dabney, letter to Dumas Malone, February 14, 1975; Dumas Malone, letter to Virginius Dabney, February 12, 1975; Virginius Dabney, letter to Dumas Malone, February 28, 1975; *Time*, March 3, 1975, 67; Dumas Malone, letter to Virginius Dabney, March 3, 1975, all five in Malone Papers.

34 Virginiua Dabney, letter to Dumas Malone, February 14, 1975; Dumas Malone, letter to Virginius Dabney, February 12, 1975; *Time*, March 3, 1975, 67; Virginius Dabney, letter to Dumas Malone, Febraury 28, 1975; Dumas Malone, letter to Virginius Dabney, March 3, 1975, all five in Malone Papers. See, in general, French and Ayers, "Strange Career of Thomas Jefferson," 418–56.

35 Dabney, *Across the Years*, 329.

36 Quoted in French and Ayers, "Strange Career of Thomas Jefferson," 418.

37 Quoted in ibid., 435.

38 Ibid.

39 Dumas Malone, quote in Dabney's book, 1981, Malone Papers.

40 Quoted in Thomas Fleming, *Intimate Lives of the Founding Fathers* (New York: Smithsonian Books, 2009), 411.

41 Brodie, *Thomas Jefferson*, 15–16.

42 Ibid.

43 T. Harry Williams, "Review: On the Couch at Monticello," *Reviews in American History* 2, no. 4 (December 1974): 526. Published by the Johns Hopkins University Press, http://www.jstor.org/stable/2701069, accessed December 29, 2010.

44 Malone, *Malone and Jefferson*, 19.

45 Thomas Robson Hay, letter to Dumas Malone, May 18, 1970, Malone Papers.

46 Nathan Schachner, *Thomas Jefferson* (New York: T. Yoseloff, 1957), 1353; Thomas Robson Hay, letter to Dumas Malone, May 18, 1970, Malone Papers.

47 Quoted in Williams, "Review," 523–29.

48 Fleming, *Intimate Lives of the Founding Fathers*, 411.

49 Williams, "Review," 523–29.

50 Malone, "The Miscegenation Legend," in *Jefferson the President.*

51 Ibid.

52 Ibid.

53 Ibid.

54 Ibid.

55 Ibid.

56 Malone, "Scholar's Way," 206.

57 Julian Boyd, letter to Dumas Malone, May 7, 1980, Malone Papers.

Chapter 16. Malone vs. CBS

1 C. Vann Woodward, "The Hero of Independence," *New York Times*, July 5, 1981.

2 Dumas Malone, "Mr. Jefferson's Private Life," *Proceedings of the American Antiquarian Society*, new ser., 84 (April 1974): 5.

3 French and Ayers, "Strange Career of Thomas Jefferson," 437–447.

4 Fleming, *Intimate Lives of the Founding Fathers*, 412.

5 French and Ayers, "Strange Career of Thomas Jefferson," 437.

6 Ibid.

7 Malone, letters to CBS executives: Robert Daley and William Paley, January 18, 1979, Malone Papers.

8 Merrill Peterson, letter to William S. Paley, January 16, 1979, Malone Papers. Malone asked Julian Boyd and Virginius Dabney to write letters to CBS as well. "There seems to be a possibility that we can stop the series," Malone wrote to Dabney, "but even if we cannot stop it, we can certainly insist that it be

presented as fiction." Dumas Malone, letter to Virginius Dabney, January 23, 1979, Malone Papers.

9 French and Ayers, "Strange Career of Thomas Jefferson," 437.

10 Ibid., 438.

11 Dumas Malone, letter to Irving Goodman, January 19, 1979, Malone Papers.

12 Blaine Harden, "Revival of 'Rumor' Disturbs Jefferson Scholars," *Washington Post*, February 13, 1979.

13 French and Ayers, "Strange Career of Thomas Jefferson," 438.

14 Ibid.

15 "Don't Do This to Jefferson," *Christian Science Monitor*, February 23, 1979, 24.

16 See, in general, French and Ayers, "Strange Career of Thomas Jefferson," 437–447.

17 Ibid., 438, 439.

18 Ibid., 439.

19 Ibid.

20 Kukla has now reversed his position and believes the Sally story; see his *Jefferson's Women*.

21 French and Ayers, "Strange Career of Thomas Jefferson," 440.

22 Virginius Dabney, letter to Dumas Malone February 14, 1975, Malone Papers.

23 Ibid.

24 Ibid.

25 Ibid.

26 Virginius Dabney, letter to Dumas Malone, December 2, 1979, Malone Papers.

27 French and Ayers, "Strange Career of Thomas Jefferson," 441.

28 Ibid.

29 Ibid., 442.

30 Ibid.

31 Ibid., 443.

32 Ibid., 444.

33 Ibid., 446.

Chapter 17. The Pulitzer Prize

1 David Herbert Donald, letter to Dumas Malone, May 5, 1975, Malone Papers.

2 Edwin M. Yoder Jr., "A Heroic Biographer," *Richmond Times-Dispatch*, January 2, 1987.

3 White House, telegram to Dumas Malone, October 4, 1981, Malone Papers.

4 Dumas Malone, letter to Harry S. Truman, May 25, 1960, Malone Papers.

5 Harry S. Truman, letter to Dumas Malone, June 26, 1960, Malone Papers.

6 Thomas Graves, address in honor of Dumas Malone, Charlottesville, VA, October 21, 1981, Malone Papers.

7 Henry Mitchell, "The Gentleman Historian: Dumas Malone, Sage of Charlottesville," *Washington Post*, January 4, 1987.

8 "My Long Journey."

9 Ibid.

10 Dumas Malone, letter to Edward Roderick, 1974; Professional Correspondence 1971–July 1975 Box: 23, 6 folders, Malone Papers.

11 Dumas Malone, "'The Taking Up of Powhatans Bones': Virginia Indians, 1585–1945," *Virginia Magazine of History and Biography* 95, no. 2 (April 1987): 243–44.

12 Thomas Adams, letter to Dumas Malone, June 7, 1972, Malone Papers.

13 Dumas Malone, letter to Thomas Adams, June 16, 1972, Malone Papers.

14 "Dumas Malone Given Bruce Catton Prize," *New York Times*, May 14, 1984.

15 Dumas Malone, letter to Paul H. Spence, 1975; Professional Correspondence 1971– July 1975 Box: 23, 6 folders, Malone Papers.

16 Letter from Malone to *Mark Twain Journal*; #12717-6, Box 24, Professional Correspondence, Malone Papers.

17 Ellen Panarese, letter to Dumas Malone, May 3, 1982, Malone Papers.

18 Malone, Phi Beta Kappa speech, 1982.

19 Lawrence F. O'Brien, letter to Dumas Malone, July 28, 1964, Malone Papers.

20 Dumas Malone, speech at the White House, September 30, 1980, Malone Papers.

21 Ibid.

22 Walter Mondale, letter to Dumas Malone, October 20, 1980, Malone Papers.

23 Bess Abell, letter to Dumas Malone, October 2, 1980, Malone Papers.

24 Dumas Malone, letter to Joan Mondale, October 9, 1980, Malone Papers.

25 Arthur Schlesinger Jr., letter to Dumas Malone, May 6, 1975, Malone Papers.

26 Dumas Malone, letter to Arthur Schlesinger Jr., May 9, 1975, Malone Papers.

27 Dumas Malone, letter to Arthur Schlesinger Jr., November 24, 1965, Malone Papers.

28 Arthur Schlesinger Jr., letter to Dumas Malone, November 27, 1965, Malone Papers.

29 Charles Warren Center, Harvard University, letter to Dumas Malone, May 8, 1975, Malone Papers.

30 Francis Lowenheim, letter to Dumas Malone, 1975; Professional Correspondence 1971– July 1975 Box: 23, 6 folders, Malone Papers.

31 Daniel J. Boorstin, letter to Dumas Malone, May 7, 1975, Malone Papers.

32 Milton Konvitz, letter to Dumas Malone, May 7, 1975, Malone Papers.

33 Columbia faculty, letter to Dumas Malone, May 6, 1975, Malone Papers.

34 James A. Bear, letter to Dumas Malone, May 6, 1975, Malone Papers.

35 William Fishback, letter to Dumas Malone, May 6, 1975, Malone Papers.

36 Julian P. Boyd, letter to Dumas Malone, May 7, 1980, Malone Papers.

37 Mills Godwin, letter to Dumas Malone, May 8, 1975, Malone Papers.

38 Linwood Holton, letter to Dumas Malone, May 22, 1975, Malone Papers.

39 Dumas Malone, letter to Linwood Holton, May 1975, Malone Papers.

40 Linwood Holton, telephone interview by the author, March 30, 2011.

41 Ibid.

42 "My Long Journey," 16.

43 Holton interview.

44 Dumas Malone, letter to Mary Wells Ashworth, May 22, 1975, Malone Papers.

45 Leonard W. Levy, "Prize Stories," *Reviews in American History* 8, no. 1 (March 1980): 1–20.

46 Ibid.

47 Ibid.

48 "Jefferson Scholar Dumas Malone Dies," *Richmond Times-Dispatch*, December 28, 1986.

Chapter 18. Fame and the Famous

1 Malone, "Scholar's Way," 200.

2 Dumas Malone, speech at UVA, Charlottesville, VA, July 3, 1981, Malone Papers.

3 John F. Kennedy, letter to Dumas Malone, February 11, 1957, #12717-6, Box 24, Professional Correspondence, Malone Papers.

4 Dumas Malone, letter to John F. Kennedy, February 25, 1957, Malone Papers.

5 Ibid.

6 "My Long Journey."

7 Letter from McGovern to Malone, 1969; #12717-6, Box 24, Professional Correspondence, Malone Papers.

8 Letter from Petersen to Malone, 1969; #12717-6, Box 24, Professional Correspondence, Malone Papers.

9 Letter from Malone to Lester Cappon, 1969 #12717-6, Box 24, Professional Correspondence, Malone Papers.

10 Linwood Holton, letter to Dumas Malone, July 26, 1972, Malone Papers.

11 Dumas Malone, letter to Linwood Holton, August 2, 1972, Malone Papers.

12 Daniel Boorstin, letter to Dumas Malone, June 3, 1976, Malone Papers.

13 Felix Frankfurter, letter to Dumas Malone, January 29, 1941, Malone Papers.

14 Dumas Malone, letter to Felix Frankfurter, January 31, 1941, Malone Papers.

15 Letter from Malone to Julian Boyd, 1969; #12717-6, Box 24, Professional Correspondence, Malone Papers.

16 Lawrence Ott, letter to Dumas Malone, November 25, 1982, Malone Papers.

17 Lawrence Ott, letter to Dumas Malone, October 14, 1983, Malone Papers (Pachter quoted in letter).

18 Lawrence Ott, letter to Dumas Malone, October 14, 1983, Malone Papers.

19 Frank Hereford, letter to John Warner, November 12, 1982, Malone Papers.

20 John Warner, letter to Frank Hereford, December 1982; Frank Hereford to John Warner, November 12, 1982, Malone Papers.

21 Cong. Rec. (1982) (statement of Sen. Warner); Congressional Record, Public Law 97-388—December 23, 1982.

22 Pub. L. No. 97-388, 96 Stat. (1982).

23 Dabney, *Across the Years*, 253.

24 Sandy Gilliam, letter to Dumas Malone, June 25, 1976, Malone Papers.

25 Sequence of events relative to the visit of HM Queen Elizabeth II and the Duke of Edinburgh, Malone Papers, July 10, 1976.

26 Buckingham Palace, letter to Dumas Malone, March 15, 1982, Malone Papers.

27 "My Long Journey," 4.

28 Ibid., 5.

29 Ibid., 6.

30 Ibid., 16.

31 Letter from Malone to Guggenheim Committee; #12717-6, Box 24, Professional Correspondence, Malone Papers.

32 Letter from Rey to Malone; #12717-6, Box 24, Professional Correspondence, Malone Papers.

33 Dumas Malone, letter to Shirley Fewell, 1974, Malone Papers.

34 Dumas Malone, letter to Auguste G. Clough, Malone Papers.

35 "My Long Journey," 4; Dumas Malone, letter to Fred S. Landess, 1974, Malone Papers.

36 Bruce Manuel, "The Sage of West Falmouth," *Christian Science Monitor*, August 10, 1981.

Chapter 19. Blindness

1 Dumas Malone, letter to Virginius Dabney, January 26, 1981, Malone Papers.

2 Dumas Malone, letter to J. Harvey Young, March 12, 1982, Malone Papers.

3 Letter from Malone to Parke Rouse, William & Mary Special Collections, Williamsburg, Virginia, Rouse Papers, November 15, 1982; Letter from Malone to Parke Rouse, in series 5, folder 2: Letters to Parke Rouse, 1950–1957, of the Parke Rouse Papers, MSS 71 R75.

4 Walter Clemons, "A Monument to Jefferson," *Newsweek*, July 27, 1981.

5 Quoted in Mitchell, "The Gentleman Historian."

6 Steve Hochman, personal correspondence with the author, June 1, 2012.

7 Dumas Malone, letter to Daniel Boorstin, June 9, 1976, Malone Papers.

8 Dumas Malone, letter to Paul Magnusson, April 1974, Malone Papers.

9 Dumas Malone, letter to Frank Bracken, October 1974, Malone Papers.

10 Dumas Malone, letter to Linwood Holton, October 21, 1972, Malone Papers.

11 Dumas Malone, letter to E. D. Kenyon, March 24, 1980, Malone Papers.

12 In July 1981 Hochman became assistant to President Jimmy Carter. He helped him research and edit *Keeping Faith: Memoirs of a President*. While working for President Carter, Hochman completed his UVA PhD dissertation, "Thomas Jefferson: A Personal Financial Biography." He currently serves as the Carter Center director of research and faculty assistant to President Carter. I am indebted to Steve Hochman for his insightful interviews and remembrances about Dumas Malone.

13 "Steve Hochman Is Emory's Resident Jeffersonian," *Emory*, July 20, 2010.

14 Steve Hochman, letter to Dumas Malone, June 14, 1968, Malone Papers.

15 "Steve Hochman Is Emory's Resident Jeffersonian."

16 Sid Moody, "Author Finishes Sixth Book on Jefferson," *Daily News-Record*, July 6, 1981.

17 Ibid.

18 Malone, *Malone and Jefferson*, 3.

19 Ibid., 4.

20 Katherine Sargeant, telephone interview by the author, November 30, 2011.

21 Katherine Sargeant, interview by the author, December 1, 2011.

22 "Personal Observations on Dumas Malone as a Biographer," undated typescript in author's collection; Steve Hochman, interview by the author, August 16, 2010; Peterson, "Dumas Malone," 237–52.

23 Morris Braun, letter to Dumas Malone, August 23, 1984, Malone Papers.

24 "My Long Journey."

25 Malone, Phi Beta Kappa speech.

26 Carl Chadsy, letter to Dumas Malone, February 4, 1981, Malone Papers.

27 Dumas Malone, letter to Carl Chadsy, February 16, 1981, Malone Papers.

28 Edwin McDowell, "Malone Rests at End of Jefferson Series," *New York Times*, June 12, 1981.

29 Ibid.

30 "My Long Journey."

31 Dumas Malone, letter to Mrs. Ayers, September 8, 1985, Malone Papers.

32 Dumas Malone, dedication to *The Sage of Monticello*.

Chapter 20. Death on the Mountain

1 Thomas Jefferson, letter to James Madison, September 6, 1789, in *Papers*, ed. Julian P. Boyd (Princeton, NJ: Princeton University Press, 1958), 15:384n2, 396.

2 Dumas Malone, speech at UVA, Charlottesville, VA, July 3, 1981, Malone Papers.

3 Helen Cripe, interview by the author, June 2011.

4 Clemons, "Monument to Jefferson."

5 Quoted in Eric Pace, "Dumas Malone, Expert on Jefferson, Is Dead at 94," *New York Times*, December 28, 1986; C. Vann Woodward, "The Hero of Independence," *New York Times*, July 5, 1981; ProQuest Historical Newspapers, *The New York Times* (1851–2006).

6 Quoted in Pace, "Malone Is Dead at 94."

7   Beddow, "Dumas Malone."

8   Smith, "In the Autumn of His Years," 8–12; Pace, "Dumas Malone, Expert on Jefferson."

9   Gifford Malone, interview by the author, December 20, 2011.

10 Pace, "Malone Is Dead at 94."

11 "Jefferson Scholar Dumas Malone Dies," *Richmond Times-Dispatch*, December 28, 1986; Smith, "In the Autumn of His Years," 8–12; Pace, "Malone Is Dead at 94"; ProQuest Historical Newspapers, *The New York Times* (1851–2006).

12 Quoted in Smith, "In the Autumn of His Years."

13 Dumas Malone, speech at UVA, Charlottesville, VA, July 3, 1981, Malone Papers.

14 David Maurer, "Set in Stone," *UVA Magazine*, Spring 2008.

Afterword

1   Katie Couric, *The Best Advice I Ever Got: Lessons from Extraordinary Lives* (New York: Random House, 2011), 104.

2   Dumas Malone, letter to Paul Horne Jr., April 4, 1980, Malone Papers.

3   Wills, "Prodigious Life."

4   Malone, *Malone and Jefferson*, 12.

5   Dumas Malone, letter to Rickie Asby, November 7, 1974, Malone Papers.

6   Malone, *Malone and Jefferson*, 9.

7   Ibid., 9–10.

8   Malone, "Reflections," 3–13.

9   Ibid.

10 Ibid.

11 Ibid.

12 Ibid.

13 Ibid.

14 Dumas Malone, letter to Anita Waddington Rice, December 18, 1974, Malone Papers.

15 Peterson, "Dumas Malone: An Appreciation," 237–52.

16 Ibid.

17 Edwin M. Yoder, "For a Heroic Biography, a Heroic Biographer," *Washington Post*, January 1, 1987.

18 Ibid.

19 Horne, "Dumas Malone," 252–56.

20 Peterson, "Dumas Malone: An Appreciation," 237–52.

21 Ibid.

22 As quoted in ibid.; Malone, *Jefferson the Virginian*, introduction.

23 Ibid.

24 Ibid.

25 Ibid.

26 Edgar Johnson, "American Biography and the Modern World," *North American Review* 245, no. 2 (Summer 1938): 364–80.

27 Peterson, "Dumas Malone: An Appreciation," 237–52.

28 Yoder, "For a Heroic Biography."

Epilogue

1 Malone, "The Scholar's Way," 212.

2 Final Report of The Jefferson-Hemings Scholars Commission, April 12, 2001.

3 See, in general, Turner, *Jefferson-Hemings Controversy*.

4 Ibid.

5 Burton, *Jefferson Vindicated*, 54; Thomas Jefferson Deposition, Buckingham Co. Court, September 15, 1815 (microfilm), Jefferson Papers, University of Virginia, Charlottesville, VA.

6 Burton, *Jefferson Vindicated*, 54.

7 Ibid., 57.

8 Katt Henry, "Jefferson Vindicated," *Cavalier Daily*, April 25, 2007, http://www.cavalierdaily.com/2007/02/28/jefferson-vindicated.

9 Jefferson, "Memoir of a Monticello Slave," 22 (referring to himself in the third person).

10 Forrest McDonald, *The Presidency of Thomas Jefferson* (Lawrence: University Press of Kansas, 1976), 31.

11 Burton, *Jefferson Vindicated*, 52–53. Burton's book is the most thoroughly detailed book I have found concerning Jefferson's younger brother, Randolph.

12 Ellen Randolph, letter to Jeff Randolph, April 21, 1808; Martha Jefferson Randolph, letter to Jeff, January 30, 1808, both in *The Family Letters of Thomas Jefferson*, ed. Edwin Morris Betts and James A. Bear (Charlottesville: University Press of Virginia, 1986); Burton, *Jefferson Vindicated*, 53.

13 See Turner, *Jefferson-Hemings Controversy*; and Burton, *Jefferson Vindicated.*

14 Bernard Mayo, ed., *Thomas Jefferson and His Unknown Brother*, with additions by James A. Bear (Charlottesville: University Press of Virginia, 1981), 21.

15 "Jefferson and Hemings Redux," *Washington Times*, July 11, 2001.

16 Sam Hodges, "Paternity Disputed: Scholars: No Proof Jefferson Fathered Slave's Children," *Mobile Register*, April 13, 2001.

17 Ibid.

18 Ibid.; Forrest McDonald, interview by the author, July 19, 2008.

19 Turner, *Jefferson-Hemings Controversy.* On the commission were the following: Lance Banning, professor of history, University of Kentucky; James Ceaser, professor of government and foreign affairs, University of Virginia; Charles R. Kesler, professor of government, Claremont McKenna College; Alf J. Mapp Jr., eminent scholar emeritus and Louis I. Jaffe Professor of History Emeritus, Old Dominion University; Harvey C. Mansfield; William R. Kenan Jr., professor of government, Harvard University; David N. Mayer, professor of law and history, Capital University; Forrest McDonald, distinguished research professor of history emeritus, University of Alabama; Thomas Traut, professor of biochemistry and biophysics, School of Medicine, University of North Carolina; Robert F. Turner (chairman), professor, University of Virginia; Walter E. Williams, professor of economics, George Mason University; and Jean Yarbrough, professor of political science, Bowdoin College.

Appendix A

1 Dumas Malone, *Virginia Quarterly Review*, Spring 1943, 161–77.

BIBLIOGRAPHY

Collections

Douglas Southall Freeman Papers, University of Virginia, Charlottesville, VA.

Dumas Malone Papers, Special Collections MSS 12712-b, SC-STKS, Albert and Shirley Small Special Collections Library, Alderman Library, University of Virginia, Charlottesville, VA.

Ellen Randolph Coolidge Papers, Albert and Shirley Small Special Collections Library, Alderman Library, University of Virginia, Charlottesville, VA.

Merrill Peterson Papers, Albert and Shirley Small Special Collections Library, Alderman Library, University of Virginia, Charlottesville, VA.

Parke Rouse Papers, Mss 71 R75, William and Mary Library, Williamsburg, VA.

Thomas A. Graves Papers, UA 2.16, Series 13: Accession 1985.037, box 1, folder 133, William and Mary Library, Williamsburg, VA.

Tyler Papers, Mss 65 T97, Group b, William and Mary Library, Williamsburg, VA.

Books

Adair, Douglass. *Fame and the Founding Fathers: Essays by Douglass Adair.* Edited by Trevor Colbourn. New York: Norton, 1974. Reprint, Liberty Fund, 1998.

Adams, Henry. *History of the United States of America during the Administration of Thomas Jefferson.* New York: Library of America, 1986.

Adams, John. *Correspondence of the Late President Adams.* Boston: Everett & Munroe, 1809.

Adams, William Howard. *The Adamses at Home: Accounts by Visitors to the Old House in Quincy,* 1188–1886. Boston: Colonial Society of Massachusetts, 1970.

————. *The Eye of Thomas Jefferson.* Washington, DC: National Gallery of Art, 1976.

————. *Jefferson and the Arts: An Extended View.* Washington, DC: National Gallery of Art, 1976.

————. *Jefferson's Monticello.* New York: Abbeville Press, 1983.

————. *The Paris Years of Thomas Jefferson.* New Haven, CT: Yale University Press, 1997.

Ashworth, Mary Wells. "Douglas Southall Freeman: The Man and the Making of a Book." In *Douglas Southall Freeman: Reflections by His Daughter, His Research Associate and a Historian.* Richmond, VA: Friends of the Richmond Public Library, 1986.

Bear, James A., Jr. *Jefferson at Monticello.* Charlottesville: University Press of Virginia, 1985.

Bear, James A., Jr., and Lucia C. Stanton, eds. *Jefferson's Memorandum Books: Accounts, with Legal Records and Miscellany, 1767–1826.* Princeton, NJ: Princeton University Press, 1997.

Bedini, Silvio A. *Declaration of Independence Desk, Relic of Revolution.* Washington, DC: Smithsonian Institution Press, 1981.

————. *Thomas Jefferson: Statesman of Science.* New York: Macmillan, 1990.

Bernstein, R. B. *Thomas Jefferson.* New York: Oxford University Press, 2003.

Betts, Edwin M., ed. *Thomas Jefferson's Farm Book.* Princeton, NJ: American Philosophical Society/Princeton University Press, 1953.

————. *Thomas Jefferson's Garden Book, 1766–1824.* Philadelphia: American Philosophical Society, 1944.

Betts, Edwin M., and James A. Bear Jr., eds. *The Family Letters of Thomas Jefferson.* Charlottesville: University Press of Virginia, 1986.

Boorstin, Daniel. *The Americans: The Colonial Experience.* New York: Random House, 1993.

————. *The Lost World of Thomas Jefferson.* Chicago: University of Chicago Press, 1948.

Boyd, Julian, ed. *The Papers of Thomas Jefferson.* 20 vols. Princeton, NJ: Princeton University Press, 1950–.

Brodie, Fawn M. *Thomas Jefferson: An Intimate History.* New York: Norton, 1974.

Bullock, Henry Morton. *A History of Emory University.* Nashville, TN: Parthenon Press, 1936.

Burns, James Macgregor, and Susan Dunn. *George Washington.* New York: Time Books, 2004.

Burstein, Andrew. *The Inner Jefferson: Portrait of a Grieving Optimist.* Charlottesville: University Press of Virginia, 1995.

———. *Jefferson's Secrets: Death and Desire at Monticello*. New York: Basic Books, 2005.

Burton, Cynthia H. *Jefferson Vindicated: Fallacies, Omissions, and Contradictions in the Hemings Genealogical Search*. Keswick, VA: Cynthia H. Burton, 2005.

Cappon, Lester J., ed. *The Adams-Jefferson Letters: The Complete Correspondence Between Thomas Jefferson and Abigail and John Adams*. Reprint, Chapel Hill and London Published for the Omohundro Institute of Early American History and Culture at Williamsburg, Virginia, 1959.

Chase-Riboud, Barbara. *Sally Hemings: A Novel*. New York: Viking Press, 1979.

Chernow, Ron. *Alexander Hamilton*. New York: Penguin, 2004.

———.*Washington: A Life*. New York: Penguin, 2010.

Coates, Eyler Robert, ed. *The Jefferson-Hemings Myth: An American Travesty*. Charlottesville, VA: Jefferson Editions, 2001.

Colbourn, Trevor, ed. *Fame and the Founding Fathers, Essays by Douglass Adair* (New York: Published for the Omohundro Institute of Early American History and Culture at Williamsburg, Virginia, by Norton, 1974).

Couric, Katie. *The Best Advice I Ever Got: Lessons from Extraordinary Lives*. New York: Random House, 2011.

Crawford, Alan Pell. *Twilight at Monticello: The Final Years of Thomas Jefferson*. New York: Random House, 2008.

Cunningham, Noble, Jr. *In Pursuit of Reason: The Life of Thomas Jefferson*. Baton Rouge: Louisiana State University Press, 1987.

———. *The Jeffersonian Republicans in Power: Party Operations, 1801–1809*. Chapel Hill: University of North Carolina Press, 1963.

Dabney, Virginius. *Across the Years: Memories of a Virginian*. Garden City, NY: Doubleday, 1978.

———. *The Jefferson Scandals: A Rebuttal*. New York: Mead, Dodd, 1981.

———. *Mr. Jefferson's University: A History*. Charlottesville: University Press of Virginia, 1981.

Dewey, Frank. *Thomas Jefferson, Lawyer*. Charlottesville: University Press of Virginia, 2005.

Durey, Michael. *With the Hammer of Truth: James Thomson Callender and America's Early National Heroes*. Charlottesville: University Press of Virginia, 1990.

Ellis, Joseph J. *After the Revolution*. New York: Norton, 1979.

———. *American Sphinx: The Character of Thomas Jefferson*. New York: Knopf, 1997.

———. *His Excellency: George Washington*. New York: Knopf, 2004.

Fleming, Thomas. *The Intimate Lives of the Founding Fathers*. New York: Smithsonian Books, 2009.

———. *The Man from Monticello: An Intimate Life of Thomas Jefferson*. New York: Morrow, 1969.

Ford, Worthington Chauncey, ed. *Thomas Jefferson and James Thomson Callender, 1798–1802*. Brooklyn: History Print Club, 1897.

Franklin, John Hope, and Alfred A. Moss, Jr. *From Slavery to Freedom: A History of Negro Americans*. 6th ed. New York: McGraw-Hill, 1988.

Freeman, Douglas Southall. *George Washington: A Biography*. 7 vols. New York: Charles Scribner's Sons, 1948–57. Volume 7 completed by John A. Carroll and Mary W. Ashworth.

———. *Lee's Lieutenants: A Study in Command*. 3 vols. New York: Charles Scribner's Sons, 1942–43.

———. *R. E. Lee*. 4 vols. New York: Charles Scribner's Sons, 1934–35.

French, Scot A., and Edward L. Ayers. "The Strange Career of Thomas Jefferson: Race and Slavery in American Memory, 1943–1993." In *Jeffersonian Legacies*, edited by Peter S. Onuf. Charlottesville: University Press of Virginia, 1993, 418–56.

Freudenberg, Ann. "Preface." In *Malone and Jefferson: The Biographer and the Sage* by Dumas Malone. Charlottesville: University of Virginia Library, 1981.

Gordon-Reed, Annette. *The Hemingses of Monticello: An American Family*. New York: Norton 2008.

———. *Thomas Jefferson and Sally Hemings: An American Controversy*. Charlottesville: University Press of Virginia, 1997.

Grunwald, Lisa, and Stephen J. Adler, eds. *Letters of the Century: America, 1900–1999*. New York: Dial Press, 1999.

Hall, Max. *Harvard University Press: A History*. Cambridge, MA: Harvard University Press, 1986.

Halliday, E. M. *Understanding Thomas Jefferson*. New York: HarperCollins, 2001.

Hitchens, Christopher. *Thomas Jefferson: Author of America*. New York: HarperCollins, 2005.

Hyland, William G. *In Defense of Thomas Jefferson: The Sally Hemings Sex Scandal*. New York: Thomas Dunne Books, 2009.

Jefferson, Isaac. "Memoir of a Monticello Slave." In *Jefferson at Monticello*, edited by James A. Bear Jr. Charlottesville: University Press of Virginia, 1967.

Jefferson, Israel Gillette. "Recollections of Israel Gillette Jefferson, Pike County Republican," December 25, 1873. In *Report of the Research Committee on*

Thomas Jefferson and Sally Hemings. Charlottesville, VA: Thomas Jefferson Memorial Foundation, January 2000.

Jefferson, Thomas. *The Life and Selected Writings of Thomas Jefferson*. Edited by Adrienne Koch and William Peden. New York: Modern Library, 1944.

———. *The Papers of Thomas Jefferson*. Vols. 21–23. Edited by Charles Cullen. Princeton, NJ: Princeton University Press, 1983.

———. *The Political Writings of Thomas Jefferson*. Edited by Merrill D. Peterson. Woodlawn, MD: Wolk Press, 1993.

———. *The Portable Thomas Jefferson*. Edited by Merrill D. Peterson. New York: Penguin, 1983.

———. *Writings*. Edited by Merrill D. Peterson. New York: Library of America, 1984.

Johnson, David E. *Douglas Southall Freeman*. Gretna, LA: Pelican Press, 2002.

Justus, Judith. *Down from the Mountain*. Perrysburg, OH: Jeskurtara, 1990.

Kimball, Marie. *Jefferson: The Road to Glory, 1743 to 1776*. New York: Coward-McCann, 1943.

———. *Jefferson: The Scene of Europe, 1784 to 1789*. New York: Coward-McCann, 1950.

———. *Jefferson: War and Peace, 1776 to 1784*. New York: Coward-McCann, 1947.

Kukla, Jon. *Mr. Jefferson's Women*. New York: Knopf, 2007.

Langhorne, Elizabeth. *Monticello: A Family Story*. Chapel Hill, NC: Algonquin Books of Chapel Hill, 1989.

Lanier, Shannon, and Jane Feldman. *Jefferson's Children: The Story of One American Family*. New York: Random House, 2000.

Lewis, Jan Ellen, and Peter S. Onuf, eds. *Sally Hemings and Thomas Jefferson: History, Memory, and Civic Culture*. Charlottesville: University Press of Virginia, 1999.

Lipscomb, Andrew A., and Albert Ellergy Bergh, eds. *The Writings of Thomas Jefferson*. Washington, DC: Issued under the auspices of the Jefferson Memorial Association of the United States, 1904–1905.

Madison, James. *James Madison: A Biography in His Own Words*. Edited by Merrill D. Peterson. New York: Newsweek, 1974.

Malone, Dumas. *Jefferson and His Time*. 6 vols. Boston: Little, Brown, 1948–81.

———. "The Pen of Douglas Southall Freeman." In *George Washington: A Biography*, Vol. 6, *Patriot and President*, by Douglas Southall Freeman. New York: Charles Scribner, 1954.

Mapp, Alf J., Jr. *Thomas Jefferson: A Strange Case of Mistaken Identity*. New York: Madison, 1987.

———. *Thomas Jefferson: Passionate Pilgrim*. New York: Madison, 1992.

Marshall, John. *The Papers of John Marshall.* Edited by Charles Cullen. Chapel Hill: University of North Carolina Press, 1984.

Mayo, Bernard, ed. *Thomas Jefferson and His Unknown Brother.* Charlottesville: University Press of Virginia, 1981.

McCullough, David. *John Adams.* New York: Simon & Schuster, 2001.

————. *1776.* New York: Simon & Schuster, 2005.

McDonald, Forrest. *The Presidency of Thomas Jefferson.* Lawrence: University Press of Kansas, 1976.

McLaughlin, Jack. *Jefferson and Monticello: The Biography of a Builder.* New York: Holt, 1988.

McMurry, Rebecca L., and James F. McMurry Jr. *Anatomy of a Scandal: Thomas Jefferson and the Sally Story.* Shippensburg, PA: White Mane Books, 2002.

————. *Jefferson, Callender and the Sally Story: The Scandalmonger and the Newspaper War of 1802.* Toms Brook, VA: Old Virginia Books, 2000.

Miller, John C. *Alexander Hamilton: Portrait in Paradox.* New York: Harper & Brothers, 1959.

————. *Crisis in Freedom: The Alien and Sedition Acts.* Boston: Little, Brown, 1951.

————. *The Wolf by the Ears: Thomas Jefferson and Slavery.* Charlottesville: University Press of Virginia, 1991.

Nichols, Frederick D., and James A. Bear Jr. *Monticello.* Monticello, VA: Thomas Jefferson Memorial Foundation, 1967.

O'Brien, Conor Cruise. *The Long Affair.* Chicago: University of Chicago Press, 1996.

O'Connor, Thomas H. *Bibles, Brahmins, and Bosses: A Short History of Boston.* Boston: Boston Trustees of the Public Library, 1991.

Onuf, Peter, ed. *Jefferson Legacies.* Charlottesville: University Press of Virginia, 1993.

Peden, William, ed. *Thomas Jefferson: Notes on the State of Virginia.* New York: Norton, 1982.

Peterson, Merrill D. *Adams and Jefferson: A Revolutionary Dialogue.* Oxford: Oxford University Press, 1976.

————. *The Jefferson Image in the American Mind.* New York: Oxford University Press, 1960.

————. *Thomas Jefferson: A Reference Biography.* New York: Scribner's, 1986.

————. *Thomas Jefferson and the New Nation: A Profile.* New York: Oxford University Press, 1970.

————, ed. *Visitors to Monticello.* Charlottesville: University Press of Virginia, 1989.

Pierson, Hamilton W., ed. *Jefferson at Monticello: The Private Life of Thomas Jefferson.* New York: Charles Scribner, 1862.

Randall, Henry S. *The Life of Thomas Jefferson.* 3 vols. New York: Derby & Jackson, 1858.

Randall, Willard Sterne. *Thomas Jefferson: A Life.* New York: Holt, 1997.

Randolph, Sarah N. *The Domestic Life of Thomas Jefferson.* Charlottesville: University Press of Virginia, 1978.

Schachner, Nathan. *Thomas Jefferson.* New York: T. Yoseloff, 1957.

Schlesinger, Arthur, Jr. *A Life in the 20th Century.* Boston: Houghton Mifflin, 2002.

Shuffelton, Frank. *Thomas Jefferson: A Comprehensive, Annotated Bibliography of Writings about Him (1826–1980).* New York: Garland Publishing, 1983.

———. *Thomas Jefferson, 1981–1991: An Annotated Bibliography.* New York: Garland Publishing, 1992.

Stanton, Lucia. *Slavery at Monticello.* Richmond, VA: Spencer, 1993.

Stein, Susan R. *The Worlds of Thomas Jefferson at Monticello.* New York: Abrams, 1993.

Thomas Jefferson Memorial Foundation. *Report of the Research Committee on Thomas Jefferson and Sally Hemings.* Charlottesville, VA: January 2000. http://www.monticello.org/site/plantation-and-slavery/report-research -committee-thomas-jefferson-and-sally-hemings

Tucker, George. *The Life of Thomas Jefferson, Third President of the United States.* 2 vols. Philadelphia: Carey, Lean, and Blanchard, 1837.

Turner, Robert F., ed. *The Jefferson-Hemings Controversy: Report of the Scholars Commission.* Durham, NC: Carolina Academic Press, 2011.

Ward, Harry M. "Douglas Southall Freeman: A Historian's Overview." In *Douglas Southall Freeman: Reflections by His Daughter, His Research Associate and a Historian.* Richmond, VA: Friends of the Richmond Public Library, 1986.

Wills, Garry. *Cincinnatus: George Washington and the Enlightenment.* Garden City, NY: Doubleday, 1984.

———. *Inventing America.* Garden City, NY: Doubleday, 1978.

———. *Negro President.* New York: Houghton Mifflin, 2003.

Wilson, L. Douglas, ed. *Jefferson's Books.* Lynchburg, VA: Progress Printing, 1986.

———. *Jefferson's Literary Commonplace Book.* Princeton, NJ: Princeton University Press, 1989.

Wood, Gordon S. *The Creation of the American Republic.* Chapel Hill: University of North Carolina Press, 1969.

———. *Empire of Liberty: A History of the Early Republic, 1789–1815.* New York: Oxford University Press, 2009.

———. *The Radicalism of the American Revolution*. New York: Knopf, 1992.
———. *Revolutionary Characters: What Made the Founders Different*. New York: Penguin, 2006.

Articles

Battle, John D. "The 'Periodical Head-achs' of Thomas Jefferson." Cleveland Clinic Quarterly 51 (1983): 531–39.

Bear, James A., Jr. "The Hemings Family at Monticello." *Virginia Cavalcade* 29 (Autumn 1979): 78–87.

Beddow, Reid. "Dumas Malone, The Sage of Charlottesville." *Washington Post Book World* 11, no. 27 (July 5, 1981).

Benet, Stephen Vincent, II. "Great General, Greater Man." *New York Herald Tribune Books*, February 10, 1935, 1.

Bradford, M. E. "The Long Shadow of Thomas Jefferson." *National Review*, October 2, 1981.

Bringhurst, Newell G. "Fawn M. Brodie: Her Biographies as Autobiography." *Pacific Historical Review* 59, no. 2 (May 1990): 203–29.

Brodie, Fawn M. "The Great American Taboo." *American Heritage* 23, no. 4 (June 1972): 4–57.

———. "Jefferson Biographers and the Psychology of Canonization." *Journal of Interdisciplinary History* 2, no. 1 (Summer 1971): 155–71.

———. "The Political Hero in America." *Virginia Quarterly Review* 40, no. 1 (Winter 1970): 46–60.

———. "Thomas Jefferson's Unknown Grandchildren: A Study in Historical Silence." *American Heritage* 27 (October 1976): 23, 33, 94, 99.

Cohen, Gary L., and Loren A. Rolak. "Thomas Jefferson's Headaches: Were They Migraines?" *Headache: The Journal of Head and Face Pain* 46, no. 3 (March 2006): 492–97.

Dabney, Virginius, and Jon Kukla. "The Monticello Scandals: History and Fiction." *Virginia Cavalcade* 29 (Autumn 1979): 52–61.

Ellis, Joseph J., and Lander, Eric S. "Founding Father." *Nature*, November 5, 1998.

Foster, Eugene A. et al. "Jefferson Fathered Slave's Last Child." *Nature* 396, no. 6706 (November 5, 1998).

Graham, Pearl N. "Thomas Jefferson and Sally Hemings." *Journal of Negro History* 44 (1961): 89–103.

Hitchens, Christopher. "Jefferson-Clinton." *Nation*, November 30, 1998.

Hyland, William G., Jr., and William G. Hyland. "A Civil Action: Hemings v. Jefferson." *American Journal of Trial Advocacy* 31 (Summer 2007): 1–68.

Jellison, Charles A. "James Thomson Callender: 'Human Nature in a Hideous Form.'" *Virginia Cavalcade* 29 (Autumn 1978): 62–69.

Jordan, Winthrop. Review of *Thomas Jefferson: An Intimate History*, by Fawn Brodie. *William and Mary Quarterly*, 3rd ser., 32 (1975): 510.

Leary, Helen F. M. "Sally Hemings's Children: A Genealogical Analysis of the Evidence." *National Genealogical Society Quarterly* 89, no. 3 (September 2001): 165–207.

Malone, Dumas. "Mr. Jefferson's Private Life." *Proceedings of the American Antiquarian Society*, new ser., 84 (April 1974): 65–74.

———. "R. E. Lee: A Biography." *American Historical Review* 40, no. 3 (April 1935): 534.

———. "Reflections." *Virginia Magazine of History and Biography* 93, no. 1 (January 1985): 3–13.

———. "The Scholar's Way: Then and Now." *Virginia Quarterly Review* 51, no. 2 (Spring 1975): 200.

Malone, Dumas, and Steven Hochman. "A Note on Evidence: The Personal History of Madison Hemings." *Journal of Southern History* 41, no. 4 (November 1975): 523–28.

Mayer, David. "The Thomas Jefferson–Sally Hemings Myth and the Politicization of American History." April 9, 2001, http://www.ashbrook.org /articles/mayer-hemings.html, last accessed January 2012; see also http:// users.law.capital.edu/dmayer/Publications/.

McClenahan, Mary Tyler Freeman Cheek. "Reflections." *Virginia Magazine of History and Biography* 94, no. 1 (January 1986): 25–39.

Mitchell, Henry. "The Gentleman Historian: Dumas Malone, Sage of Charlottesville." *Washington Post*, January 4, 1987.

Morgan, Marie, and Edmund S. Morgan. "Jefferson's Concubine." *New York Review of Books*, October 9, 2008.

Neiman, Fraser D. "Coincidence or Causal Connection? The Relationship between Thomas Jefferson's Visits to Monticello and Sally Hemings's Conceptions." *William and Mary Quarterly* 57 (2000): 205.

Onuf, Peter S. "The Scholars' Jefferson." *William and Mary Quarterly*, 3d ser., 50 (1993): 671.

Peterson, Merrill D. "Dumas Malone: An Appreciation." *William and Mary Quarterly*, 3d ser., 45, no. 2 (April 1988): 237–52.

———. "Dumas Malone: The Completion of a Monument." *Virginia Quarterly Review*, Winter 1982, 26–31, http://www.vqronline.org/articles /1982/winter/peterson-dumas-malone/.

Phelps, Mary Ellen, "Jefferson Biographer Wins Freedom Medal." *Cavalier Daily*, January 21, 1983.

Pyles, Thomas. "In Memoriam, Kemp Malone, Onomatologist." *Journal of the American Names Society* 21, no. 3 (September 1973).

Sandburg, Carl. "Douglas Southall Freeman: 1886–1953." *Proceedings of the American Academy of Arts and Letters and the National Institute of Arts and Letters*, 2nd sess., no. 5 (1955).

Shuffelton, F. "Being Definitive: Jefferson Biography under the Shadow of Dumas Malone." *Biography* 18, no. 4 (Fall 1995): 291–304, http://muse.jhu.edu/journals/bio/summary/v018/18.4.shuffelton.html.

Smith, Jeffrey. "In the Autumn of His Years, Dumas Malone Reaps a Rich Harvest." *Emory Magazine* 58 (December 1981): 8–12.

Smith, W. Thomas, Jr. "A Rite of Passage Unlike Any Other: S.C. Boot Camp Readies Marine Recruits for War." *Washington Times*, October 10, 2005.

Wenger, Mark R. "Thomas Jefferson, the College of William and Mary, and the University of Virginia." *Virginia Magazine of History and Biography* 103, no. 3 (July 1995): 339–74.

Wills, Garry. "The Aesthete." Review of *The Worlds of Thomas Jefferson*, by Susan R. Stein. *New York Review of Books* 40 (August 12, 1993): 6–10.

———. "Prodigious Life, The Sage of Monticello." Review of *Jefferson and His Time: The Sage of Monticello*, by Dumas Malone. *The New Republic*, August 1 and 8, 1981, 32–34.

———. "Uncle Thomas's Cabin." Review of *Thomas Jefferson: An Intimate History*, by Fawn Brodie. *New York Review of Books* 21 (April 18, 1974): 26.

Wilson, Douglas L. "Thomas Jefferson and the Character Issue." *Atlantic* 27, no. 5 (November 1992), digital edition, http://www.theatlantic.com/past/docs/issues/96oct/obrien/charactr.htm.

———. "Thomas Jefferson's Early Notebooks." *William and Mary Quarterly*, 3rd ser., 42, no. 4 (October 1985).

Wiltrout, Kate. "What Would Make Someone Sign Up for This?" *Virginian-Pilot*, December 12, 2004.

Yoder, Edwin. "The Sage at Sunset." *Virginia Quarterly Review*, Winter 1982, 32–37, http://www.vqronline.org/articles/1982/winter/yoder-sage-sunset/.

Newspapers and Journals

Cavalier Daily
New York Times
Pike County Republican
Richmond News Leader
Richmond Recorder
Richmond Times-Dispatch

Virginia Gazette (Williamsburg)
Washington Federalist
Washington Gazette
Washington National Intelligencer
Washington Post
Washington Times

Personal Interviews

Herbert Barger
Cynthia Burton
Helen Cripe
Sandy Gilliam
Steve Hochman
Linwood Holton
Edward A. Leake
Gifford Malone
Forrest McDonald
Katherine Sargeant
Robert F. Turner
Ken Wallenborn

INDEX

Vaughan, Joseph L., 43
Vidal, Gore, 155–56, 168
Viking Press, 165–66
Virginia Magazine of History and Biography,
    140
Virginia Quarterly Review, 49, 77, 100–101,
    152, 216–17, 218, 221
Virginia State Library, 168, 204
Visualtek, 202–3
von Bismarck, Otto, 23

Walker affair, 159, 161
Wallenborn, Ken, 198
Ward, Judson C., Jr., 35
Ward, William Arthur, 213
Warner, Augustine, 190–91
Warner, John, 189–90, 202
Warner, Mildred, 191
Warren, Charles, 68
Washington, George
    about, 72, 74, 113, 121, 191
    Freeman's biography of, 136–38, 141, 143,
        144, 145
Washington Post, 67–68, 166, 187
Wayles, John, 150, 161
Wayles, Martha, 159
We Americans (Anderson), 90
Webster, Daniel, 72, 186
Wertenbaker, Thomas Jefferson, 123
West Falmouth, 60–61, 64. *See also* Cape Cod
White House invitations, 1–3, 79, 82, 173,
    178–79, 186–87
*Who's Who among Students in American
    Universities and Colleges,* 200
Who's Who in America, 85

Wilbur L. Cross Medal, 8, 37
Will, George, 147, 171
William and Mary College, 125, 126, 128–
    29, 155, 174
Williams, Alan D., 166
Wills, Garry, 1, 160, 213
Wilson, Woodrow, 44, 47, 72–73, 74, 121–
    22, 218
Woman of the Year, 157
Woman's College of Oxford, 13
women, Malone on, 73
Woodson, Thomas M., 154
Woodward, C. Vann, 163, 209
World War I, 23, 29, 72–73
World War II, 100–101
writing
    Malone on, 40–41, 55, 71, 107, 108, 214–
        16
    Malone's process and style, 107–10, 138–
        39, 201–2
    Malone's yearn for, 23
writings of Malone, 243–44. *See also specific
    writings*
Wyatt, John, 59–60, 176
Wyllie, John, 120
Wynn, Ed, 82
Wythe, George, 124, 126, 129–30, 193, 204

Yale Divinity School, 21–23, 38
Yale News, 17
Yale University, 17, 29, 37–42, 53, 69, 123
Yale University Press, 51
Yoder, Edwin M, Jr., 157, 173

Zanski, Charles, 100

About the Author

William G. Hyland Jr. is an author, historian, and professor of law. His previous book, *In Defense of Thomas Jefferson* (2009), was nominated for the Virginia Literary Award. His publications have also appeared in the law journals of the University of Texas, University of Alabama, and the *American Journal of Trial Advocacy*. Hyland has lectured nationally on CSPAN-Book TV, Colonial Williamsburg, and the National Archives. He lives and works in Tampa, Florida.